THE
BASEMENT
BUGGER'S
B·I·B·L·E

THE PROFESSIONAL'S GUIDE TO CREATING, BUILDING, AND PLANTING CUSTOM BUGS AND WIRETAPS

SHIFTY BUGMAN

PALADIN PRESS • BOULDER, COLORADO

The Basement Bugger's Bible:
The Professional's Guide to Creating, Building,
and Planting Custom Bugs and Wiretaps
by Shifty Bugman

Copyright © 1999 by Shifty Bugman

ISBN 1-58160-022-4
Printed in the United States of America

Published by Paladin Press, a division of
Paladin Enterprises, Inc.,
Gunbarrel Tech Center
7077 Winchester Circle
Boulder, Colorado 80301 USA
+1.303.443.7250

Direct inquiries and/or orders to the above address.

Visit our Web site at www.paladin-press.com

Table of Contents

Part I: In the Lab

Part II: In the Field

Appendices

A Note from Shifty

Let's get a few things straight. First, despite its matador's cape of a title, this book is not an advertisement for, an enticement to, or a promotion of illegal wiretapping, which happens to be called that because it's illegal. Grim sequelae are many and include federal prosecution and time in the joint, along with horrendous legal bills and loss of greens privileges at Winged Foot. The scope of the term embraces pretty much any form of unauthorized eavesdropping; and, yes, this book profiles wiretapping of the most sordid sort. It also makes the point here to distinguish between bugging and reading about bugging. Read; don't bug.

The book presents technical background as nonfiction that holds as close to the original tools as I can get without spilling trade secrets. In many cases I have updated devices because the original parts are no longer sold. The reader should understand that anyone who duplicates or attempts to duplicate these devices, or merely buys parts to build them, might be inviting strange repercussions. Episodes purporting to describe field use of tools invoke a fictive format whose full aspect is a product of my imagination.

This mixed presentation brings bugging to life in a way that is beyond the reach of strict nonfiction, besides being the only way to make the point without soiling my own digs.

Irrespective of whether the capers occurred, sufficient time has elapsed for the several statutes of limitation to absolve all who might have participated. No account describes events more recent than 1987. All hardware shown in photographs has been destroyed.

Neither the publisher nor I guarantee anything about this book, including the accuracy or safety of its information, the suitability of that information to a particular purpose, or the legality of the episodes recounted, whether stated or implicit in the text or inferred by the reader. The publisher and I specifically disclaim any and all liability and responsibility to any person or entity for damage or loss caused, or alleged to be caused, directly or indirectly, by the use, misuse, negligent use, or inability to use information contained in this book. We present this book "as is" and without expressed or implied warranty of any kind.

—Shifty Bugman
Las Cruces, California

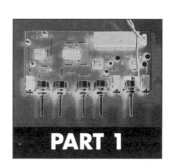

PART 1

In the Lab

CHAPTER 1

The Unified-Field Theory

Typical treatments take off at a trot, tossing out tools as if every buyer could grade them on the fly like so many damsels dancing by. In fact, few can name the traits of proper bugging tools or tell the real thing from fluff, a state unsurprising and probably inevitable in an air of incessant hype: "Isn't this little bug adorable?" "We're experts; believe what we say!" "What you see is all there is." Brainwashing may explain the benightedness of many who think they know the facts.

A pro views the game as a gestalt, not a galaxy of gadgets. Constant practice gives him a gut-level grasp of the principles involved. They convey readily because they flow from crude physics and common sense.

Studio recordings happen in dead quiet, at an unhasty pace. They use fixed apparatus weighing tens of pounds, capturing the full audio spectrum. Hardware depreciates over decades; the number of retakes is infinite. But bugging—eavesdropping, snooping, spying, wiretapping—seeks only to intercept speech, usually of parties who prefer not to be heard, often in settings hostile to the task. The agent must go where the action is and surmount a wall of noise. He favors hidden gear running on a Ray-O-Vac® and set up in a rush.

Retakes? Not on the menu.

The task defines its tools, explaining why the student cannot tap mixing-board lore for guidance.

THE NATURE OF COVERT INTERCEPTS

The literature of hearing loss holds a rich vein on what makes speech intelligible.

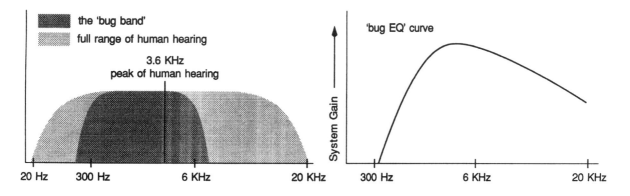

Audiology codified what veteran buggers learned through years in the trenches.

The spectrum of human hearing stretches from 20 Hz to 20 KHz, but the spectrum of human speech tops out at 7 KHz, with most energy focused between 300 and 6,000 Hz.

Information in speech resides in two types of sounds. The first is known as a formant, the sound made by tightened vocal cords vibrating in a stream of air—the vowel sounds aaaah, eeeeh, and so on. If cord vibration frequency is viewed as a carrier, speech contains amplitude modulation and frequency modulation. The second distinctive component is called unvoiced energy. It originates with air traversing the throat without vibrating the cords, then through the mouth and lips. It includes explosive venting, as the k in kick or the p in pop, and air passing through the teeth, as the s in hiss. Unvoiced energy conveys so much information that it remains fully intelligible as whispering.

These observations reveal a narrow, skewed band where the intelligence in speech resides, what one might call the "bug band," laying the basis for an equalization curve suited to covert intercepts. The curve banishes bass tones to allow high gain in the presence of low-frequency ambient noise and accents the spectra of unvoiced energy. It extends from just above 300 Hz to about 6 KHz. The low end rolls off more sharply than the top end. Buggers tune their tools here to suit Willie Sutton's rule: Go where the money is.

With this clear objective in mind, covert audio lays itself out in a chain that begins with a microphone.

MICROPHONES

A microphone or "mic" changes sound to electricity. To pick the right mic for the job, the agent must know the traits of them all.

Condenser Mics

Condenser mics juxtapose a pair of conductive plates—one fixed, one movable and serving as the mic's diaphragm. Plates in proximity can hold a charge, hence the name

condenser mic. The type explains itself through three equations:

$$W = \frac{V^2 C \times 10^{12}}{2}$$

where:

W is stored energy in joules
V is potential in volts
C is capacitance in picofarads

$$C = \frac{.22 K A}{d}$$

where:

C is capacitance in picofarads
K is dielectic constant of the medium between the plates
A is area of one plate in square inches
d is distance between plates in inches

Rearranging and solving for distance:

$$d = \frac{V^2 K A \times (1.1 \times 10^{11})}{W}$$

Sound shifts distance between plates, which alters voltage. Mic sensitivity is a function of applied plate voltage, distance between plates, their area, and other factors, such as compliance of the diaphragm. Raw signal at the plates is not usable due to its extremely high impedance. In a complete microphone, one plate ties to the gate of a field-effect transistor (FET). Diaphragmatic movement causes a drain current to flow through a DC-biased external resistor. Thus, condenser mics are not primary generators.

Studio condenser mics charge the plates through an external bus. The industry standard is 48V. Some, like the Bruel & Kjaer 4000 series, use 130V to give a small diaphragm the sensitivity of a large one.

Electret condenser mics place a permanently polarized plastic slab known as the "electret" between a metal plate and a conductive diaphragm. This obviates external plate bias. All

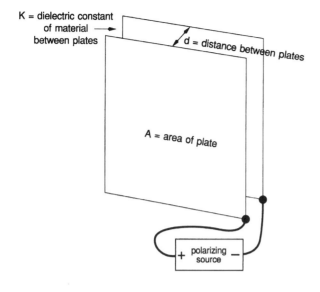

K = dielectric constant of material between plates →

d = distance between plates

A = area of plate

+ polarizing − source

hobby-grade condenser mics use an electret and are often called, simply, electrets.

Electrets have dominated bugging since *Blade Runner*. They're cheap, tiny, sensitive. They draw a fraction of a milliamp. DC bias present at their outputs requires capacitor coupling into most circuits.

Cheap electrets' chief flaw is noise. Most claim a signal-to-noise (S/N) ratio > 40 dB, which is 12 dB noisier than a vinyl LP. Lately, the Panasonic line upped this claim by 20 dB. S/N specs would tell the user a lot more if they added "relative to what?" The 40 dB S/N ratio might hold for tones that generate 2 mv from the mic. If those tones were softened and mic output dropped to 500 µv, S/N ratio would sink to 28 dB, a case more typical of covert work.

Condenser mics' great bass response, prized in the studio, is something the bug designer must defeat. Here bug equalization (EQ) comes into its own, for it ignores bass coming off the mic.

Cheap electrets are readily hacked in that the user can manipulate supply voltage and drain resistance. Package directions specify 1K for the Radio Shack 270-090 electret mic. They do not point out that raising the bias resistance to 10K and keeping bias voltage between 6V and 10V will boost mic output by more than 12 dB. Thermal noise of the bias resistor rises from 4 nv / rtHz at 1K to 12.8 nv / rtHz at 10K, a factor of 3.2, which is less than the fourfold rise in gain. By these factors alone, raw mic output has a better S/N ratio with the higher bias resistance. (The mic might or might not mate more quietly to the amp, depending upon the amp's input noise current. These matters are detailed in a later section.)

Given that the bias resistor is the mic's effective impedance, electrets function as high-impedance devices. Studio condenser mics have low impedances, because they couple raw mic output to a step-down transformer. They can afford the voltage loss because studio capsules typically measure an inch across, giving them many times the area, and, by the condenser equations, many times the output of a tiny electret.

The occasional electret suffers low output or high noise or both. Professionals usually audition a mic before soldering it to that once-in-a-lifetime contract bug.

Piezoelectric Mics

Piezoelectricity means voltage generated in a material by the application of force, and vice versa. Quartz, Rochelle salt, barium titanate, and other substances share the property. Every click lighter uses piezo ignition.

Piezo mics exist as crystal and ceramic types that ruled the hobby scene prior to the emergence of cheap electrets. The design sandwiches a piezo wafer between metal electrodes, then links the sandwich to an aluminum foil diaphragm. That assembly is housed in a cuplike metal case.

Ceramic mics are not polarized in the sense of an electret, but the negative (case) lead should always tie to ground to minimize hum. The fact that the output terminals do not present a DC path means they can couple directly to most amplifier inputs. Hobby types are large, 3/4″ to 2″ in diameter, which can be a plus in applications requiring a wide pickup area. Ceramic mics would be a lot more pervasive if they were smaller. Only high-output types, -55 dB or better, still belong in surveillance.

High impedance figures often quoted for the type—7K to 25K ohms—should be taken with a grain of salt. The impedance varies with frequency, falling as frequency rises. In the bug band ceramic mics behave as medium-impedance devices. Their impedance peaks at low frequencies, partly explaining their susceptibility to hum.

The best ceramic mics are quieter than electrets by virtue of not generating FET self-noise. They can be a hair more sensitive on midrange peaks, a tinny sound that mirrors their foil heritage. They have practically no output in the deep bass and high treble, meaning their feeds need little equalization.

Piezoceramic mics have been waning since the introduction of polyvinylidene fluoride (PVDF), a piezoplastic sold by Amp Corporation under the name Kynar®. Common plastics such as nylon and PVC exhibit piezoelectricity at a vestigial level that was never enough to spur commercial pursuit. PVDF and its copolymers generate 10 times the output of piezoceramics or other piezoplastics. To dramatize this trait, Amp makes a promotional goodie that wires a neon bulb to the end of a Kynar® strip. Waving the thing gently back and forth will generate the 90V neon lamp trigger.

PVDF is waterproof and possesses natural density that couples vibration to air and water a lot more efficiently than ceramics do. It can be made into almost any size and shape, or applied to objects impractical for brittle solids. Its physical frequency response extends from 0.01 Hz to 2 gigahertz, making PVDF the current material of choice for ultrasonic transducers used in hydrophones, sonar, and ultrasonic transducers.

Bare PVDF sheets make poor mics. Placing them in a stressed state—wrapped around a 1″ diameter cylinder, for example—turns the material into a suitable microphone. A conformal coating of PVDF can turn any surface into a mic.

Raw PVDF sheets are available from Amp Corporation.

Dynamic Mics

A copper or aluminum coil placed in a magnetic field will move when current flows through the coil. Conversely, movement of the coil in the field generates current in the coil. Dynamic speakers and dynamic mics share this operating principle. The distinction is purely semantic, for speakers make dynamite mics for special bugging gigs.

Buggers rarely use true dynamic microphones. At best, they're 20 dB less sensitive than an optimized electret. They lean to large size, 1″ or so, and cost $5–$10. A mic's magnetic field can attract metal debris strongly enough to puncture its diaphragm. These mics are inherently subject to hum from magnetic fields that surround power transformers.

Despite drawbacks of the breed, loudspeakers used as microphones offer unique advantages. They're big, but exist in disguise. Their negligible impedance suits ultralow-noise applications; their limited response minimizes low-frequency ambient noise. Step-down transformers meant to drive speakers become step-up transformers for speakers used as mics.

Others

While electret, piezo, and dynamic mics will meet 99 percent of the modern bugger's needs, he should at least be aware of two other types.

Prior to the breakup of AT&T, domestic telephones used a drop-in carbon microphone cartridge, basically a pack of carbon granules sandwiched between conductive plates. Sound pressure alters the resistance of the pack and thus its conductivity. An external DC bias provided through a transformer makes the thing a microphone. The type is found in pre-1980 telephones.

Less a separate type than a special design, noise-canceling mics occasionally surface in bugging applications. Their design is predicated on the notion that ambient noise is likely to suffuse the environment. A mic built to expose both sides of a diaphragm equally to sound registers little output from this noise because noise impinges equally on both sides of the membrane, thus canceling. But sound originating very near to, and only on one side of, the membrane does not cancel and thereby generates a signal. The theory worked; aircraft and mobile radio sets use noise-canceling mics.

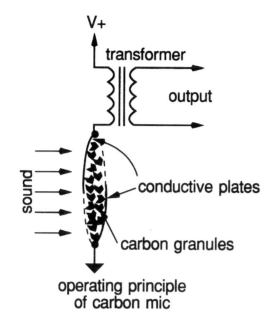

operating principle
of carbon mic

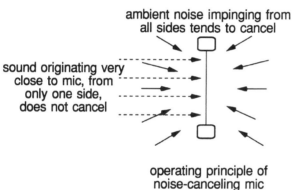

operating principle of
noise-canceling mic

MICROPHONE SENSITIVITY

Mic sensitivity is usually stated in "-dB." The less negative the number, the more sensitive the mic; -68 dB is 29 dB more sensitive than -97 dB. Assuming the reference to be 0 dB=1 volt, a sound that generates 1 mv from a -68 dB mic would produce only 36 µv from the -97 dB mic. The amp must make up what the mic fails to produce.

A mic rated -60 dB or better qualifies as sensitive. The bugger should seek the most sensitive model he can get.

Optimized electrets are the most sensitive, followed closely by piezo mics. Dynamic mics average the least sensitive, due in part to the fact that they're designed to work inches from the sound source.

MIC CONNECTION MODES

Mics tie to preamps in three distinct modes:

* unbalanced
* balanced
* pseudodifferential

Common mic elements produce an unbalanced output; common preamps sport unbalanced inputs. Unbalanced means two terminals, one of which is ground, treated as a reference that does not bear a signal. The other conductor bears a signal relative to ground. Unbalanced feeds work okay for runs up to several feet. Practical length of an unbalanced run depends on impedance of the mic and the severity of local interference.

Balanced lines and stages are also called *differential*. These three-conductor feeds contain ground and two signal lines. Both lines carry signal in balanced form: equal amplitude and out of phase. The point of balanced transmission flows from the fact that a differential amplifier amplifies only the difference between the input terminals. It ignores signals present equally in both lines. For example, a line might bear a legitimate 1 mv signal and an interfering signal several volts peak-to-peak (V_{p-p}). A differential amp can ignore the interference and boost the true signal.

Balanced mode resists hum because induced voltages tend to have equal amplitude and phase in both signal conductors. The differential amplifier, or a transformer winding, will ignore them, where an unbalanced amp will not. Balanced feeds also favor low impedance. The lower the impedance, the lower the voltage dropped by an induced current.

Pseudodifferential mode can be thought of as differential without the ground terminal. A dynamic mic feed could be coupled by single-ended or pseudodifferential means.

In choosing a connection mode, the bugger must weigh distance, impedance, and local interference. The longer the cable run required, the more it suits low impedance—and the more the designer should favor balanced transmission.

MIC CONNECTION MODES

A) A ubiquitous setup in bugging gear: electret mic connecting to input of op amp. Connection is unbalanced, through single-conductor shielded cable, either dedicated microphone cable or RG174/U coaxial cable. C1 is necessary to prevent a large DC offset at op amp output due to DC bias at mic output.

B) Setup is identical but for the fact that microphone bias travels in center conductor of mic cable, one type of phantom power for an electret, practical in runs of several feet, but only in interference-free settings.

C) A true differential setup typical of studio gear. Here the source is the secondary winding of T1. Signal travels in twisted pair. Shield lead ties to T1 center tap. At the amplifier input, signal feeds to SSM2017 differential preamp (discussed in some detail later). Note that the input terminals are able to reach ground through T1 center tap, which also ties to circuit ground. This eliminates the need for external biasing network and helps preserve amp's common mode rejection ratio (CMRR).

D) Setup resembles "C," but in this case the transducer is a dynamic microphone, or a transformer winding without a center tap. Balanced transmission is still used, but the amplifier inputs have to get their DC bias through an external path supplied by R1 and R2. In this case, CMRR may suffer unless R1 and R2 are perfectly balanced. These connection modes appear in most bugging devices.

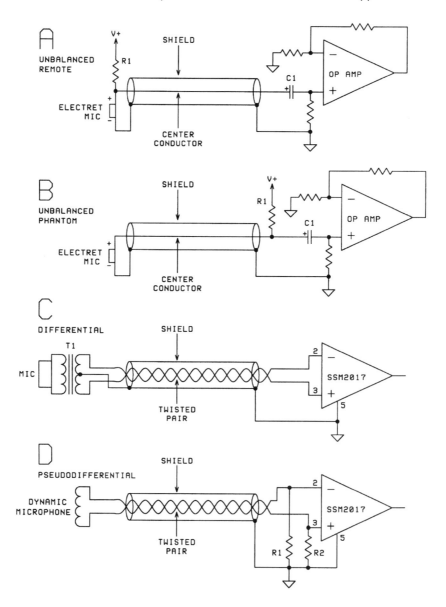

ELECTRET CONDENSER MICS

- predominant mic in bugging tools
- impedance: determined by value of bias resistor; medium to high
- output terminal is a DC path with highly positive DC offset; therefore, most electrets couple through capacitors
- fantastic frequency response extending <5 Hz to >15 KHz
- sensitivity: good to excellent; manufacturer's rated output can be increased by more than 10 dB through manipulation of bias resistance and supply voltage
- sizes: 6 mm and 9.7 mm diameter
- cost: $.50 on the surplus market to $7 retail
- sources: Digi-Key, Mouser, Hosfelt, many surplus vendors

A) Schematic symbol of electret mic w/bias resistor. The positive DC offset present at electret mic output demands capacitor coupling into most circuits.

B) What's happening inside an electret mic. The "electret" is a permanently polarized plastic membrane that maintains a charge between metal plate on FET gate and the grounded metal film applied to one side of the electret. Diaphragmatic movement caused by sound alters distance between plates of this condenser. Field-effect transistor steps down enormous impedance; effective mic impedance becomes value of bias resistor. Chief noise source of an electret mic is the voltage noise generated by the FET. Electrets are the most sensitive mics commonly available.

C) See-through side view of common electret mic. FET source lead can be isolated from ground by shearing trace on back of case, allowing interposition of an impedance network between source and ground.

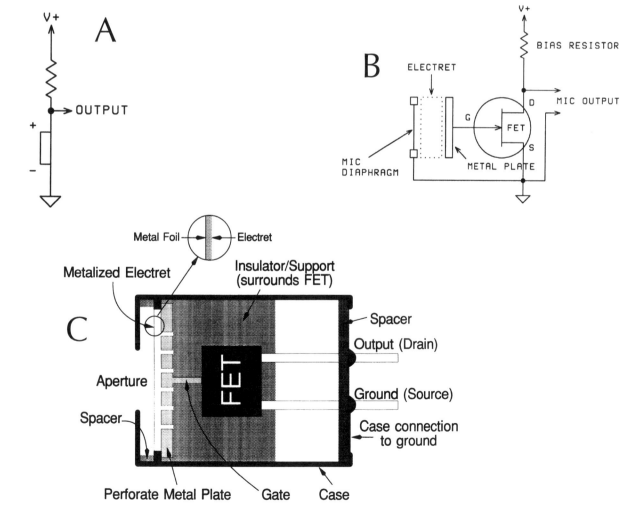

ELECTRET CONDENSER MICS

Photos show representative electret mics. Ground terminal is identified by connection to case.

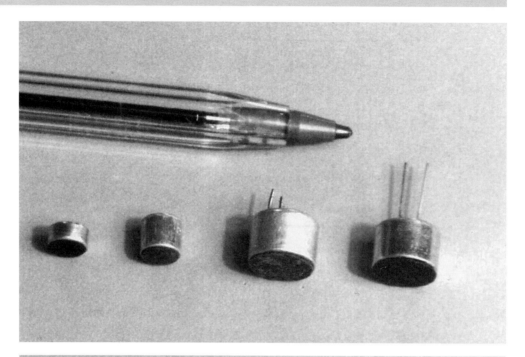

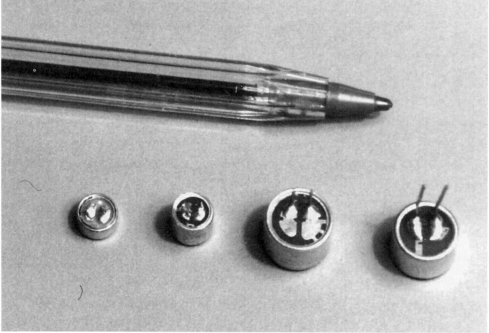

ELECTRET CONDENSER MIC

Top photo shows electret mic disassembled by prying up crimp on rear of case. Perforate metal plate normally attached to FET gate has been removed to show the FET, which bears a common Japanese semiconductor part number. Careful technique enables electret hacking. Options include replacing the FET with a low-noise type, such as PF5102, and disconnecting the drain lead from the case, making all three FET terminals independently accessible. The possibilities presented by this flow from the nature of single-transistor audio amplifiers. Bottom photos show the two smallest electret mics currently available in open channels. Larger of the two is Panasonic WM-62A, smaller is Mouser (Kobitone) 25LM046; the latter measures .197" x .098".

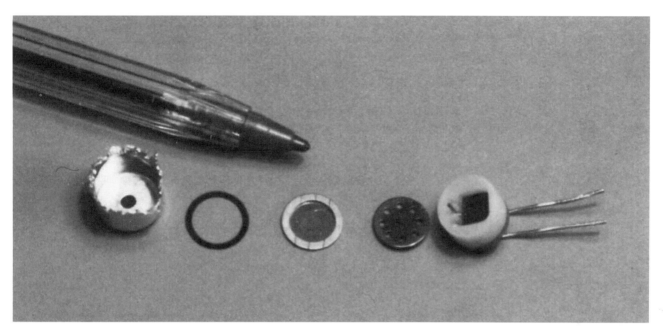

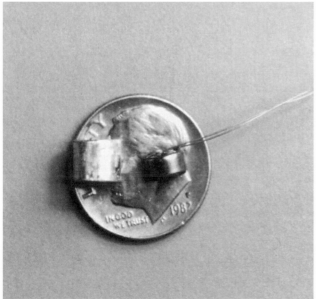

CRYSTAL/CERAMIC MICS

- piezoelectric
- sensitivity: good to mediocre, -55 to -75 dB
- impedance: nominally high, 7K–25K; actually medium, ~1K in the midrange
- frequency response: poor at high and low extremes, irregular in the midrange; speech-band peaks can help
- coupling to preamplifiers: not a DC path, therefore coupling capacitors are not needed

- size: 3/4"–2"
- cost: $3–$5
- sources: Mouser is the chief source in hobby price range

Top photo shows three common ceramic mics. Bottom photo shows mic with cover removed, revealing metal foil diaphragm.

CRYSTAL/CERAMIC MICS

Photo shows ceramic mic with metal foil diaphragm cut away to expose yoke, piezo wafer, and output contacts. Mic has not been destroyed; gluing an extension to the yoke converts it to a contact microphone. Diagram illustrates construction details of typical ceramic mic.

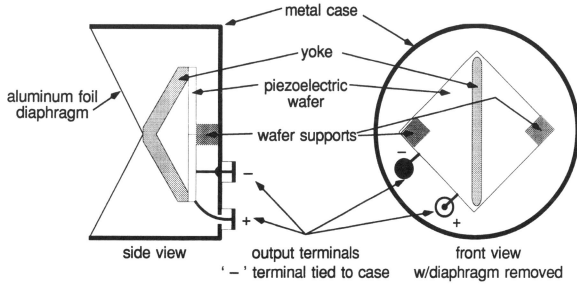

metal case

yoke

piezoelectric wafer

aluminum foil diaphragm

wafer supports

− +

side view

output terminals
' − ' terminal tied to case

front view
w/diaphragm removed

DYNAMIC MICS

- two key subtypes: dedicated dynamic mics and loudspeakers used as mics
- sensitivity: fair to poor: -68 to -97 dB
- impedance: extremely low to medium, 400–600 ohms
- susceptible to hum from AC power fields frequency response: adequate for bugging; tends to be flat in the midrange
- a DC path; can conduct bias potential for discrete transistor or op amp
- type couples readily to step-up transformer 8:200, 8:500, 8:1200, etc.
- size: ~1"–8"
- cost: $1 and up
- sources: Mouser is the chief source of raw dynamic mic capsules; dynamic speakers are available through many outlets

Diagram shows operating principle of dynamic mics and dynamic loudspeakers. Current flowing in a magnetic field induces a force, causing cone or diaphragm to move; movement of diaphragm induces flow of current in coil. Photos illustrate common dynamic microphones.

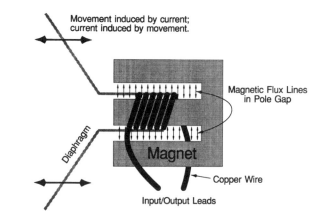

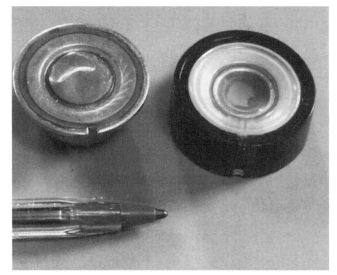

PIEZOPLASTIC SENSORS

Sensor consists of a polyvinylidene fluoride membrane sandwiched between layers of thin metal foil. Stressing the plastic generates a voltage; application of a voltage causes plastic to move.

Top photo shows collection of Kynar® sensors sold by Amp Corporation in an evaluation kit.

A, B, and F are unspecialized sensors in various sizes and with various types of edge connectors.

E has an FET built into the connector to serve as a remote preamp/impedance match, not unlike an electret condenser mic.

C is a subassembly used to make "touch-sensitive" keyboards in electronic musical instruments: the harder the player plays, the greater the sensor output and the louder the note.

D shows a neon bulb wired on the end of a 3" piezo strip. Holding this by the end opposite the bulb and flipping it gently back and forth readily generates the 90 volts needed to fire the neon bulb.

Bottom photo shows piezo speaker used to make musical greeting cards and other novelties; also works as a microphone.

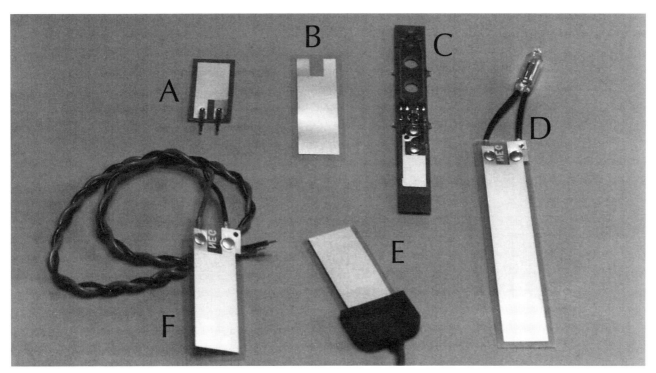

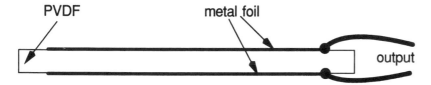

MICROPHONE RESPONSE PATTERNS

Microphone sold at retail means a microphone element mounted in a case to protect it from damage and shield it from hum. The case also controls the direction from which it accepts sound. This latter characteristic is known as response pattern and is plotted in polar coordinates, 0 degrees being straight ahead, 180 degrees being directly behind the microphone, viewed from above. Mic case alters directional response using dampers and phase-canceling slots. None of the types amplify sound. In fact, removing the element from the case will usually boost sensitivity. Of many possible response patterns, a handful have proven useful:

- **omnidirectional**—mic responds equally to sound originating anywhere in a sphere around the mic
- **cardioid**—most common pattern; heart-shaped; has a notch directly behind the mic; common hand-held mics exhibit this plot
- **hypercardioid/supercardioid**—increasing frontal preference and rejection of sound to the sides
- **shotgun**—exaggerated, frequency-dependent frontal preference
- **figure-of-eight**—equal acceptance to front and rear, nearly complete rejection to sides

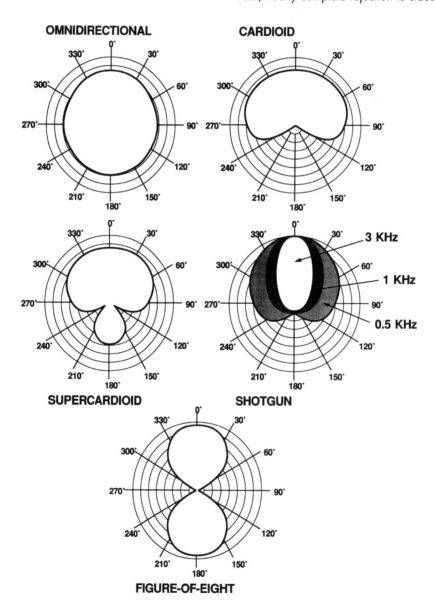

OMNIDIRECTIONAL

CARDIOID

3 KHz

1 KHz

0.5 KHz

SUPERCARDIOID

SHOTGUN

FIGURE-OF-EIGHT

CHAPTER 2

Audio Amplification in Bugging Gear

Microphone feeds are faint things that measure microvolts to a few millivolts. They must grow to several hundred millivolts to become useful, but because turning up the gain means turning up the noise, audio amplification in covert gear must take noise into account.

Noise comes in two key species, ambient and electronic. Ambient noise originates in the environment and is readily seen on an audio spectrum analyzer (SA) to predominate at low frequencies, often below 20 Hz. Though still perceptible, subsonic tones do not overwhelm to the extent implied by their spectral predominance. Human hearing inured itself to this rumble. Broadband amps do not discriminate, and for that reason seem to exaggerate bass. Electronic noise issues from three discrete sources. First, each amplifying device generates what's known as input noise voltage, E_n. E_n gets amplified along with any other signal present at the input. Amplifiers also produce input noise current, I_n. I_n generates noise only as it drops a noise voltage passing through a source impedance (R_s) connected to an input. Noise so produced is known as "$I_n \times R_s$ noise." The third source of electronic noise is called thermal agitation or Johnson noise. Each resistance or impedance generates a characteristic amount of noise that depends on ohmic value and temperature. For calculation, systems are assumed to be at room temperature, so thermal noise is treated as a function of resistance or impedance.

Electronic noise terms seem awkward initially but quickly grow familiar. E_n is specified in nanovolts per root Hz (nv/rtHz); I_n in picoamps per root Hz (pa/rtHz). Op amp and transistor data sheets list these values, usually at 10 Hz and 1,000 Hz, and also print characteristic curves of E_n vs. frequency (example illustrated in the graph on page 19; curves redrawn after manufacturer's data). As a universal trait, electronic noise tends to hold constant above 1,000 Hz and to rise below a frequency known as the "noise corner," which has significance mainly for devices that apply high gain near DC. Familiarity with noise terms allows comparison of what's quiet with what's noisy and useful projections of how the several noise variables are likely to interact.

Calculating total noise involves identifying each separate noise source, then adding them in quadrature, the square root of the sum of the squares. The algebraic sum (2 + 2) is 4. Quadrature summation looks like this:

$$[(2^2) + (2^2)]^{0.5} = [4 + 4]^{0.5} = 2.83$$

The expression for total noise is:

$$\text{total } E_n = [\{(\text{amplifier noise voltage})^2 + (I_n \times R_s \text{ noise})^2 + (\text{thermal noise})^2\} \times BW]^{0.5}$$

NOISE DEMO

To experience ambient noise through the ears of wideband gain, breadboard Circuit A. Microphone response extends below 1 Hz, amp response extends below 20 Hz. Power up, don wide-range headphones, slowly increase gain (R4). Common (and usually subliminal) sounds, such as fridge and air handler, leap to the fore. Open a window to get a feel for outdoor ambient noise. Blow gently on the mic. Despite high gain and low noise, this amp would bomb in the field. Bass overwhelms useful spectra. Yet this spectral skewing tells the designer how to banish noise in the preamp. Rather than filtering bass once it has been amplified, build the bug EQ curve into the preamp by configuring it to boost only frequencies of interest. Power down, change C2 to 2.2µF. Power up and listen again. Skewing the response has neutralized 80 percent of ambient noise typical of otherwise quiet environments. In this newly contoured form the demo amp has definite potential. Circuit B demonstrates several aspects of electronic noise. Breadboard circuit, connect U1 output to oscilloscope, set sensitivity to 20 millivolts per division. First, make Rx 10 ohms. U1's E_n (and a minor contribution from the RC network at inverting input) has been amplified by ~60 dB, over a bandwidth limited by amp response and capacitor values. Now replace Rx with a 100K resistor; note increase in noise.

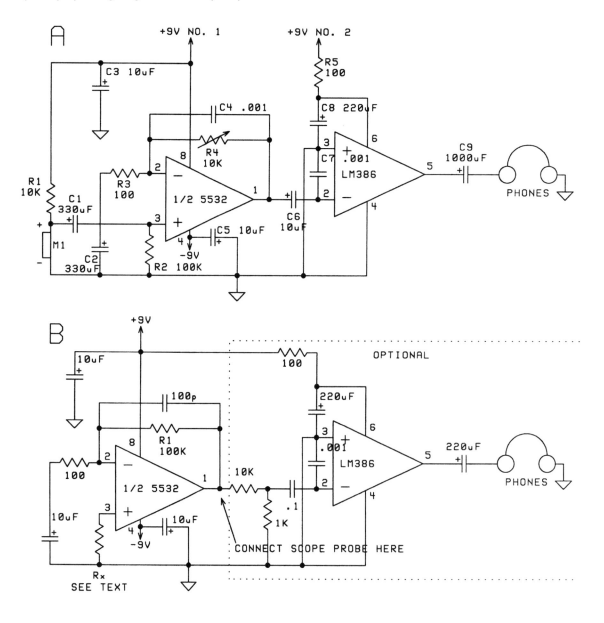

NOISE DEMO

This demonstrates graphically that source impedance can be the key noise determinant. If no oscilloscope is available, the experimenter can hear the difference by adding the audio driver shown inside the dotted line. Replace R1 with a pot to allow gain control. One obvious upshot of this observation: given two mics with equal output but differing impedances, choose the one having the lower impedance.

Graph shows generic example of E_n vs. frequency curves that appear in op amp data sheets. Note that E_n rises at very low frequencies and tends to flatten above 1,000 Hz.

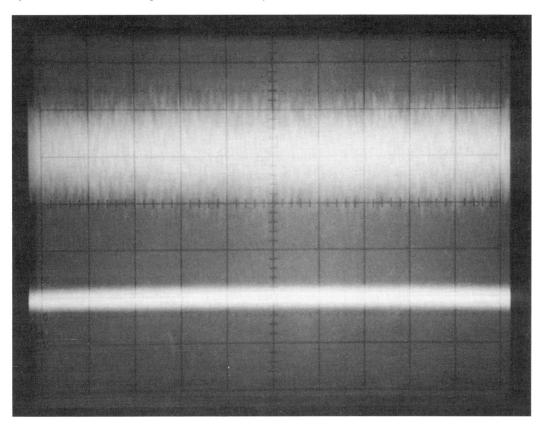

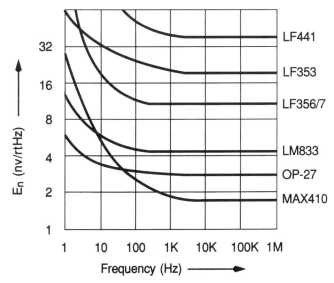

BW means bandwidth, the frequency range over which amplification applies. The observation that noise varies as the root of bandwidth holds the key to an advanced amplifier technique detailed later in the book.

WHAT'S QUIET?

In descending order, this table lists E_n and I_n @ 1,000 Hz for commonly available semiconductors.

Generally, devices at and below the NE5532 (5 nv) are considered very quiet—suitable for covert work. Devices that generate 25 nv or more make noisy preamps but can serve as line-level buffers.

AMPLIFIER TECHNIQUES

Three types of blocks amplify audio in bugging gear: discrete transistors, dedicated pre-

DEVICE	E_n	I_n
LM348 (quad 741)	45 nv	—
TL061	45 nv	0.01 pa
LF441	35 nv	0.01 pa
TL081/LF351	25 nv	0.01 pa
TL071	18 nv	0.01 pa
LT1055	15 nv	0.002 pa
MAX439	14 nv	0.07 pa
LT1008	14 nv	0.005 pa
LF356/7	12 nv	0.01 pa
LT1001	9.6 nv	0.12 pa
NE5532	5.0 nv	0.6 pa
LM833	4.5 nv	0.7 pa
NE5534A	3.5 nv	0.6 pa
OP-27/37	3.0 nv	0.4 pa
MAX427	2.5 nv	0.4 pa
LT1007/1037	2.5 nv	0.4 pa
MAX410	1.8 nv	0.2 pa
SSM2017	0.95 nv	2.0 pa
LT1028	0.90 nv	1.0 pa
MAX4106	0.85 nv	—
(E_n only 0.75 nv above 10 KHz; video amp)		
LM394	<0.8 nv	>1 pa
(discrete transistor pair; I_C = 2 ma or higher)		

(Data taken from manufacturers' data sheets.)

amplifier integrated circuits, and operational amplifiers. Each uses distinctive means to maximize gain, minimize noise, and shape response. Properly designed stages can do the same things. Selection is dictated by cost, supply voltage, board space, and so on. Tricky hybrids crop up occasionally, but they are not considered here.

DISCRETE TRANSISTOR AMPS

Overwhelmingly, covert audio prefers the common-emitter amplifier, discussed elsewhere in this chapter. This design accommodates low- to high-impedance sources, offers good voltage and current gain, and costs pennies to implement.

The chief gripe with discrete transistors is that inter-sample variation keeps one transistor from behaving exactly like the next. An exception occurs in premium matched pairs, such as MAT-02, SSM2210, LM394, etc. These pieces exhibit very high beta; very low noise voltage, usually <1 nv with collector current >1 ma; and close electrical match. They're useful in differential amps. Their cost of up to $10 per pair is justified in supercritical applications and with transducers having less than 31 ohms impedance.

Ordinary transistors suffice in most applications. Practical designs incorporate measures to immunize them to differences between individual transistors and ensure that they tolerate reasonable changes in supply voltage.

The difficulty of using transistors has been overblown. Design of bugging gear requires no grasp of transistor theory, only a few basic principles.

Like op amps, discrete transistors have characteristic input voltage noise and input current noise. E_n falls as the root of collector current; I_n rises as the root of collector current.

BIPOLAR TRANSISTORS VS. FIELD-EFFECT TRANSISTORS

The bipolar transistor (BPT) vs. field-effect transistor (FET) "controversy" recalls vile, contrived VHS vs. Beta "shoot-outs" that once plagued the video monthlies. Some MOSFETs and JFETs can beat BPTs on noise above 100 KHz; BPTs keep an edge below 100 KHz. At many frequencies the types tie, depending on collector current (or drain current) and other factors. Pros use FETs as tools, no trendier than a hacksaw. Hucksters invoke them as fire-gods to wow chumps. Yes, the mind drifts back to a tipsy Gene Hackman boasting in *The Conversation*: " . . . a MOSFET amplifier of my own design . . ."

The serious designer should remember these facts:

- BPTs show higher transconductance than FETs, meaning barely half the gain per FET stage compared to a BPT stage.
- FETs' vestigial noise current suits them to very high source impedances that bugging tools rarely need.
- While both types require high current to minimize voltage noise, the average FET takes several times the current of an average BPT to achieve comparable bug-band input noise voltage.
- FETs hit their stride at significantly higher voltage than do BPTs, making FETs more practical in 15V circuits than in 5V circuits.
- BPTs are dirt-cheap; FETs are not. In quantity, prime 3904s can be had for a nickel each. The cheapest FETs cost half a buck.
- FETs excel in nonamplifier applications that need voltage-variable resistance with lower ON resistance than BPTs can give.
- FETs are voltage-activated devices; BPTs are current-activated devices. This translates to FETs' ability to avoid loading signals from very high-impedance sources.

To coin a phrase, choose the right transistor for the job.

DEDICATED PREAMP CHIPS

As a class, preamp ICs are now a quarter-century old. They evolved to meet needs that had been clumsy to realize in discrete circuits, specifically the massive gain and tight-tolerance equalization required of magnetic phono and analog tape preamplifiers. The requirement for EQ died as digital science embraced consumer audio. What had been sensational fixtures in the days of Kolchak live on as fit but dated players, definite seconds to op amps for covert work.

Despite what was for the time phenomenally high gain and low noise, many non-engineers found these chips hard to use. Maximum headroom of an amplifier running on a single supply demands that its output be biased at 1/2V+. Preamp chips achieved this by a resistive divider involving feedback resistors and input resistors. The fact that these resistors also determined gain made getting the desired gain without shifting the DC offset a tricky affair. And, once fixed, all variables were frozen, because changing the supply voltage shifted the output potential.

Chief examples of the breed are the LM381, LM382, and LM387 (NE542), all two-channel single-supply chips. Their availability has waned of late, with only the 387 still being stocked by its native number; the LM381 lives on as NTE942. Thousands of these chips still languish in covert junk boxes.

A new generation of preamps debuted about the time the Stones wrapped up their "Steel Wheels" tour. They're as quiet as the quietest op amps and a lot easier to use with balanced, low-impedance lines that rule the studio. These chips run off dual supplies, and they sport very low input noise voltage and very high input noise current. They excel with source impedances under 250 ohms. They should not be used with source impedances higher than 1.5K. They include SSM2015 (E_n 1.3 nv), SSM2016 (E_n 0.8 nv), and SSM2017 (E_n 0.95 nv).

OPERATIONAL AMPLIFIER PREAMPS

Op amps offer many advantages over discrete transistors. They give higher gain at low voltage, that gain being largely independent of supply voltage. They require fewer parts to realize equivalent EQ curves. Their inter-unit uniformity enables the designer to treat them as

PREAMPLIFIER NOISE ANALYSIS

The purpose of calculating total input noise is to derive an objective measure of absolute noise and an index for comparison. Total input noise is expressed as nanovolts per root Hertz, at a frequency of 1,000 Hz.

For any amplifier, calculating total input noise involves the quadrature sum of noise sources:

- amplifier noise voltage, E_n
- $I_n \times R_s$ noise
- thermal noise

Amplifier E_n is found in the manufacturer's data sheet for op amps and dedicated preamp chips. For discrete transistors, a curve of E_n vs. collector current is usually supplied in the data sheet. E_n varies directly as the root of collector current (or drain current in the case of an FET).

Amplifier I_n is also found in the manufacturer's data sheet but must be multiplied against each impedance present at an amplifier input to yield a noise voltage.

Thermal noise of a resistance (or impedance) in isolation is found through this formula:

$$\text{thermal noise} = [\text{resistance} \times (1.64 \times 10^{-20})]^{0.5}$$

Despite apparent complexity, these calculations take less than two minutes on a pocket calculator.

Take a specific example, the preamp shown on this page. From the data sheet, LM833 E_n = 4.5 nv/rtHz @ 1 KHz.

To calculate $I_n \times R_s$ noise, get I_n from the data sheet: I_n = 0.7 pa/rtHz = 7×10^{-13} amps. Multiply this by the impedance present at each input. R1 in series with C1, and the ceramic mic in parallel with R3, simplify to net impedances using Ohm's law and the formula for an RC series impedance. (Strictly speaking, the net impedance of R1 and C1 should be paralleled with R2, but since R2 is very much greater than R1, the difference is small enough to ignore, and the ceramic mic impedance is mostly capacitive reactance.)

Net impedance of C1 in series with R1 at 1 KHz = 101 ohms.

Net impedance of 9K ceramic mic in parallel with R3 = 8,257 ohms.

Multiplying these net impedances by I_n gives the noise voltages:

$$101 \times (7 \times 10^{-13}) = 0.07 \text{ nv}$$

$$8,257 \times (7 \times 10^{-13}) = 5.8 \text{ nv}$$

Next, determine thermal noise of the net impedance at each input of the LM833:

$$[101 \times (1.64 \times 10^{-20})]^{0.5} = 1.3 \text{ nv}$$

$$[8257 \times (1.64 \times 10^{-20})]^{0.5} = 11.6 \text{ nv}$$

We now have five noise sources:

1. Op amp E_n = 4.5 nv
2. $I_n \times R_s$ noise for 101 ohms = 0.07 nv
3. $I_n \times R_s$ noise for 8257 ohms = 5.8 nv
4. Thermal noise of 101 ohms = 1.3 nv
5. Thermal noise of 8257 ohms = 11.6 nv

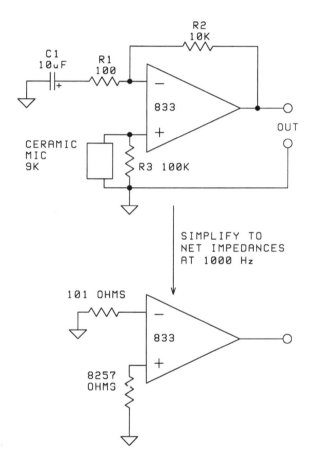

PREAMPLIFIER NOISE ANALYSIS

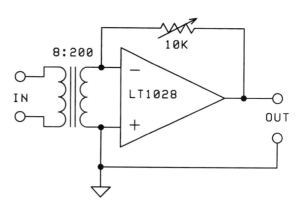

Add these terms in quadrature, the root of the sum of the squares:

$$[(4.5 \times 10^{-9})^2 + (0.07 \times 10^{-9})^2 + (5.8 \times 10^{-9})^2 + (1.3 \times 10^{-9})^2$$
$$+ (11.6 \times 10^{-9})^2]^{0.5}$$

$$= \quad [(2.0 \times 10^{-17}) + (4.9 \times 10^{-21}) + (3.4 \times 10^{-17}) + (1.7 \times 10^{-18}) +$$
$$(1.3 \times 10^{-16})]^{0.5}$$

$$= \quad 13.6 \text{ nv/rtHz}$$

Not bad. The ceramic mic sounds quieter than an electret having the same impedance because it generates no FET self-noise.

The exercise also enables calculation of what each source contributes to total noise. This assessment must take place while each term is squared. Summing all squared noise terms and ranking them for percentage of total:

Total of squared noise terms	=	1.9×10^{-16} nv^2	= 100%
thermal noise of 8,257 ohms	=	1.3×10^{-16} nv^2	= 68%
$I_n \times R_s$ noise of 8,257 ohms	=	3.4×10^{-17} nv^2	= 18%
E_n of LM833	=	2.0×10^{-17} nv^2	= 11%
thermal noise of 101 ohms	=	1.7×10^{-18} nv^2	= 1%
$I_n \times R_s$ noise of 101 ohms	=	4.9×10^{-21} nv^2	= 0%

(Percentages do not total 100% due to rounding.)

The culprit is revealed. If the agent required a quieter system, the most effective measure would be to lower the source impedance, which would also reduce the second most important noise source, $I_n \times R_s$ noise. Only if these two indices' total dropped below 4.5 nv would a quieter chip reduce noise significantly.

Quick second example, the LT1028 speaker-mic preamp shown below.

$$E_n = 0.9 \text{ nv}; \ I_n = 1 \text{ pa } R_s = 200 \text{ ohms.}$$

$$[(0.9 \times 10^{-9})^2 + (1.8 \times 10^{-9})^2 + (2 \times 10^{-10})^2]^{0.5}$$

$$= \quad [(8.1 \times 10^{-19}) + (3.2 \times 10^{-18}) + (4 \times 10^{-20})]^{0.5}$$

$$= \quad 2.0 \text{ nv/rtHz}$$

Notice that the source is a DC path that serves as the inverting input resistance and that grounding the unused input has eliminated two noise terms compared to the prior example.

Two nanovolts total—plus 14 dB of transformer gain? Now we're cookin' . . .

black boxes whose performance closely matches prediction. On the downside, they cost more than transistors and tend increasingly to leave an acquisition trail.

Some op amps come in series whose part numbers share a common prefix, coupled with a final digit to distinguish single, dual, or quad. For example, "TL07X series" means that TL071 (single), TL072 (dual), and TL074 (quad) types exist.

The builder can choose any op amp, including types not discussed in this text. But, before chancing the unknown, he should read the op-amp data sheet and note the following variables:

- E_n and I_n
- "absolute maximum ratings," which specify supply or input voltages that will damage the amp
- a nonstandard pinout
- stability requirements
- special features, such as pins devoted to offset trim, bias, etc.

Data sheets are available individually from the manufacturer of the chip, usually free of charge; but the serious builder should front $60 or so to get a set of databooks containing data sheets for hundreds of op amps and related parts. Databooks are bursting with circuits that have immediate bugging applications.

OP AMP SUBTYPES

Op amps come in so many species that some parts catalogs resemble op-amp boutiques. These subtypes are categorized in many ways, the most useful to the bugger being:

- low noise
- low voltage
- low power
- micropower
- high speed
- high power

Specialization grew out of the impossibility of optimizing everything in one device. Ultralow noise dictates that the internal transistors run at high collector current. That, in turn, means high supply current but also coincides with the option to incorporate high speed. An op amp built to run on low current sets the minimum noise level by virtue of the inverse relationship between E_n and I_c, and also limits maximum speed.

LOW NOISE

Up to the end of the 1970s, common op amps generated more noise than the thermal noise of their source impedances. Buggers worked around high noise by creating low-noise hybrids that preceded the op-amp input with a differential amp made from discrete transistors.

The first "super-low-noise" op amps, Signetics' 5534A/5532 series, gave E_n 3.5 nv and 5 nv, respectively. These amps were among the first to generate significantly less noise than common source impedances. Combined with their ability to drive a 600-ohm load, they quickly became an audio standard. Op amps have been getting quieter ever since, with E_n currently hovering around 800 picovolts.

A useful guide in choosing a low-noise op amp is the value of source impedance whose thermal noise equals the chip's E_n. Common values include the following:

- LF347/TL084   39,000 ohms
- TL071   20,000 ohms
- LM833/5532   1,250 ohms
- OP-27   550 ohms
- MAX410   200 ohms
- LT1028   61 ohms
- MAX4106   44 ohms

Choosing a transducer with an impedance greater than the value listed makes transducer thermal noise the predominant source of noise in the system.

Many op amps older than five years are *second sourced*, meaning that the firm that originally designed, and perhaps patented, the amp has licensed manufacture to others. Second-sourcing has made bargains of older chips. The latest high-performance single might give twice the performance of an old standard but cost several times as much; compare the OP-27/37 (E_n 3 nv, ~\$2) to the LT1028 (E_n 1 nv, ~\$9). A source impedance >500 ohms makes the difference moot.

LOW POWER

Low-power op amps draw significantly less than 1 milliamp each. The LF44X, TL06X, and MC3317X series each clock in at about a quarter-milliamp per amp; one milliamp or less per quad. Low power incurs relatively high noise, so these chips suit buffers, active filters, and control-voltage generators. A preamp should use a quieter chip. Note that current refers only to that drawn by the amp itself, not current the amp sources into a load.

MICROPOWER

Micropower op amps draw <100 µa apiece. In keeping with unavoidable semiconductor behavior, noise is higher and speed lower than in low-power op amps. Micropower op amps are useful in sensor applications that generate only a DC output, such as comparators to sense a phone to be off the hook. Their use in the signal path is usually accompanied by intrusive noise. Micropower op amps enable the design of bugs whose life is measured in years, because op amp current is less than the leakage current of some batteries. Life of the device equals shelf life of the battery.

The MAX478 dual draws 17 µa per op amp, with E_n 49 nv, I_n .01 pa. The amp can provide up to 30 dB of gain at 1 KHz. The MAX406 draws 1.2 µa quiescent current; it can source 600 µa, sink 200 µa, and carries E_n of 150 nv/rtHz. It, too, can provide up to 30 dB of gain at 1 KHz.

LOW SUPPLY VOLTAGE

Most op amps are characterized while running off a ±15V supply. While many will function down to ±3V, some do not deliver rated specs at low voltage. Low-voltage denotes types that are either optimized for low voltage or maintain high-voltage specs at low voltage. The LM324 and the Motorola MC3317X series will function down to ±1.5V

The MAX41X series will run off ±2.4-5V (>10V will damage the chip) yet delivers E_n 1.8 nv, I_n 1.2 pa, and has enough speed for ultrasonic gain stages. An ideal choice for battery-powered gear and low-impedance sources.

The LM4250 op amp can run off as little as 2V and contains a bias-select pin to program the amp for low-power or micropower operation. For single-cell applications, the LM10 will run off 1.1V.

HIGH SPEED

The bugging scene is strewn with tools needing gain applied over the range 20 KHz to the low megahertz. Op amps comfortable here are defined as high-speed. Speed shows up in slew-rate (SR) and gain-bandwidth product (GBW), not always helpful figures for nonengineers. To assess the suitability of an op amp for ultrasonic gain, go to the open-loop gain curve; read gain vs. frequency off the graph.

Some well-known op amps are sold in two versions: the standard "compensated" type, which is stable at unity gain, and a high-speed "uncompensated" version, which often requires more than unity gain for stable operation. The OP-27 is compensated and is stable at unity gain; the OP-37 is an uncompensated '27, requiring minimum gain of 5 for stable operation, or requiring an external stability network. Uncompensated types average 10–20 dB more high-frequency gain than their compensated twins.

Instability parallels speed. The higher the speed of the op amp, the more the user should limit bandwidth to the frequencies of interest and take special care in bypass. The fastest amps demand ground-plane construction.

Op amps useful into the ultrasonic include OP-37, LT1028, and MAX437.

HIGH OUTPUT CURRENT

A laser emitter hidden atop the Seagram Building will beam audio from a bug directly to a satellite. The laser needs half an amp of drive current. Controlling that current is easily managed by an op amp driving a power transistor. But an op amp with enough drive power could run the diode directly, saving board space in size-critical applications.

Power op amps are optimized for drive current and noise and are speed secondary, though high current and high speed often coincide. The LT1010 will drive 250 milliamps; the LH0101, 2A continuous current, 5A peak. The LM12 can put ±10A @ ±35V into a 4-ohm load, 150 watts RMS, up to 800 watts peak. The LM12 comes in a TO-3 case and demands a substantial heatsink.

DISCRETE-TRANSISTOR AMPS

- *cheapest, most versatile audio amp*
- *cascadable to boost gain or sharpen frequency contour*
- *noise: when run at collector current (I_C) ~1 ma, common small-signal transistors can be as quiet as low-noise op amps (OP-27, 5534, etc.)*

A) NPN transistor as common-emitter amplifier. R1 and R2 bias the transistors into an ON state; R4 determines collector current, R3 determines "emitter degeneration." Theoretical gain = R4 / R3; gain somewhat lower in practice. To work up this configuration on the breadboard, choose supply voltage; choose collector current (approximated by $I_C = [1/2V+] / R3$); choose gain, approximated by R4/R3; for theoretical maximum gain let R3 = 0. Then, using a 100K pot with wiper tied to base and the ends to V+ and ground, measure collector voltage, adjust pot until it reads roughly 1/2V+. Substitute closest value standard resistors for wings of pot; test for gain on breadboard. Experimentation will show that available one-stage gain rises with supply voltage and that transistors with different DC current gain ("beta") will require different bias resistors.

B) Another common-emitter amplifier, but base is biased from positive DC potential at collector, through R1. Because output taken at collector is inverted compared to input at base, R1 supplies negative feedback. This results in slightly less gain than two-resistor base bias but also tends to even out differences among transistors and tolerates variations in supply voltage better than two-resistor bias. To work up this type on breadboard, choose supply voltage and collector current as above; choose desired gain, approximated by R2 / R3; for maximum gain let R3 = 0. Place 2 meg pot between base and collector, attach voltmeter to collector; adjust pot until collector is at 1/2V+. Note that, in low-voltage circuits (<3V), bias may have to come through a single resistor tied to V+.

C) Ratio of collector impedance to emitter impedance approximates gain of common-emitter amp. This circuit sets DC bias as in "B," but emitter impedance has been markedly reduced by bypass capacitor C2. Thus, gain of this stage rises above a point that depends on relative values of C2 and R3; specifically, transition frequency f = 1 / (6.28RC), where R is in ohms and C is in farads. For example, if R2 = 2.2K, and R3 = 1K, DC gain is roughly 2.2. But if C2 = 1µF, then gain rises at 6 dB per octave above 160 Hz. This shows one means to implement the bug EQ curve in the preamplifier.

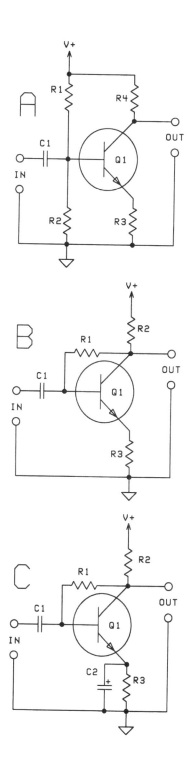

DISCRETE-TRANSISTOR AMPS

D) Two identical stages coupled by C4. Note polarity: Q1 collector is at a higher DC potential than base of Q2; therefore, connect positive cap terminal to Q1 collector. Gain contour from low to high frequencies will depend in part on transition frequencies of R2–C2 and R6–C5. Gain slope now 12 dB/octave, twice as steep as single stage. In practice, this gain continues to rise into ultrasonic and RF ranges unless actively suppressed. C3 shows one way, in parallel with feedback resistor; C6 shows a second way, in parallel with collector resistor.

E) Putting theory into practice. Chosen supply 7.5V. Q1 is 2N5089, a high-beta low-noise type. Collector current for both transistors chosen is fairly high, between 1 and 2 ma. DC gain is 2.2, set by the ratio of R3 to R2. Emitter bypass cap C2 gives treble gain that approaches the transistor's beta. Second stage configured to boost output by ~20 dB. Also, a different transistor has been used, requiring different bias; collector feedback found to be 617K, 620K closest standard value.

On the breadboard, device measured 27 dB of gain at 100 Hz, 45 dB at 4 KHz. High gain and presence of several active devices on same power bus demand bypass cap C8. Stably coupling this preamp to a power driver, such as an LM386, will demand even stronger bypass. Transistor amplifiers can be much more complex, yet these few unfastidious rules let the designer work up the audio gain stage he needs empirically, in minutes.

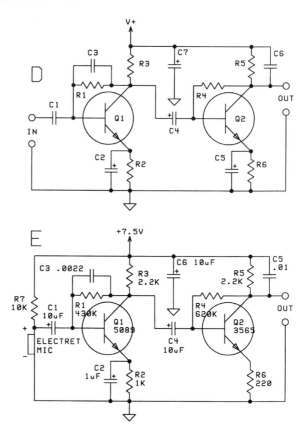

LM381

- single supply, 9–30V (40V for "A" version)
- 14-pin DIP
- dual channel
- asymmetrical supply terminals
- noise: ~5 nv/rtHz (comparable to 5,532/833 op amps)
- bias output at 1/2V+ for maximum headroom
- collector of input transistor externally accessible (pins 5 and 11)
- open loop gain 85 dB @ 1 KHz; hot performer
- a legend in bugging circles, the "Ultralow-Noise Preamplifier," realized by optimizing collector current ("B" below)
- availability: NTE942, ~$10

Exportable audio preamps based on LM381.

A) Standard, single-ended configuration, biased for 9.0V (not alkaline or nicad; a true 9.0V). Gain and low-frequency response selectable by choice of R1 and C1; 10 ohms and 33µF give a hot performer.

B) The "ultralow-noise" configuration. R2 and R3 tie directly to collector of internal input transistor, raising collector current to lower input noise voltage (but raising input noise current); 10µF cap at their juncture decouples this path. Trim 10K pot to give 1/2V+ at output.

C) Working with source impedances greater than 1K, which most bugging tools do, defeats the point of special collector bias. This circuit bypasses R1 with C2 to skew the gain heavily into the treble; realizes bug EQ in single, low-noise stage. In all cases, if signal source has DC offset more positive than that of pin 1, reverse polarity of 10µF input coupling cap, or use a bipolar cap. Ceramic mics need no coupling cap. In all three circuits, the 0.001µF cap across pin 1–pin 3 is an RF shunt.

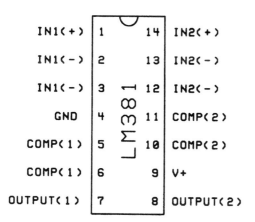

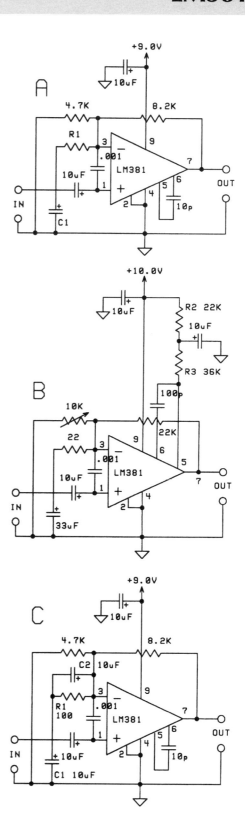

LM387

- single supply, 9–30V (40V for "A" version)
- dual channel
- 8-pin DIP
- input noise: ~7 nv/rtHz
- bias output at 1/2V+
- internally the same as LM381, but true single-ended use is not possible
- cost: ~$2
- availability: Digi-Key; NTE824

Exportable audio preamps built around LM387.

A) Manufacturer's circuit: flat 20–20,000 Hz, gain 60 dB. Not much use in covert work; 600-ohm series resistor adds noise.

B) Covert-ready building block; bug EQ built in, taps 387's maximum open-loop gain, biased for true 9.0V, compensated for stray capacitance and shunted for RF. Piezo transducers may omit 10µF coupling cap into pin 1. Reverse polarity of 10µF input cap for electret condenser mic.

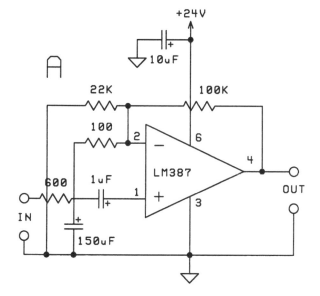

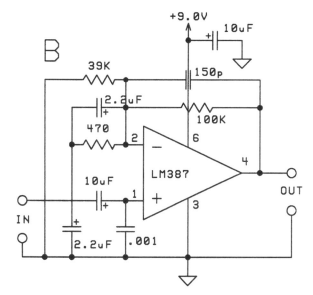

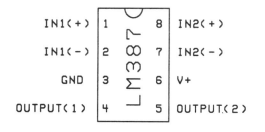

SSM2017

- dual supply, ±6–22V
- single channel
- 8-pin DIP
- noise: E_n 0.95 nv / rtHz (extremely low); I_n 2 pa/rtHz (very high)
- thermal noise of 75-ohm source exceeds chip's E_n
- $I_n \times R_s$ noise predominates with source impedances >2K ohms
- counterproductive to use this chip with source impedances greater than 1.5K ohms
- gain determined by single resistor or pot, 0–70 dB
- current consumption: typically 11 ma, both supplies
- bandwidth >1 MHz; needs RF-quality bypass
- output needs to see load >2K
- shunt inputs w/cap to prevent high-frequency oscillation
- availability: scarce; PAiA Electronics
- cost: ~$4

Exportable preamps using SSM2017.

A) Inputs biased in pseudodifferential mode; dynamic mic couples directly; let R1 = R2 = 10 times microphone impedance. R3 sets gain at 40 dB.

B) Inputs biased in single-ended mode, dynamic mic couples directly. Note that if value of R3 is lowered to raise gain, a significant DC offset can develop at output, necessitating offset trim network; thus, this configuration suits only moderate gain.

C) True differential input configuration. No external biasing network needed, gain can be set by single pot or resistor R3; only a small DC offset occurs, even at maximum gain. In all circuits, the 0.01µF cap across inputs prevents high-frequency oscillation and shunts RF. Cap value suitable for source impedance up to 1K. Also, source impedance (or transformer secondary winding impedance) should not exceed 1.5K to avoid excessive $I_n \times R_s$ noise. Chip gives least total noise with source impedances <250 ohms.

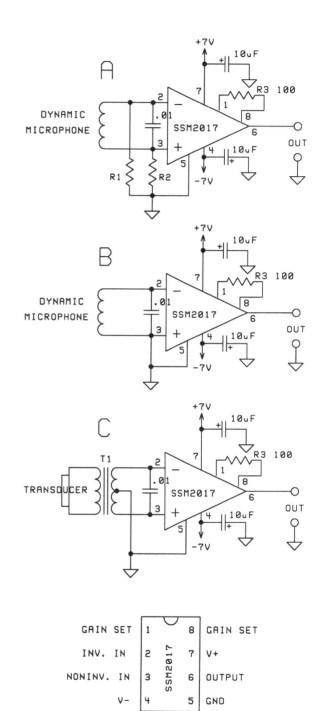

OP-AMP BASICS

A) Standard op amp schematic symbol. Observe polarity of bypass capacitors. For simplicity, power supply terminals and bypass capacitors are often omitted from op amp schematics. Standard pinouts of op amps in dual inline packages:

B) single

C) dual

D) quad. Package orientation per notch, pit, white stripe, or some combination of those on one end. Note that quad op amp power supply pins are reversed compared to single and dual packages.

E) The most common method to power an op amp, true dual supply. Value of positive and negative supplies (V+ and V-, respectively) should be equal.

F) To run an op amp from a single supply, it is necessary to create a bias potential equal to half the value of V+. A resistive voltage divider, such as R1–R2, is one common means to do this. This "rail splitting" creates an "artificial ground," merely a bias potential the op amp needs to place it in a linear operating mode. The battery negative terminal becomes V-. Divider biasing will suffice for circuits of low to moderate gain. "Bypass capacitors" are usually necessary to stability in op amp circuits.

Graph shows open-loop gain curves for several common devices. To determine what gain an op amp can supply at a given frequency, consult the open loop gain curve. An LM324 might give 52 dB at 1 KHz; an LM381, about 85 dB. Virtually all op amp data sheets print open loop gain curves. LF353 is a common FET-input op amp. LM359 is a high-speed current-differencing (Norton) amplifier. (Curves redrawn after manufacturers' data.)

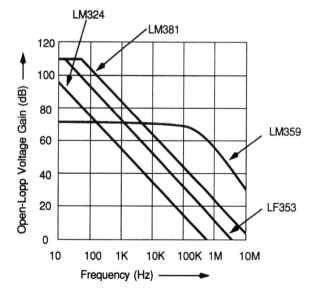

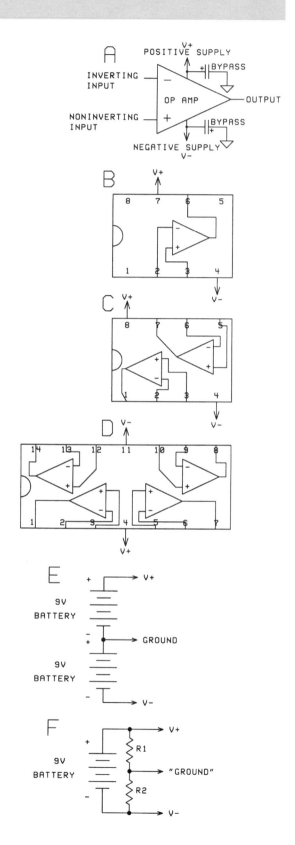

OP-AMP BUILDING BLOCKS

Eighty percent of analog bugging gear can be constructed from these op-amp building blocks. To get the most out of them, and to suggest new possibilities, think of substituting frequency-dependent impedances for the resistors. This holds the key to selective gain control.

A) standard inverting amplifier
B) noninverting amplifier
C) differential amplifier, also known as a subtractor. To attain peak common mode rejection of which a differential amp is capable, resistor match must be perfect. Since this proves impractical without resorting to expensive matched resistors, R4 is often made a trimpot. Apply common mode signal to both inputs; trim R4 for best common-mode rejection.

D) summing amplifier (inverting type), also known as a mixer

E) DC voltage follower
F) AC voltage follower supplies its own bias through R1; AC signal couples through C1. Voltage followers are often used as buffers. A buffer is a device with high input impedance, low output impedance, used to drive tape outputs or match a high source impedance to a low-impedance stage.

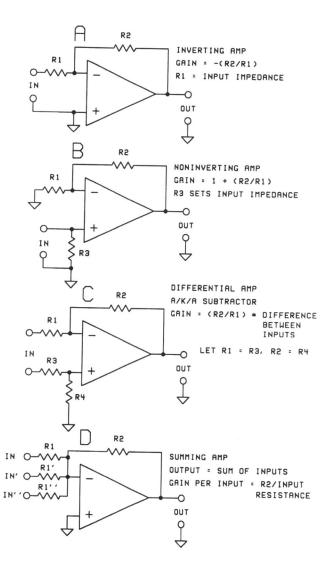

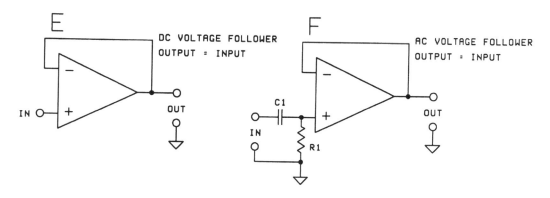

OP-AMP PREAMPS

A) Generic noninverting configuration can meet >90 percent of covert preamp needs. Gain = 1 + [[impedance 2) ÷ (impedance 1)]]. Because both impedances are frequency-dependent, control of low- and high-frequency gain can be achieved in one stage. Sequential caps C1 and C2 give theoretical impedance near zero at a frequency dependent on their values. At that point the op amp delivers maximum gain, in keeping with open loop gain curve. This high-frequency emphasis destabilizes many op amps, making C3 do double duty as stray-capacitance compensation and as a high-frequency gain limiter. R3 sets input impedance; choose value 10 times source impedance to minimize loading losses.

B) Concrete embodiment of op amp preamp; has countless uses: spike mics, hose mics, boundary mics, contact mics, inductive probes, RF transmitter preamps, optical bug preamps, etc. Omit C1 if maximum gain is not needed.

C) Differential amp useful for balanced inputs, such as studio microphone. Obvious drawback is noise of two 1K series resistors. Still, with quiet op amp, this type of circuit is useable with low-impedance transducers (<200 ohms) at up to 40 dB of gain.

D) Inverting amp that uses transducer impedance to set gain. Most useful for inductive probes, conventional dynamic mics, speakers used as microphones, and transformer secondaries.

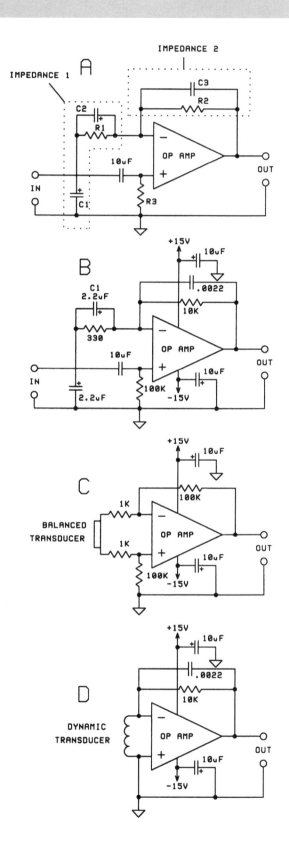

CHAPTER 3

Dynamic Control

In amplitude terms, the difference between a sigh and a gunshot may span 100 dB. Professional bugging gear must handle it. Trouble is, a system tweaked to hear cheerleaders cooing in the other end zone will make a sneeze sound like Hendrix at Monterey. The disparity conveys an intuitive rationale for dynamic control.

Dynamic management avoids overloading transmission/storage media. It frees the operator from having to ride the gain. Veteran field operatives praise the comfort factor. Nothing takes the agent out of his game quicker than constant cacophony.

This function settles comfortably into four categories: clip limiting, compression, non-clip limiting, and automatic gain control.

CLIP LIMITING

Clipping has much to commend it. It's the simplest, cheapest way to cap dynamic range, and it's the stingiest in terms of printed circuit real estate. It consumes no power. For those reasons clipping is probably the predominant form of dynamic control in bugs.

Two diodes will implement clipping. They fit conveniently at two points in the signal path: (1) as a cap-coupled path to ground, or (2) in the feedback loop of an op amp.

Silicon small-signal diodes turn on at about 0.6V, germanium diodes at about 0.35V. The clip level is twice the turn-on voltage: $1.2V_{p-p}$ for silicon diodes, $0.7V_{p-p}$ for germanium diodes.

The designer who needs a higher clip level can wire several diodes in series or use diodes that have higher voltage drops. Red, green, and blue light-emitting diodes (LEDs) turn on, respectively, at about 1.7V, 2.2V, and 3.4V. LEDs used for clipping should be coated with black paint or otherwise shielded from light.

A clipped waveform resembles a squarewave, rich in odd-order harmonics that lend speech a Donald-Duckish tenor that doesn't necessarily detract from intelligibility. Some aircraft/spacecraft communications systems clip as part of speech-enhancement processing.

The fact that clipping generates high-frequency harmonics becomes significant in systems in which clipped audio feeds an ultrasonic FM stage. Harmonics can cause aliasing of a frequency modulator and, for that reason, should be removed by a lowpass filter.

COMPRESSION

Compression cramps the waveform without chopping it off. The result sounds a lot more natural than clipping.

Most compressors are voltage-controlled amplifiers (VCAs) that change gain on the fly. They derive a control voltage by sampling audio at some point in the signal path, then rectifying it or taking the root mean square (rms), sometimes the log of the voltage. The resultant varying DC feeds a VCA control port. Sampling signal before compression runs the compressor in parallel mode; sampling the output of the compressor itself runs it in feedback mode. In practice, the action of a parallel control loop tends to be more conspicuous than that of a feedback loop.

Compressors activate at a level known as threshold. The amount of gain reduction above (or boost below) threshold is defined by a compression ratio, which may be stated in linear terms or in dB.

Compression comes in many flavors, the most common being downward-only or "single-ended." In this mode signals below threshold pass at unity gain. Signals above threshold are diminished according to the compression ratio. For instance, if threshold is $1V_{p-p}$ and linear compression ratio 4:1, a $2V_{p-p}$ input will emerge from the compressor as $1V + (1V \div 4) =$

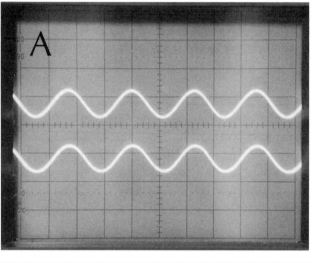

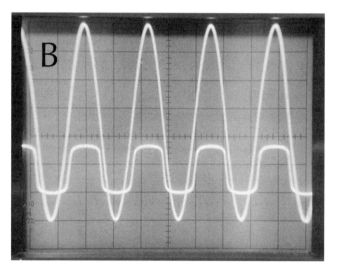

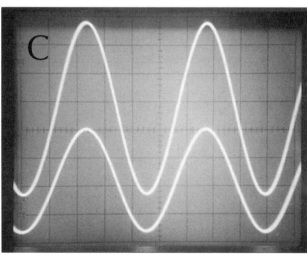

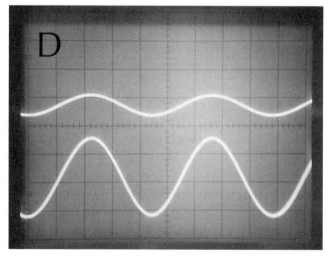

A) top trace diode clipper input, bottom trace clipper output, scale 0.5V/div., germanium diodes

B) top trace input, bottom trace shows clipped output; does not exceed ~800 mv$_{p-p}$

C) scale 1V/div.; top trace shows input to 570 compressor, bottom trace shows output

D) As in C, but scale changed to 200 mv/div.; top trace input, bottom trace output. Double-ended compression makes loud sounds softer, soft sounds louder.

$1.25V_{p-p}$. If threshold were lowered to $0.5V_{p-p}$, and ratio to 3:1, the same $2V_{p-p}$ input would emerge as $.5V + [(2V - 0.5V) \div 3] = 1V_{p-p}$.

Double-ended compression limits signal above threshold but also boosts signal below threshold in keeping with the compression ratio. For threshold set at $2V_{p-p}$ and linear ratio at 4:1, an input of $1V_{p-p}$ would emerge as $1V + [(2V - 1V) - (1V \div 4)] = 1.75V_{p-p}$. Double-ended compression tries to keep the signal at threshold; the compression ratio determines how hard it tries. High threshold combined with high compression ratio gives the sound typical of hard rock FM stations, which squeeze practically all dynamic range out of their feeds.

Unlike clip limiting, compression takes time to kick in, known as attack. The time compression takes to cease once signal has fallen below threshold is known as decay. Due to the nature of sonic transients, attack should happen faster than decay. Typical attack times range from a few hundred µs to 10 ms. Decay happens more slowly, 50 ms to several seconds.

Attack and decay determine what frequencies a compressor can process while keeping a natural sound. Mismatch between time constants and frequency can cause the compressor to decay between individual cycles of signal, with resultant distortion. Slow attack and release make compressor action audible as "breathing" or "pumping."

Attack, decay, threshold, and ratio are independently adjustable on most studio compressors. Bugging gear has simpler needs. For covert intercepts, attack and release should suit the midrange from about 500–4,000 Hz. Bass should be sharply attenuated before the feed gets to the compressor to avoid modulating the midrange.

Non-clip limiting is a special form of single-ended compression with a fixed, infinite compression ratio. Signal is not allowed to increase once it passes threshold. In practice, a linear compression ratio >15:1 is considered limiting.

Automatic gain controls (AGCs) are double-ended compressors that attack slowly and decay very slowly. They're meant to hold average system output constant over a wide range of inputs. Rather than dealing with signal on a millisecond-to-millisecond basis, they look at a longer average. Release times range from several hundred ms to one minute.

CLIP LIMITING

- *cheapest, simplest means to control dynamics*
- *clip level selected in choice of drop per diode*
- *cost: pennies*
- *availability: universal*

   Four examples of diode-clipped stages.
   A) Typical transistor stage cap-coupled to dual diodes, in turn coupled through C2 to next stage.
   B) Some stages poorly tolerate the loading effect of diodes; R1 relieves load; diode pair cap-coupled to ground.
   C) Typical op amp stage, diodes in feedback loop. In this case clipping sounds smoother than signal-path clipping because what's actually happening is logarithmic amplification. Signal will continue to rise above the nominal clip threshold, but at that point it is well into the flat part of the log curve, so little increase in output level occurs. In all cases that use double parallel diodes, clip level roughly equals twice diode drop—0.7V for germanium, 1.2V for silicon.
   D) Zener diodes in series give clip level roughly twice zener voltage plus one silicon diode drop. Many other means exist to implement diode clip-limiting.

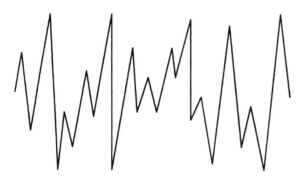

RAW AUDIO IN

CLIPPED AUDIO OUT

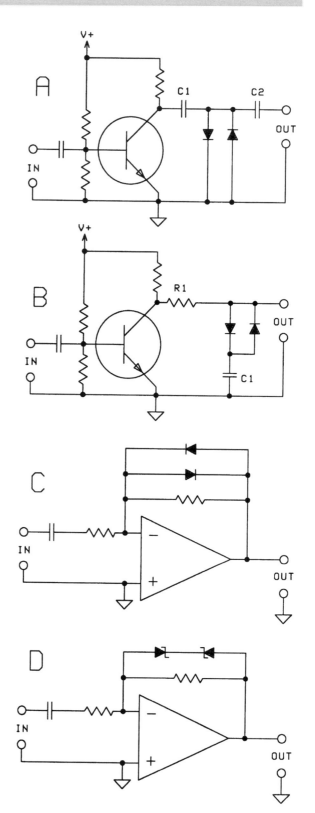

NE570/571

- 16-pin DIP
- single supply, 6–18V (NE571), 6–24V (NE570)
- dual channel
- power consumption <4 ma; suits battery-powered gear
- built-in compression function approximates x0.5; expansion approximates x2
- internal op amps comparable to 741 type
- boost performance by using external op amps
- must bias output at 1/2V+
- trimmable functions: harmonic distortion, DC envelope bounce, low-level mistracking; these trims are not used in most covert gear
- must know DC offsets to orient polarized capacitors properly: pins 2 (15), 3 (14), 5 (12), 6 (11), and 8 (9) are at about +1.8V; pin 1 (16) is slightly above ground; pin 7 (10) should be at 1/2V+
- availability: good—DC Electronics, Hosfelt
- cost: $1.90–$4.00

Exportable 570/571 circuits (only one channel shown).

A) The databook standard compressor configuration. Note orientation of polarized caps. Changing V+ will necessitate change in values of R1 and R2, because those values also set DC bias of output pin 7. Alternatively, a trim potential can be applied to pin 5 (12).

B) The databook AGC schematic. Device "tries" as hard as it can, within gain limits of internal op amp, to keep applied signal at threshold. The only difference between AGC and compressor is that AGC takes rectifier input directly off the input signal, making control loop parallel, compared to feedback control loop in compressor.

C) Identical to B, but external op amp gives device greater maximum gain. Use DC trim network R2–3 to set DC output of U2 at 1/2V+. Threshold of all three circuits is ~2V$_{p-p}$.

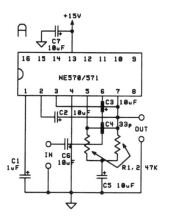

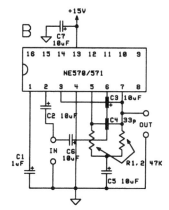

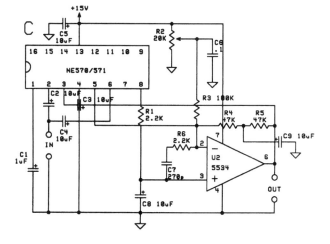

CHANNEL 1			CHANNEL 2
RECTIFIER CAPACITOR	1	16	RECTIFIER CAPACITOR
RECTIFIER INPUT	2	15	RECTIFIER INPUT
GAIN CELL INPUT	3	14	GAIN CELL INPUT
GND	4	13	V+
OP AMP INPUT	5	12	OP AMP INPUT
20K RESISTOR TO PIN 5	6	11	20K RESISTOR TO PIN 12
OP AMP OUTPUT	7	10	OP AMP OUTPUT
THD TRIM	8	9	THD TRIM

NE570/571

NE570/571

A) Non-clip limiter follows Signetics' databook design. Gain of internal op amp set at unity by ratio of 100K resistors. Output sampled by two comparators, one biased at (1.8V − .5V), the other at (1.8V + .5V). Audio that exceeds $1V_{p-p}$ trips either or both comparators, turning Q1 on, activating gain cell, all in <1ms. Attack determined by time constant of R1 and C1, decay by C1 and 10K resistance inside the 570/571.

B) The Basement Bugger's version of same circuit more practical for battery-powered gear, simplified by

elimination of one comparator. Delay in detecting first half-cycle of transient goes unnoticed in covert applications. Also, comparator bias has been made adjustable by 10K pot, and independent of system supply by 5V regulator. Threshold adjustable from $\sim 1.1V_{p-p}$ to $\sim 5V_{p-p}$. Note that resistance values have changed to keep DC bias of output pin 7 at 1/2V+. System tuned for "9V" nicad, which averages 7.5V. Circuit works superbly to limit sudden, loud peaks; its operating mode makes it a poor choice for limiting constant tones, however.

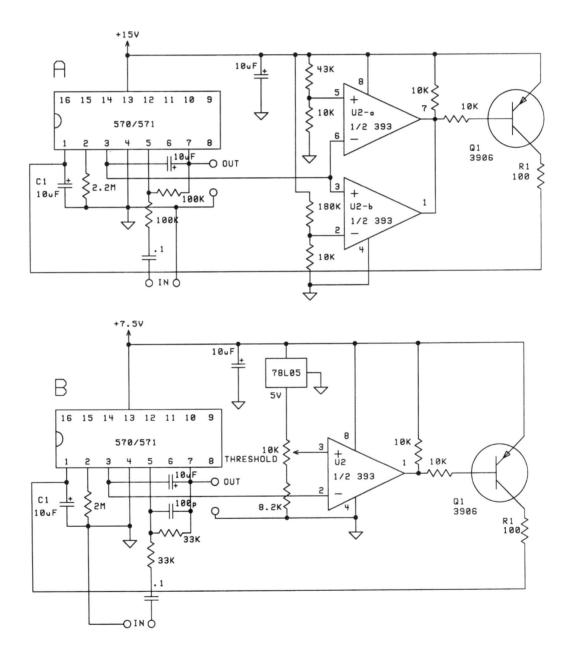

SSM2120

- 22-pin DIP (0.3" spacing; sockets rare)
- dual supply, ±5–18V
- current consumption <12 ma both supplies
- dual channel
- studio quality; suits bench gear more than portable
- can be configured as compressor, AGC, expander, noise gate, or dynamic filter
- requires external op amp
- availability: scarce in hobby channels; PAiA Electronics is one source
- cost: ~$15 with shipping

Exportable downward-only compressor using one channel of SSM2120. Feedback control loop. R8 varies compression ratio over the rough range 1.4:1-10:1. R2 varies threshold from several hundred millivolts to several volts$_{p-p}$. C2 controls (mainly) decay time. Small value shown suits bug-band intercepts. Increase C2 for signals of wider bandwidth. Although chip will function over the supply ±5–18V, changing supply voltage will necessitate changing values of several resistors to avoid shifts in threshold and ratio. High-frequency oscillation sometimes noted at control-out terminal; can be suppressed with cap in parallel with R7. The 2120 operates so smoothly that the average listener may not hear it in action, despite a dB compression ratio greater than 2:1.

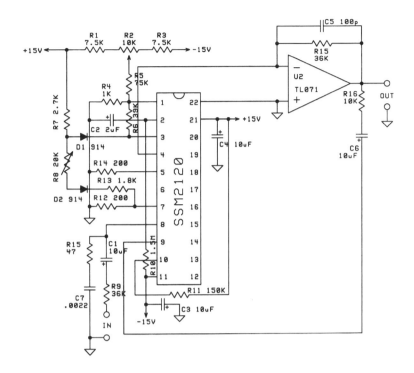

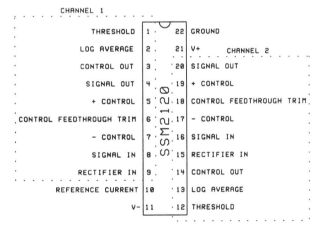

CHARGED PUMP DEVICES

- *The five dynamic controllers following this page derive control voltage from a charge pump.*
- *Charge pump generates positive or negative DC from an audio feed.*
- *Use control voltage to activate chips, FETs, or bipolar transistors to alter gain.*
- *Generally, charge pump should be driven by its own amplifier.*

A and B) simple, exportable charge pumps. Audio couples through C1 to diode pair configured as halfwave rectifier; diodes typically 1N914; use germanium (1N34A, 1N60, 1N270, etc.) for low-level applications. Observe polarity of output capacitor C2.

C and D) block diagrams of common automatic gain controls that use a charge pump

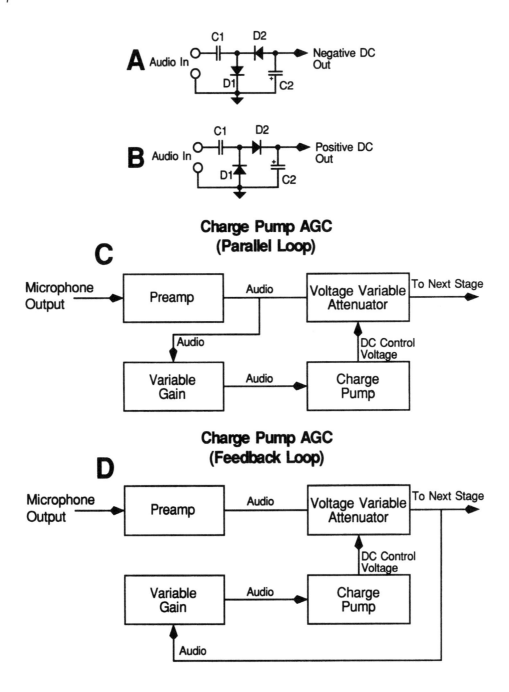

FET DIVIDER AGC

- field-effect transistor drain-source path serves as a shunt to ground at high-impedance node
- simple, cheap; can be implemented in a variety of ways
- performance: very good, downward-only compression
- examples below use N-channel JFETs
- P-channel JFETs use control voltages of opposite polarity to those of N-channel JFETs
- availability: excellent; most FETs will work
- cost: $0.50–$1.00

A) Generic example of FET divider principle. With FET gate held at V– in resting state by R3, drain-source path is essentially an open circuit. Has no effect on signal traversing R1 and C1. As a progressively higher positive voltage is applied to FET gate through R2, drain-source channel resistance falls, bottoming out at ~10–250 ohms, depending

on FET. Coupled through C2 to "high-impedance node," this makes an AC voltage divider with R1. Since R1 impedance is many times that of FET drain-source resistance, audio amplitude is reduced by divider action.

B) Exportable device. Circuit inside dotted line is a preamp with roughly 60 dB of gain at 3 KHz. Its output is taken off collector biased through 4.7K resistor, a "high-impedance node." Signal at that point feeds a positive charge pump made up of Q1 and associated components. Variable voltage is available through wiper of R4, tied to gate of Q2, held low in resting state by R5. Note that, in this single-supply circuit, Q2 source has been biased at 1/2V+, so gate is fooled into thinking that R5 is tied to a negative voltage. As audio level rises, Q2 drain-source path turns on, shunting audio through C1 at a high-impedance node, which is also the take-off point for the next stage. This configuration has high distortion but is simple and adequate for covert work.

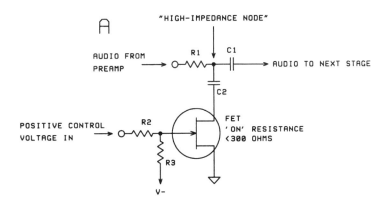

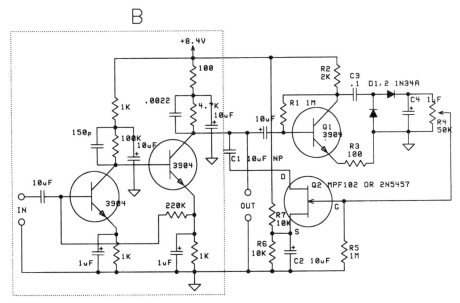

MC1350

- *8-pin DIP*
- *single supply, 6–15V*
- *single channel*
- *a/k/a MC1490 (8-pin DIP) and MC1590 (metal can case; pinout differs)*
- *bandwidth >100 MHz; originally designed as RF/IF amp and AGC*
- *availability: good—Hosfelt Electronics, DC Electronics*
- *cost: $1*

The 1350 is meant for balanced inputs and outputs that occur in IF strips; it proves slightly tricky to use for audio AGC. Line-level signal is reduced 34 dB by divider R3–4. Audio couples to one input through C5; other input is grounded through C3. In resting state, with no AGC applied, net input-output gain is ~6 dB because AGC terminal is held near ground by R5. Audio taken off one output (pin 8) couples to variable positive charge pump made up of Q1 and surrounding components. As positive voltage fed to pin 5 through R6 increases, 1350 gain decreases. Values shown allow minimum threshold ~150 mv_{p-p}. Ratio is high enough to qualify as a limiter.

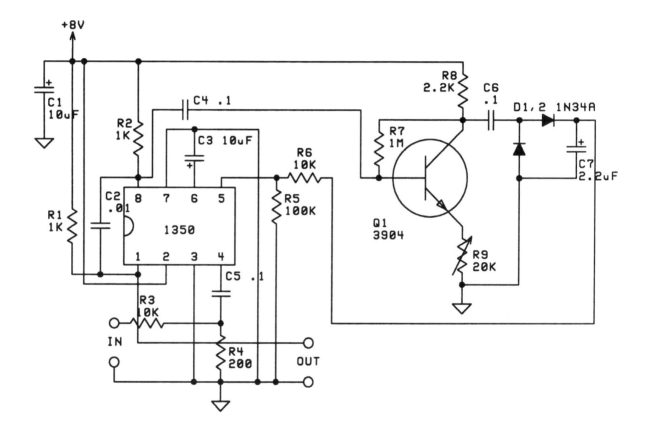

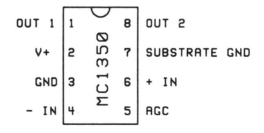

MC3340

- 8-pin DIP
- single supply, 9–18V
- single channel
- availability: Hosfelt Electronics, DC Electronics; also available as NTE829
- cost: $1.50–$2.00

The 3340 works like this: Line-level signal enters pin 1, emerges from pin 7. When pin 2 is at ground potential, chip applies its maximum gain of ~14 dB. As resistance between pin 2 and ground increases, attenuation of signal increases. While it is possible to apply a control voltage directly to pin 2, the tactic proved unsatisfactory due to high distortion. The exportable circuit shown here takes a different approach. Input network R1-2 divides the signal by ~5. Q1 in resting state is biased ON by R3, making drain-source resistance minimum, enough to run 3340 at maximum gain. Net effect of divider R1–2 and maximum

chip gain is unity gain in resting state. C3 couples a sample of audio output to Q2, configured as a common-emitter amplifier by R5-7, gain variable from –13 dB to +35 dB by R7. Q2 output couples through C4 to negative charge pump made up of D1-2 & C5. Thus, as 3340 audio output rises, the charge pump generates an increasingly negative potential coupled to gate of Q1 through R4. Negative voltage tends to pinch off Q1 drain-source channel, making it appear an open circuit to pin 2, increasing 3340 attenuation. Result: a downward-only compressor with threshold variable by R7 from several volts$_{p-p}$ to ~40mv$_{p-p}$. Signals below threshold pass unchanged. C5 affects attack and decay times; value can be reduced or increased as desired, but lower value will increase distortion. Value of C2 determines high-frequency response limit of chip. Increase C2 to lower the response. C3 decouples the supply. Smooth performer . . .

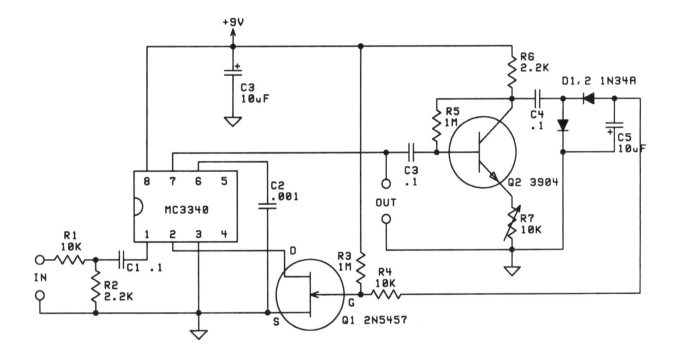

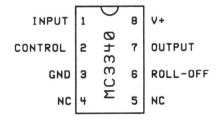

LIGHT-DEPENDENT RESISTORS

- *4-pin case, TO-39 style (VTL2C2) and irregular (CLM6000)*
- *LED and light-variable resistor potted together*
- *when LED intensity is HIGH, resistance goes LOW*
- *availability: Hosfelt Electronics*
- *cost: ~$4*

Two light-dependent resistors are commonly available in hobby channels, the Clairex CLM6000 and the VacTec VTL2C2. Both types contain a light-variable resistor whose dark value measures in excess of 20 megohms. With 17V fed to the LED through a 1,000-ohm resistor, my samples of each measured ~300 ohms. This reveals an extremely wide resistance range that, effectively, can be controlled by a voltage. Circuit shows a compressor that could function as a freestanding unit or incorporate into another piece of gear. Line-level signal couples through C1 to op amp configured as an inverting amplifier with a nominal gain of 10, set by ratio of R2/R1. C2 limits high-frequency response and provides stray-capacitance compensation. The CLM6000's light-variable resistor is wired in parallel with R2. With no current applied to LED, enormous resistance has no effect on U1-a gain. U1-a output couples through R3 to U1-b, an inverting amp with gain variable by R4 from 0-4. U1-b output couples to positive charge pump made up of D1-2 and C4-5. Charge pump output couples through current-limiting resistor R5 to anode of LED in CLM6000. In operation, increasing R4 feeds more audio to charge pump, generating greater positive voltage. This lights the LED in the CLM6000, causing light-variable

resistance to fall. That, in turn, reduces gain of U1-a. Compression threshold is variable from infinite to ~500mv$_{p-p}$. Linear compression ratio is between 10:1 and 20:1, making this unit a "compressor/limiter," in studio lingo. Behavior of this type of compressor is often described as "smooth." U1 is a common dual op amp, such as TL082. Circuit also works with VTL2C2.

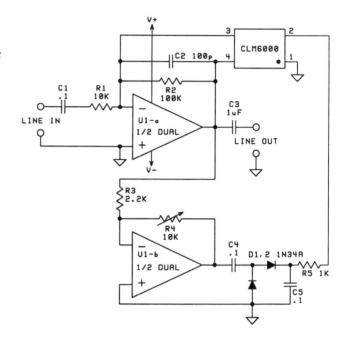

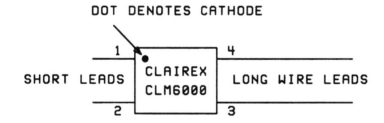

DOT DENOTES CATHODE

SHORT LEADS — CLAIREX CLM6000 — LONG WIRE LEADS

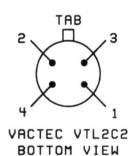

TAB

VACTEC VTL2C2
BOTTOM VIEW

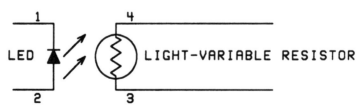

LED — LIGHT-VARIABLE RESISTOR

INTERNAL SCHEMATIC OF
BOTH LIGHT-VARIABLE RESISTORS

LM3080

- 8-pin DIP
- operational transconductance amplifier
- single channel
- dual supply, ±2–18V; or single supply w/artificial ground
- availability: Mouser, Digi-Key, Hosfelt, DC Electronics
- cost: $1.50–$2.00

The 3080 transconductance amplifier lets the user vary gain by a current applied to an output biasing network at pin 5. Audio input couples through divider R1-2, which converts voltage to current. Resting output gain is set by series resistance R4–5 from pin 5 to V+. Values

shown give gain close to unity. Output takes the form of a current, which drops a voltage across R6. C4 limits high-frequency response. Because the output impedance is very high, signal is buffered by voltage follower U2-b, which easily drives variable charge-pump amplifier U2-a. Charge pump C5–6 and D1–2 generates a NEGATIVE control voltage that couples to the R4–5 juncture. As potential supplied to this point grows less positive, bias current into pin 5 drops, reducing U1 gain. Result: a downward-only compressor/limiter with threshold variable by R8 from infinity down to ~180 mv$_{p-p}$. If supply voltage changes, values of R4 and R5 will have to change also. Can work as freestanding limiter or incorporate into another circuit.

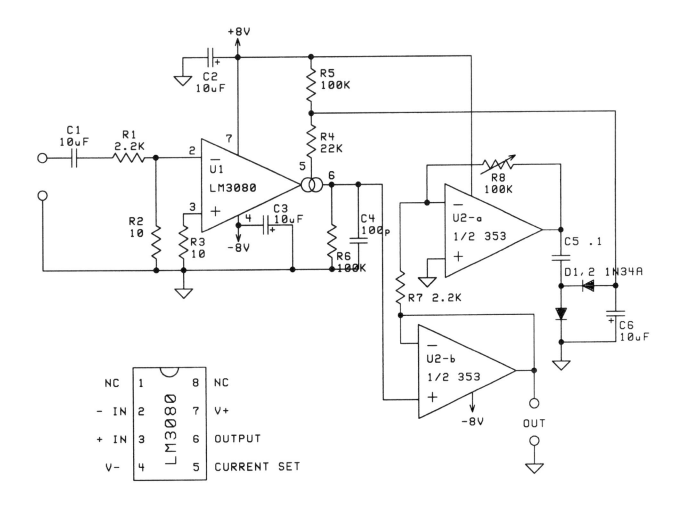

CHAPTER 4

Filtering and Equalization

Filtering and equalization denote post-preamp frequency adjustment. Consensus has accepted an artificial distinction that defines filtering as the attenuation of frequencies above and/or below the band of interest and EQ as the manipulation, by boost or reduction, of frequencies within the band of interest. This text defines the band of interest as 300–6,000 Hz.

While a proper intercept will be equalized upon creation, improper intercepts remain a fact of life. These benefit from filtering and EQ. Classic bass/treble tone controls are useless in bugging gear because they act outside the band of interest.

Though intuitive concepts, filtering and EQ flow from mathematic relationships whose inclusion would tend to opacify the point. The text focuses on exportable building blocks that have proven useful in a wide range of surveillance gear.

FILTERING

Filters attenuate tones above or below the band of interest. The band of interest is called the *passband*; the band where attenuation takes place is called the *stopband*. The point at which the passband ends and the stopband begins is known as the *cutoff frequency*, f_C, which denotes the point that voltage has fallen by about 30 percent.

Filters used in surveillance include highpass filters, which attenuate frequencies below f_C; lowpass filters, which attenuate frequencies above f_C; bandpass filters, which attenuate frequencies above and below two separate cutoff points; and band-reject (notch) filters, which attempt to attenuate a single frequency but affect adjacent frequencies to some extent.

Allpass filters, not discussed here, alter phase but not amplitude. They come into play in encoding and decoding multichannel bug feeds.

Passive resistor-capacitor filters exhibit lackluster behavior, remedied by adding gain and positive feedback. Such filter/amplifier hybrids are known as active filters. They can be built from transistors or op amps, but op amps' inter-unit uniformity enables paper design of filters that transfer to hardware without additional tuning.

EQ

Equalization happens within the band of interest, boosting signals, attenuating noise, or both. The process affects three variables: gain, center frequency, and bandwidth. Gain can be positive (boost) or negative (cut). The center frequency is the one at which EQ exhibits greatest effect. Bandwidth refers to the frequencies adjacent to the center frequency that are affected by EQ. The narrower the bandwidth, the less the adjacent frequencies are affected. The electronic literature states bandwidth in terms of "Q." Bandwidth = center frequency/Q; Q = center frequency/bandwidth. If bandwidth is 1/3 octave, Q = 3. Wide bandwidth means low Q, narrow bandwidth means high Q.

Graphic equalizers debuted in consumer audio products in the mid-'1970s. Their spread paralleled the availability of cheap solid state amps that gave high performance at low cost. Most consumer graphic equalizers today are stereo devices that offer fixed center frequency and bandwidth, variable boost/cut, generally ±12 to ±18 dB. For bugging, their utility rises directly as the number of bands on the equalizer. Commercial devices are available with 30 or more bands. The bugger can easily build a custom graphic EQ having any number of bands and centered on any frequencies desired.

True parametric equalizers confer continuous control over boost, bandwidth, and frequency. The most common parametric EQs are based on something called a state-variable filter. This seemingly complex circuit reduces to a circuit board not much bigger than a priority mail stamp. Parametric EQ's superior versatility suits it to bugging.

TRACKING FILTERS

Tracking filters tune themselves to track specific tones over a limited range of shift. Like compressors, they generate a control voltage from audio; the voltage tunes the filter continuously. Originally built for constant tones, they were adapted to speech by canny buggers. Tuned to a specific voice, the tracking filter will try to pull that voice out of the background.

Tracking boost can easily be made a tracking notch, useful to kill, say, a whistler on an RF intercept.

SWITCHED CAPACITOR FILTERS

Mathematically, filters are transmission lines whose behavior conforms to equations called transfer functions. These same transfer functions can be implemented in ways other than continuous-time (analog). Switched capacitor systems represent discrete versions of continuous-time functions that approximate analog. Their resolution is limited by the sampling (clock) rate. Switched capacitor filters have reached a level of simplicity, performance, and cost that make them practical alternatives to analog filters.

Perhaps the biggest drawback is the need for a clock, the source of squarewaves that switch the capacitor in the filter, usually at 10 to 100 times the frequency of interest. This added circuitry injects digital noise that is sometimes difficult to exclude from the analog signal path.

HOW TO APPLY FILTERING AND EQ

- Audition the intercept.
- If the track needs no filtering, don't filter it. Each pass through a line-level stage adds noise.
- If the tack needs filtering, define the reasons: speech too weak, noise too high, or some combination of flaws. EQ is largely an intuitive process, quickly learned. A typical analog processor contains highpass, lowpass, and parametric functions.
- If the material needs more than one pass of EQ or filtering, archive the feed on media that degrades the S/N ratio as little as possible, such as VHS Hi-Fi, mini-disc, or DAT.

FILTERS

Lowpass

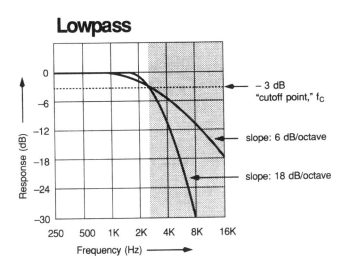

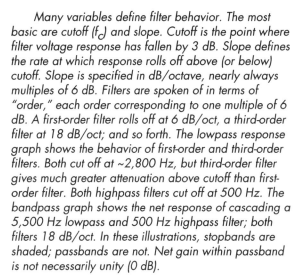

- − 3 dB "cutoff point," f_C
- slope: 6 dB/octave
- slope: 18 dB/octave

Many variables define filter behavior. The most basic are cutoff (f_C) and slope. Cutoff is the point where filter voltage response has fallen by 3 dB. Slope defines the rate at which response rolls off above (or below) cutoff. Slope is specified in dB/octave, nearly always multiples of 6 dB. Filters are spoken of in terms of "order," each order corresponding to one multiple of 6 dB. A first-order filter rolls off at 6 dB/oct, a third-order filter at 18 dB/oct; and so forth. The lowpass response graph shows the behavior of first-order and third-order filters. Both cut off at ~2,800 Hz, but third-order filter gives much greater attenuation above cutoff than first-order filter. Both highpass filters cut off at 500 Hz. The bandpass graph shows the net response of cascading a 5,500 Hz lowpass and 500 Hz highpass filter; both filters 18 dB/oct. In these illustrations, stopbands are shaded; passbands are not. Net gain within passband is not necessarily unity (0 dB).

Highpass

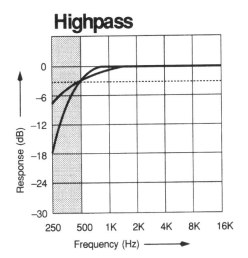

Bandpass

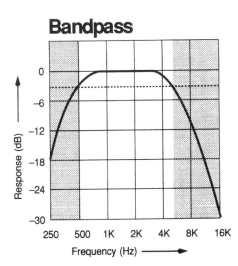

FILTERS

Exportable lowpass and highpass filters based on op-amp voltage follower.

A) 12 dB/octave lowpass filter, R1 = R2, C1 = C2. Cutoff = 1/6.28RC, where R is in ohms and C is in farads = 7,200 Hz. To change cutoff frequency, scale R1 and R2 up or down, or scale C1 and C2 up or down, or both. Impedance = value of R1. Critical to note that, in this configuration, input must DC-couple to prior stage to bias op amp in an ON state. Where that is not possible, circuit B must be used. Input now has a DC path to ground (or 1/2V+ in single-supply circuits), and coupling cap C3 has been added.

C) Highpass filter is constructed exactly the same as lowpass, but capacitors and resistors have swapped places. This circuit's cutoff point is ~160 Hz. Highpass filter "automatically" biases op amp (through R2).

D) Circuit identical to "A," but cutoff has been made variable by dual pot in series with R1 and R2. Here cutoff is variable from ~7,200 Hz when pot resistance is minimum, to ~1,200 Hz when pot resistance is maximum. Technique applies equally well to highpass filter.

E) Simple way to attain sharper roll-off, "quasi-18 dB/octave" configuration. Identical to "C," but for addition of C1 and R3, C1 being ten times the value of C2; R3 one-tenth the value of R1. Input impedance lowered to value of R1.

F) Configuration of "E" has been swapped to make lowpass, quasi-18 dB/oct filter; resistors have been scaled to give cutoff of ~72 Hz. Bias potential must be available at input of R1. A bandpass filter is achieved by cascading lowpass to highpass filter (place lowpass first). Component tolerances not critical: 5 percent resistors and 10 percent or better capacitors, preferably of temperature-stable type. Op amp type also not critical; TL081 or 071 make excellent choices. These circuits are exportable and can meet ~80 percent of filtering needs in surveillance audio gear.

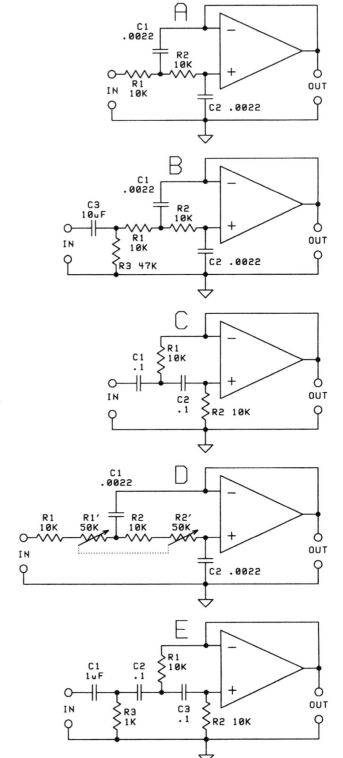

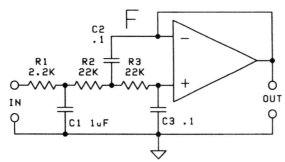

EQUALIZERS

Differences between graphic equalizer and true parametric equalizer. In graphic equalizer, center frequency and bandwidth are fixed; boost/cut is variable. Top figure shows response curves that result when individual bands are set at full boost/cut while other bands remain centered. Some graphic EQs provide for limited bandwidth/frequency changes via switching capacitors. High performance is so readily achieved with cheap solid state amps that the number of bands has no practical limit. The true parametric equalizer confers seamless control over boost/cut, bandwidth, and center frequency. Many analog designs are based on the state-variable filter.

Graphic Equalizer

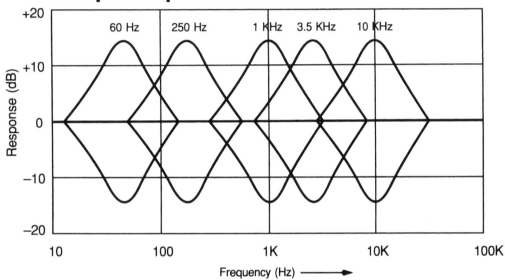

Parametric Equalizer

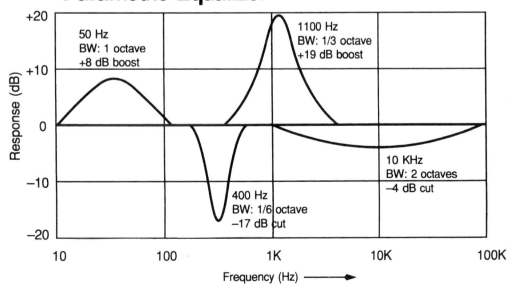

EQUALIZERS

A) Signetics' databook 5-band graphic equalizer, similar to several published in the late 1970s, when high-performance op amps became available at low cost. Values of C1 and C2 determine center frequency for each band. In all cases, C2 = 10 x C1. For center frequency of 794 Hz, C1 = 0.0015µF; C2 = 0.015µF. Other frequencies found by simple ratio, e.g., if C1 = 0.0018µF and C2 = 0.018µF, center frequency drops to 662 Hz. 50K pot controls boost/cut, 250K pot serves as master volume control. Change 20K resistor to 11K if number of bands is increased to 10. Op amp type not critical; 5532, 833, 07X series, etc. Power supply and bypass not shown.

B) A wholly different approach. The LM13600 (or LM13700) dual transconductance amplifier configured as a voltage-tunable narrow bandpass filter with >20 dB gain, at the center frequency, over the range 180–7,000 Hz. Device is sensitive to variations in supply voltage, so keep close to ±8V. Has proven extremely effective after preamp of moderate gain.

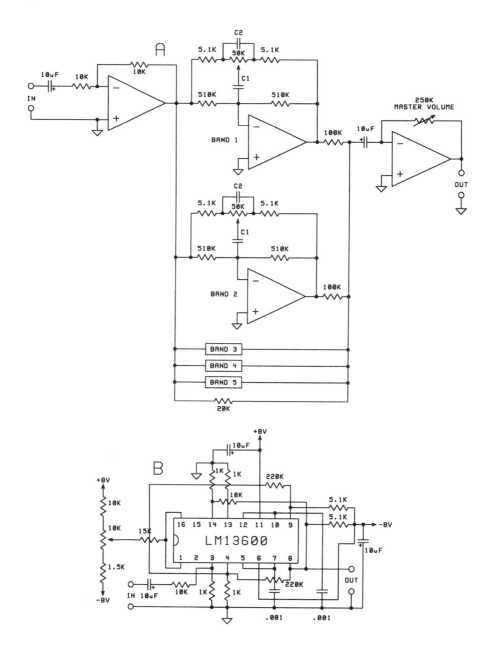

EQUALIZERS

This "super tone control" dates from the early days of FET-input op amps; circuit adapted from manufacturer's databook. Input buffer rolls off above 15 KHz because treble boost extends well into the ultrasonic otherwise. Can boost/cut bass and treble up to 20 dB, boost or cut

midrange centered on ~1 KHz nearly as much. Curves approximate response with other controls in flat position. Op amp type not critical; power supply lines and bypass not shown.

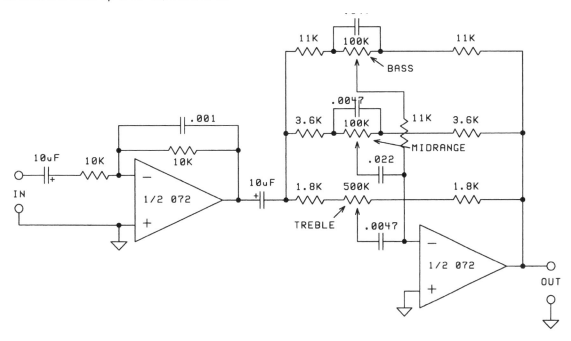

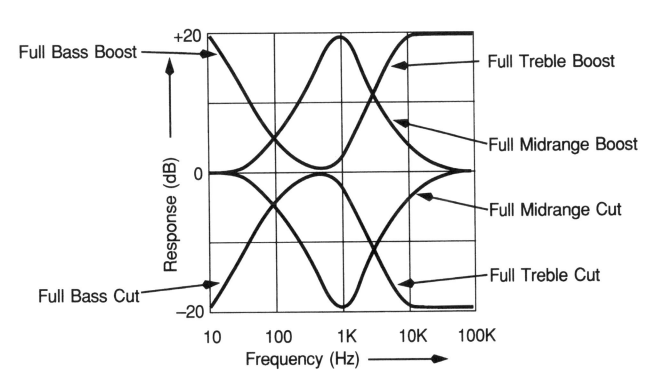

55

TRUE NOTCH FILTERS

A) One of the earliest (1969) op-amp-based high-performance fixed-notch filters. Difficult to tune; notch depth depends upon perfect match among resistors and capacitors. Values shown tune 60 Hz. Response curves adjacent show effect of bootstrapping on Notch Q.

B) Modern, high-Q, tunable notch filter. Switched-capacitor design. Notch depth typically ~40 dB without trimming; can be increased by trimming, mainly R2. Let R1 = 10K; make R2 a 10K trimpot to tune. Requires tunable source of 5V squarewaves, such as NE566. (Circuits and illustrations redrawn after manufacturers' data.)

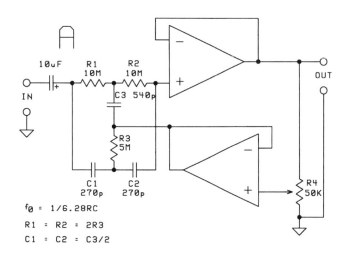

$$f_0 = 1/6.28RC$$
$$R1 = R2 = 2R3$$
$$C1 = C2 = C3/2$$

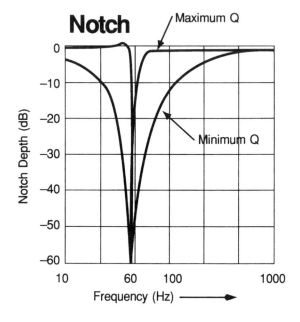

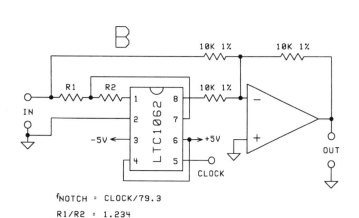

$$f_{NOTCH} = CLOCK/79.3$$
$$R1/R2 = 1.234$$

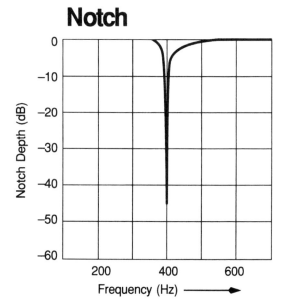

CHAPTER 5

Getting the Message Out: Power Amps

At some point an audio feed must connect to a speaker or a set of headphones. Preamps won't drive these low-impedance loads and will not satisfactorily drive high-impedance headphones. The most expedient solution is a device that

- can drive low-impedance headphones and small speakers,
- can run off a low-voltage single supply,
- costs little,
- comes in a small package, and
- is widely available.

These traits exist in a class of integrated circuits known as audio power drivers. Of several dozen options, three chips fill three specific bugging niches.

LM386

If stocking status at Radio Shack defines ubiquity, the LM386 owns the category. This chip is found in many small consumer electronic products and is widely second-sourced. It has 26 dB of built-in voltage gain that rises to 46 dB by addition of a capacitor. It offers inverting and noninverting inputs—an important stability option in many bugging circuits. The unused input should be grounded

to exclude interference. The chip biases its output at 1/2V+ from an internal divider, so coupling to the load requires a capacitor. The 386 runs off 4–15V and will drive loads of 4–32 ohms. It comes in N-1, N-3, and N-4 subtypes, in ascending order of power output and supply voltage. The 386's quiescent current runs 4–8 ma, this value being somewhat dependent on supply voltage.

On the downside, the 386 suffers noticeable and occasionally intrusive noise, 5–10mv$_{p-p}$ measured at the output with both inputs grounded—the noisiest of the three chips under discussion.

All 38X power chips are subject to instability, suppressed by an output shunt known as a "snubber." The 386 uses a 10-ohm resistor in series with a 0.1μF ceramic cap. The data sheet states that this is needed only with the 386N-4, but veteran designers use it on all versions of the chip.

LM380

The 386's predecessor put out more power but required a 10–22V supply. Built-in voltage gain is fixed at 50 (34 dB). A properly heatsinked 380 will put two watts into an 8-ohm load. The chip comes in 8- and 14-pin versions. The latter devotes the extra space to an internal copper lattice that sinks heat through six pins into the circuit board. The output stage has thermal shutdown and short-circuit protection not found in the 386.

Like the 386, the 380 has inverting and noninverting inputs and requires a snubber (2.7 ohms in series with 0.1µF).

MC34119

Motorola designed this 8-pin dual inline package (DIP) to run off as little as 2V, for use in speaker phones powered off the phone line. The output stage is unique among small audio drivers, consisting of a pair of power op amps in bridge-tied load (BTL) configuration. Antiphase outputs double the voltage across the load and obviate an output coupling capacitor. A chip running on 2V can show the phones ~$4V_{p-p}$. The output does not usually require a snubber, but output leads should be tightly twisted. Quiescent current can be reduced to 65µa by tying pin 1 to V+.

The 34119 sometimes demands a load greater than 8 ohms for stability. A small resistance in series with each output meets this

requirement. Both outputs are biased at 1/2V+ and must be treated as floating.

THREE NICHES

The LM386 is the quintessential portable 9V power driver, suitable for headphones or small speakers. The LM380 suits table-model gear running off an AC-derived supply and driving small-to-medium speakers. The MC34119 suits dual-AA-battery devices or applications that demand less noise than the 386. Also, its op-amp heart allows manipulation of gain and frequency response the same as any op amp would.

OTHER USES FOR POWER DRIVER ICs

All three chips can drive LEDs, laser diodes, ultrasonic transducers, and line-locator transmitters. Because the 380 and 386 automatically bias their outputs at 1/2V+, they can serve as an artificial ground for high-power single-supply circuits. The 34119's unique output suits it to true amplitude modulators.

LM386

- *8-pin DIP, also available in surface-mount package*
- *single supply, 4–12V (LM386N-1 and N-3); 5–15V (LM386N-4)*
- *single channel*
- *drive power: up to 1W*
- *quiescent current ~6 ma; operating current variable, up to several hundred milliamps*
- *noisy: 5–10mv$_{p-p}$ at output w/shorted inputs; audible, occasionally intrusive*
- *output automatically biased at 1/2V+*
- *built-in voltage gain: 20 (26dB); 200 (46 dB) selected with cap from pin 1 to pin 8*
- *option to reduce voltage gain with external resistive divider*
- *will drive speaker or low-impedance phones (4–32 ohms) through cap of 100–1,000μF*

- *will drive high-impedance phones through matching transformer*
- *availability: universal, practically all mail order vendors and Radio Shack*
- *price: $0.50–$1.50*

This exportable circuit will meet 90 percent of output driver needs for covert audio gear. The most common means to reduce chip's 26 dB of gain is voltage divider R1–R2, attenuating signal before it enters 386. Chip tends to rectify strong AM radio signals; C3 helps exclude those signals. Terminals 2 and 3 are reversible, to invert polarity of output; can help stability in some high-gain circuits. R4-C5 is a snubber (an ultrasonic shunt that aids stability). Use of C4 raises 386 gain to 46 dB, a noisy move that is usually inadvisable. Supply decoupling network R3–C2 proves so often necessary that the designer should include it routinely.

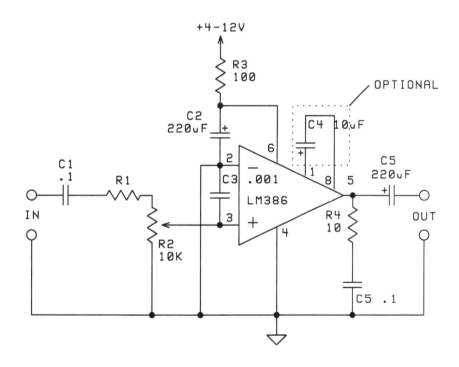

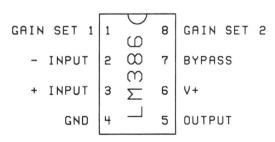

LM380

- *14-pin DIP (LM380N); 8-pin DIP (LM380N-8)*
- *single supply, 10–22V; not suited to 9V operation*
- *single channel*
- *quiescent current: ~10 ma; operating current variable, can exceed 1A*
- *output noise: 1–2 mv$_{p-p}$ w/shorted inputs*
- *output automatically biased at 1/2V+*
- *will drive speaker or low-impedance phones (4–32 ohms) through cap of 100–1,000µF*
- *output short-circuit and thermal shutdown protection*
- *built-in voltage gain: 50 (34 dB)*
- *availability: good; Digi-Key, Mouser, many other mail order retailers*
- *cost: $1.20–$2.50*

Exportable LM380 audio drivers. Because chip requires higher supply voltage and more external parts than 386 or 34119, its best use is as an audio driver in devices that need to produce substantial volume from a loudspeaker. In 14-pin DIP, pins 3, 4, 5, 10, 11, and 12 are internally connected to ground and a copper heatsink. Printed circuit layout should place as much copper as possible in contact with these pins, preferably by direct soldering rather than use of a socket. For use near chip's power limit, attach an external heatsink (for example, a Staver V-7). Resistive divider R1-R2 determines what percentage of line-level signal gets to input. If no attenuation is desired, omit R1. Choose R1 = 470K to divide out chip's built-in voltage gain. C2 is an RF shunt, and C3 keeps noise out of unused input, whose high impedance readily picks up noise. R3–C6 forms a snubber.

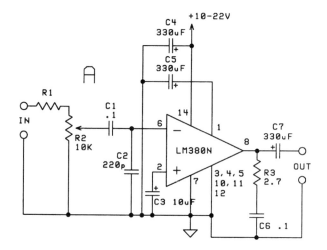

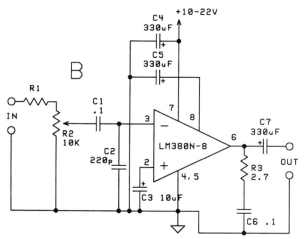

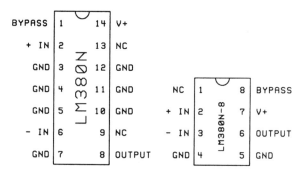

MC34119

- 8-pin DIP
- single supply, 2–16V
- single channel
- quiescent current ~4 ma; operating current variable, up to several hundred milliamps
- mute: pin 1 to V+ through resistor; quiescent current drops to 65µa
- balanced, floating outputs; DC-couple to speaker or phones, insulate from ground
- load impedance 16–100 ohms; prefers higher impedance than do 386/380 types
- significantly lower output noise, when configured for unity gain, than 386
- voltage gain variable 0–1,000 at 1 KHz
- availability: DC Electronics, Hosfelt
- cost: <$2

Exportable MC34119 audio power drivers.
A) Generic; B) circuit performance resembles that of LM386; C) power driver has essentially unity gain. In all cases, both output terminals are automatically biased at 1/2V+ and thus must be isolated from ground. V+ applied to pin 1 shuts down chip and reduces quiescent current to ~65µa.

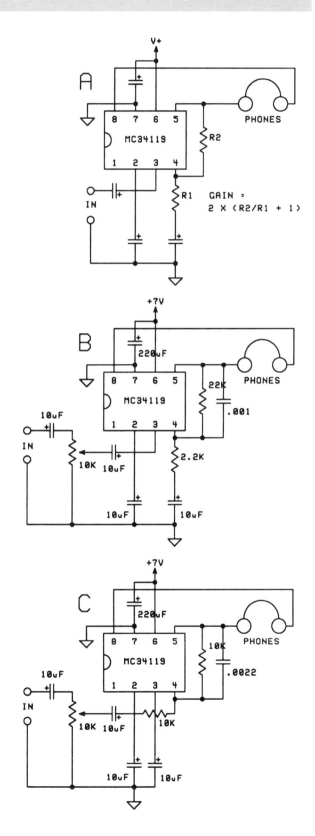

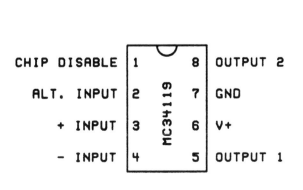

CHIP DISABLE	1		8	OUTPUT 2
ALT. INPUT	2		7	GND
+ INPUT	3	MC34119	6	V+
- INPUT	4		5	OUTPUT 1

CHAPTER 6

Headphones

Critical/discreet listening requires headphones. Ideal phones are light, low-impedance, sealed, on-the-ear or around-the-ear designs. Open-air (Sennheiser®) types are prone to feedback when used with exposed mics and high gain. Good mono phones are scarce, and great stereo phones abound. Common practice is to convert stereo to mono with an adaptor plug that parallels the transducers, such as Radio Shack p/n 274-368. Dozens of adaptors are available through major electronics suppliers.

Peak performance also calls for impedance match between output stage and headphones. High-impedance phones sound weak when driven from a low-impedance output because the output stage cannot generate sufficient voltage. Low-impedance phones driven from a high-impedance output sound weak because the output can't muster enough current. Low-impedance stages are designed to drive 4–16 ohms; high-impedance stages, 300–2,000 ohms. Commercial pieces usually label outputs as "high-Z" or "low-Z" to indicate impedance of

the output stage. If you built the piece, you know the output configuration. The 380, 386, and 34119 are low-impedance drivers.

To drive low-Z phones from a high-Z output, couple phones to output through a matching transformer. Driver transformers are available in 8:100, 8:200, 8:300, 8:600, 8:1000, and 8:1200 ohms, and with 75-, 200-, and 400-milliwatt power ratings. Choose the impedance closest to that of the output stage. "Halfway" values can be had by using the transformer center tap. For instance, if the phones rate 500 ohms, use the center tap of an 8:1K transformer.

The same process applies to high-impedance (>100 ohms) phones, running off a low-impedance stage. Simply reverse the transformer connection.

If the phones' impedance isn't known, measure the drivers' DC resistance. This is usually close enough to the impedance to match. Wiring the drivers in parallel halves the impedance. Wiring the drivers in series doubles the impedance.

HEADPHONE COUPLING

A) Plug wiring used by most stereo headphones.

B) Method of converting stereo phones permanently to mono by soldering to mono plug in parallel mode. Resultant impedance equals half the impedance of each driver.

C) Method of converting stereo phones permanently to mono by soldering to mono plug in series mode. Resultant impedance equals twice the impedance of each driver. Once converted, B and C can be inserted in standard mono jack.

D) Method of wiring stereo jack to drive stereo phones in parallel mono mode.

E) Method of wiring stereo jack to drive stereo phones in series mono mode; note that, in this case, the sleeve terminal must be insulated from ground. D and E alter the jack to accept unmodified stereo headphones.

F) One possible wiring scheme to mate high-impedance phones to 386 or 380 output.

G) Coupling balanced output of 34119 to transformer. This chip is sometimes unstable driving an 8-ohm load; R1 and R2 cure instability with little effect on volume. 8:1200 transformer used for illustration; 8:200, 8:300, 8:500, and other ratios also available. The small 75-mw Mouser transformers are adequate for most phones.

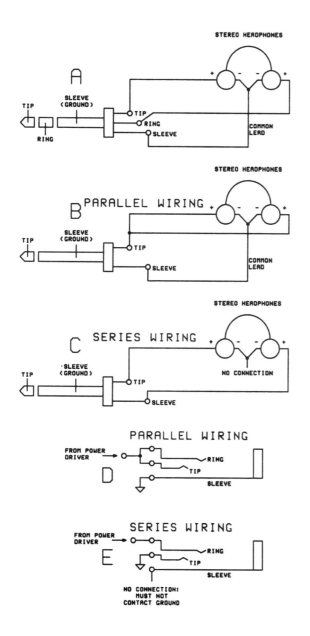

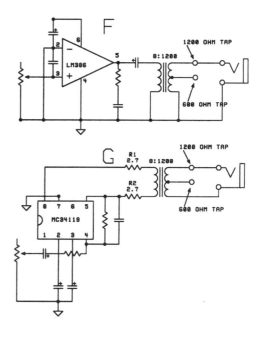

CHAPTER 7

Power: Tips and Techniques

BATTERIES

Maybe 75 percent of bugging gear is battery powered. Since the dawn of the transistor radio, the American consumer has shown a preference bordering on monomania for products that run off 9V "transistor" batteries, developed specifically for early portables. This fixation so suffused the culture that every Mom 'n Pop grocery story is likely to stock 9V batteries. Unfortunately, "9V" tells as much about a battery as "red" tells about a radish. Nine volts is an expedient marketing tag that ignores the behavior of batteries under load. Fresh 9V batteries measure close to 9 volts. Voltage falls under load, but 9V batteries still meet the supply requirements of many bug-friendly semiconductors. Op amps are specified at ±15V, but many will function down to ±3.5V.

A discharge curve allows projection of battery life at a given current drain, down to a specific voltage. From the curves printed in this chapter, a device that draws 24 ma and shuts off at 7V will run for 3, 13, and 39 hours, respectively, from carbon-zinc, alkaline, and lithium batteries. The curves also predict double the life at half the current, or half the life at double the current. Extrapolations hold so long as current consumption does not exceed the battery's maximum.

If no discharge curve is available, plot your own. Wire a resistor across the battery terminals, measure voltage at appropriate intervals, plot the curve. If a device draws 20 ma from a 7.4V battery, choose a standard resistance close to 7.4V/0.02A = 370 ohms to test the battery. For higher current and larger batteries,

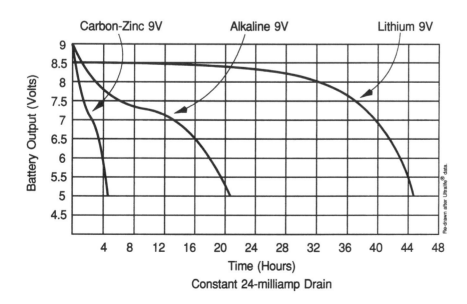

Constant 24-milliamp Drain

the energy dissipated through the resistor might demand a metal-oxide power type. Power in watts = voltage × current. When testing a four-D-cell nicad pack @ 150 ma drain, 5V × 0.15A = 0.75W. Use a 33-ohm metal oxide power resistor rated at least 1W. Do not touch the resistor during the test, because it may get hot enough to cause a burn. The curve resulting from this test will not show constant current, because current through the load falls with voltage. The curve will typify a real-world load enough to be useful. As an alternative to the resistive load, use the device itself as the load.

Avoid unreasonable discharge rates. For instance, no 9V batteries are rated to deliver 200 ma continuously. Most battery manufacturers specify the maximum recommended discharge rate.

RECHARGEABLE BATTERIES

With alkaline 9V batteries now priced around $2.50 each and lithium types $7–$10 each, and with carbon-zinc batteries continuing to constitute a waste of resources, rechargeables are the only sane option for heavy battery users.

Alkaline batteries possess several times the capacity of nicads. A nicad recharged 100 times might replace, say, 33 alkaline batteries costing $2.50 each, or $82.50 worth. Assuming the 9V nicad and a charger cost $20, the savings come to $62.50. And 100 recharging cycles is a conservative estimate.

Modern nicads have beaten the memory effect, so the user does not have to periodically discharge them all the way. Energy density continues to rise, with late-model nickel metal hydride "AA" cells offering 1,200 mah, eclipsing "C" cells of the past. Nicads of lower capacity can be had as surplus bargains.

Rechargeables specify capacity in milliampere-hours (mah), or ampere-hours (ah) for high-capacity types. This multiplied by the average voltage gives total available power in watts.

ODD BATTERY SIZES

At least check the batteries in the watch and hearing-aid case at the drugstore. Some batteries are hard for guys over 50 to see but supply 1–3V, with enough current to drive an RF bug.

DC-TO-DC CONVERTERS

Certain high-performance circuits demand a dual supply at a total voltage in excess of 10V. Getting this in portable gear meant at least two batteries until the arrival of small DC-to-DC upconverters.

Converters are miniature switching supplies. They convert DC to ultrasonic AC, step up the AC in a transformer and/or voltage multiplier, and then convert the stepped-up AC back to DC. Each converter is about the size of a couple sticks of Dentyne®. Recent models deliver 2W. Ultrasonic switching pulses leak into the power bus but don't usually affect audio gear. The most popular versions run off a nominal 5V input (4.5–5.5V); they supply a regulated 5, 10, 12, 15, or 17 volts. At press time they sold for $9 each from Digi-Key. Dual-supply models furnish ±5V to ±17V, at a cost of $14–$25 each (Digi-Key and Mouser).

Wasted power is the price of conversion. Efficiency of this type of converter falls in the 60- to 75-percent range.

VOLTAGE REGULATORS

The occasional circuit has to be biased so delicately that the voltage shift that occurs with battery aging will upset performance. The designer is wise to run these pieces off a regulated supply. The cheapest regulator is a zener diode, available in fractions of a volt from 1.8–200V, and with a power rating of 1/2W to >10W. Low-power zener regulators take up maybe 0.25 in² of board space but are best considered soft in that their output will change slightly with changes in supply and changes in load.

A three-terminal regulator (3TR) costs pennies more than a zener, but offers rock-solid voltage regulation, superior ripple rejection (in AC supplies), plus built-in thermal shutdown.

Three-terminal regulator usually means a member of the 78XX (positive) and 79XX (negative) series. The Xs tell voltage: 05, 12, 15, etc. These regulators come in TO-220 cases; high-current versions in TO-3 cases. Presence of an L in the part number (78L08, etc.) denotes a TO-92 case.

All 3TRs exhibit a trait called dropout, the number of volts higher than the output that the input must see in order to hold the output at the rated voltage. For example, a 7805 has a dropout of ~2.6V, making the minimum input 7.6V to meet specified regulator behavior. In light-duty circuits, which includes much bugging gear, the input can be a fraction of a volt more than 5V. Dropout varies among regulators and is specified in the data sheet. Ultralow-dropout regulators can be had, such as the Zetex ZLDO series, which incurs less than 100 mv of loss.

TO-92 regulators generally support a top current of 100 ma; TO-220 types 0.5–1.5A, depending on capacity of their heatsink.

BENCH SUPPLIES: THE WALL WART

Wart, not *Mart*; a black cube, maybe a couple of inches on a side, that contains an AC step-down transformer and plugs directly into the AC outlet, delivering AC at some manageable level, 5–20V being typical. Wall warts eliminate the need for batteries in bench gear while freeing the builder from having to work with high-voltage AC wiring.

Wall warts come in AC and DC types. AC types provide raw, stepped-down AC; DC types vary greatly in what they mean by "DC." Some contain well-regulated DC supplies whose output is usable raw; others provide the unfiltered output of a rectifier. Both types can be had for $3–$15; many surplus bargains.

DESIGNING BATTERY-POWERED GEAR

Anticipating that a battery-powered piece will see a change in supply voltage during normal operation, check performance in the breadboard stage while varying supply over the expected range. Measure current consumption at top and bottom ends of this range. These values, combined with a battery

discharge curve, allow realistic projection of operating life.

Buggers who build hardware to spec learn quickly that customers bring unstated expectations. Veterans of this market query their customers:

- What are the maximum acceptable dimensions of the device?
- How long must it operate continuously?
- Can the user replace the battery?
- If the device mates to headphones, what is their impedance? Mono or stereo? Plug size?

Sometimes the customer cannot anticipate the trade-offs dictated by his specs. For example, he may specify dimensions that prohibit the best battery for the job. You can build a piece that meets his specs and might run off a penlight cell. The customer does not realize that this sticks him with 20 times the electronic noise of a 9V system.

Though the design of 9V battery terminals keeps the user from connecting the battery backwards, a momentary backwards connection during replacement is not unusual. This can destroy critical parts. The prudent designer "idiot-proofs" the battery leads with a series rectifier diode. No current flows unless the battery is connected properly, but available voltage falls by ~0.6V.

USING DC–DC CONVERTERS

- *input voltage: +4.5–5.5V; four-cell nicad pack ideal*
- *output voltage: single supply +5–17V; dual supply ±5–17V*
- *power: 1–2 watts, more than enough for most portable bugging gear*
- *current: inversely proportional to voltage, e.g., 100 ma at 5V, 33 ma at 15V*
- *output contains ultrasonic switching pulses that don't usually affect audio gear*
- *efficiency: ~70 percent*
- *cost: $9–$25*
- *availability: Digi-Key, Mouser, Hosfelt*

Schematics show common converter circuits. A) Portable uses 4-cell nicad pack; battery drain can exceed 160 ma; choose cells rated to deliver at least this much continuous current. B) Using a wall wart having DC output >7V and rated 200 ma or more. C) An AC wall wart requires rectifier and filter capacitors. In B and C, note that converter output ground is isolated from 5V power input ground and that 5V regulator should be the TO-220 version and will require a heatsink. Photos show typical converters; large device obtained on the surplus market. Smaller models bought at retail are the type described here, and the ones whose pinouts are given in schematic "D."

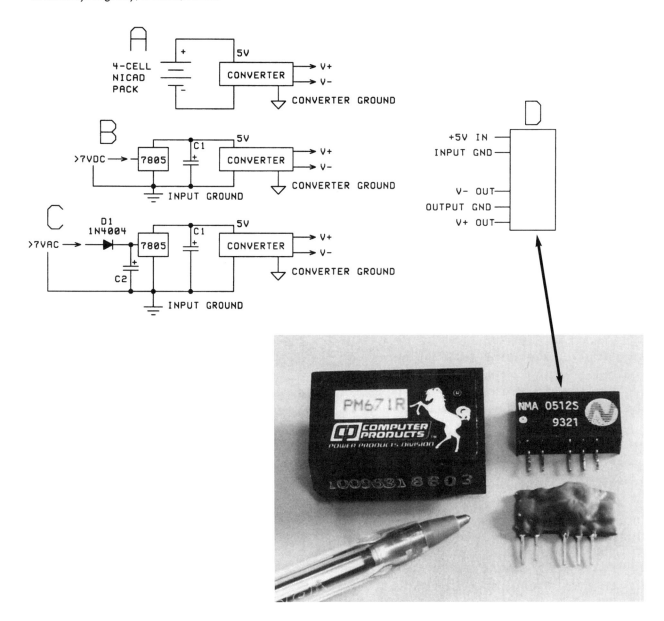

POWER OPTIONS

A) Standard zener diode regulator setup. Zener diodes are available from ~2–100V, 5 percent tolerance; 1/2W and 1W types common. One way to approximate the value of R1 is:

R1 = (supply voltage - zener voltage) ÷ (1.1 × maximum load current)

B) Three-terminal regulator, or "3TR," provides regulation that holds up under load better than zener diode. Fixed output types include 7805, 7812, 7815 positive; negative series 7905, etc. Supply voltage should be at least 2.6V greater than output voltage for tightest regulation. Devices will shut down if they overheat. Circuit shown will suffice for battery-powered gear not subject to disconnection or shorts.

C and D) two of countless examples of supplies possible using discrete power converter integrated circuits. "C" generates a substantial 12V supply from a couple of alkaline cells. "D" shows how a complete piece of bugging gear can run off an aging nicad cell. Though these power converters use ultrasonic switching, they generate audio-band supply ripples that can affect operation of bugs.

E) Pinouts of common 3TRs in TO-220 and TO-92 cases. Heatsink TO-220 case.

F) Buggers who build hardware to go find it wise to "idiot-proof" the power bus by inserting a rectifier diode between the power switch and the circuit board. This way, if battery is momentarily connected backwards, as often happens when replacing a 9V under time pressure, no damage occurs. A second diode (inside the dotted line) is needed for protection of a device running off a dual supply. Technique does not suit circuits that are working near lower supply limit because of the 0.6–1V forward drop of each rectifier.

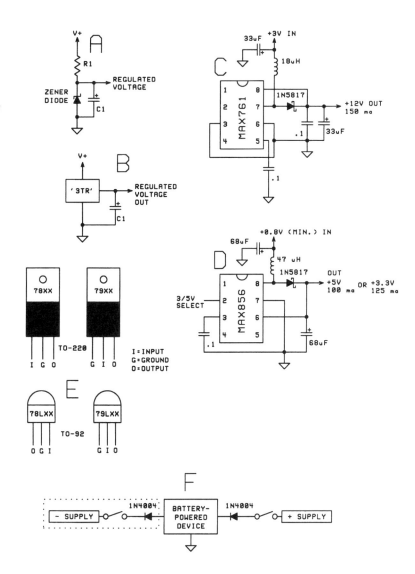

CHAPTER 8

Stability in High-Gain Circuits

Circuits illustrated so far are meant to work in concert in high-gain systems. Gain walks hand in hand with instability, which manifests as oscillation, distortion, or unexplained muting. The higher the gain, the greater this penchant to crap out. Circuits with 60 dB of gain present at least the potential for instability. Bugging systems frequently exceed 80 dB of gain; 100 dB is not uncommon. Rare cases require more than 120 dB. Because instability results from myriad factors, solutions to the problem tend also to be many.

Perhaps the most common explanation for instability roots in the notion of bypass. Rather than serving as a passive source of electrons, the power supply is an active element. Signal permeates the supply as well as the signal path. Bypass capacitors store a reservoir of current that the rest of the circuit can draw to avoid loading the supply. If circuit demand exceeds capacitor storage, instability results from signal modulating the supply. This explains the universal use of bypass capacitors. Instability due to insufficient bypass is cured by heftier bypass. A circuit unstable with 10µF of bypass might even out with 100 µF or 220µF, an empiric move readily tested on the breadboard.

Sometimes upping the value of bypass capacitors exacerbates the matter. Here the problem lies not with insufficient capacity but in the need to isolate individual circuit segments through resistor-capacitor (RC) networks. Each stage is supplied off the end of a lowpass filter, better isolating it from the supply bus. A common example is the standard 100-ohm-resistor decoupling network used on the LM386. High-gain 386 circuits often seem impossible to stabilize without the resistor. With the resistor, the chip can work stably in systems whose total gain approaches one million. Electret mics running off the amplifier power bus present another case responsive to RC decoupling.

The use of op amps whose gain reaches well into the RF can sometimes cause instability cured by supplementing conventional bypass with capacitors that exhibit low impedance at high frequencies, such as tantalum capacitors or 0.1-0.001µF ceramic discs, placed as close as possible to the power leads.

Instability can originate in layout. Juxtaposition of input and output lines naturally promotes feedback through antenna effects. High-gain circuits should use a linear, spacious arrangement that maximizes separation of input and output. Wiring should be kept neat and short. Some systems benefit from board-mounted pots and jacks and shielded cable between the board and the signal ports. Twisting unshielded leads can help, too.

Watch the phase of input relative to output. The definition of an oscillator includes an output in phase with the input. Feedback oscillation defies bypass. Simply inverting phase at some point in the signal path will stabilize the system. Here the choice of inverting/noninverting inputs on a power driver can save the day.

Op-amp circuits that are unstable when biased off a simple resistive divider often firm up when the bias is fortified by an active ground, such as the output of an op-amp voltage follower.

Audio power drivers, such as the 386 or 34119, occasionally cause instability when their current drain is reflected through low-current preamp segments. Such instability is sometimes cured by giving the power driver and the preamp separate return paths to ground.

If instability manifests as ultrasonic or RF oscillation, the cure can be as easy as limiting bandwidth of each stage to, say, 10 KHz.

Interstage isolation using transformers is one of the most effective antidotes to instability and can lighten the load on semiconductors by providing voltage gain. Optocouplers are a bit more cumbersome to use but can both isolate stages and replace an amplifier stage with optocoupler gain.

Many unruly circuits even out when stages run off independent supplies. Designers try to avoid this inelegant resort, which is sometimes unavoidable in systems whose response extends below 20 Hz.

Muting noted in the final few degrees of travel of a volume-control pot feeding a 386 from an op amp usually traces to ultrasonic oscillation in the op-amp output stage. In this case, 100–1,000 ohms' resistance in series with the op-amp output can cure the problem without materially affecting gain.

The higher the system frequency, the greater the stabilizing influence of a *ground plane*, a layer of copper on the component side of a printed circuit board, unbroken but for lead holes, tied at multiple points to circuit ground. A ground plane enhances stability in systems running at several hundred kilohertz and up.

Stabilizing high-gain circuits involves so many factors, so much trial and error, as to qualify better as art than science. Yet these techniques, singly or in combination, can stabilize any practical piece the bugger cares to build.

STABILITY

A) Designer has come up with a dynamite circuit for directional mics, hose mics, etc. The electret is biased for optimum output. Preamp U1 has the bug EQ curve built in. Noise-wise, U1 is among the best choices for the 10K source impedance; by the open loop gain curve, it gives between 65 and 85 dB in the bug band. Couples to an LM386 power driver, properly shunted for RF and equipped with a snubber. Total gain, depending on frequency, will approach 100 dB.

Too bad circuit "A" proved violently unstable when built. Compare changes in version "B": (1) Microphone is now decoupled from the power bus by lowpass network R9–C10. (2) Instead of getting its "artificial ground" from a

resistive divider, U1 biases off the output of U3, an op amp configured as a DC voltage follower, whose input is biased at 1/2V+ by divider R5–R6. An op amp output stage can source and sink current; a resistive divider cannot. (3) U2 is now decoupled by lowpass network R10–C13. (4) Essentially all the 386s built-in gain has been neutralized by divider action of R11–R7. Total system gain remains substantial and more than many applications are likely to need. (5) C11 limits U1's active bandwidth to frequencies of interest. (6) Finally, in "A," the circuit path is noninverting from input to output, making feedback oscillation likely. "B" uses U2's inverting input, making the net gain inverting. Built on a clean, open board, "B" is stable as a fireplug . . .

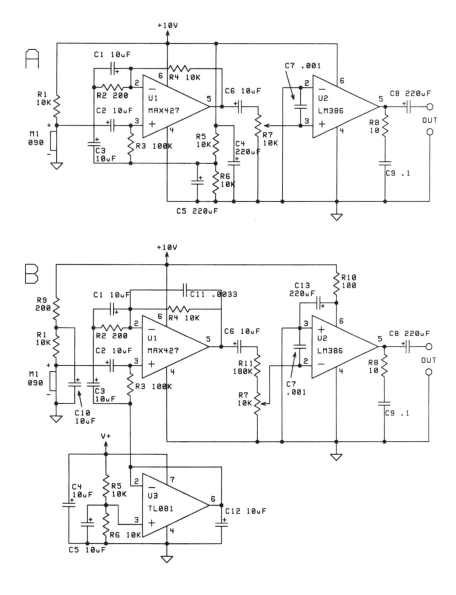

CHAPTER 9

Directional Microphones

Directional mics exist as two species: those that amplify, and those that don't.

AMPLIFYING DIRECTIONAL MICROPHONES (ADMs)

ADMs boost sound at the membrane. They come in five flavors: reflectors, horns, boundary mics, resonators, and combinations of these four.

Reflectors

Reflectors are best known as parabolic microphones that have graced the sidelines of every pro football game since platform soles. Their essence is intuitive, seen in solar reflectors and satellite dishes. Gain relates loosely to the ratio of frontal dish area to microphone area. The approximate gain of an RF dish is:

$$\text{Gain} \cong \frac{19.7\, r^2}{(\text{wavelength})^2} \cong 5D^2$$

where:

r is dish radius

D is dish diameter in multiples of the wavelength of the frequency of interest

Audio antennas don't reap the spectacular gain of RF dishes, in part because sonic wavelengths loom long relative to the span of the dish. Assuming the speed of sound to be 1,050 feet per second, a 1,000-Hz tone has a wavelength of 1,050 / 1,000 = 1.05'. For an 8' dish, gain predicted by the first equation is:

$$19.7(4)^2 / (1.05)^2 = 285.9 = 49.2 \text{ dB}$$

Gain predicted by the second equation is:

$$5(4 / 1.05)^2 = 290.25 = 49.34 \text{ dB}$$

Assuming the 8' dish to focus on a 6" spot and using the relative-area concept, gain is:

$$3.14(48)^2 / 3.14(3)^2 = 256 = 48.24 \text{ dB}$$

The three methods agree closely enough to use any one of them to estimate dish gain. The RF equations also suggest that the reflector offers another means to attenuate low frequencies relative to midrange and high frequencies.

Construction of parabolic mics is obvious from inspection, with the caveat that the mic should be big enough to cover the focus, which dwarfs the diameter of an electret in dishes bigger than about 6" across. The mic must reside precisely at the focus. Although formulas exist for fixing foci, the builder will find it prudent to optimize placement empirically.

In the mid-'60s, the Chicago Museum of Science and Industry maintained an exhibit that drove home the principle that a pair of co-focused reflectors (segments of an ellipse, if memory serves; by definition, an ellipse has two foci). The foci were some tens of feet apart. One patron stood at each focus, facing the reflector. Each patron could hear the other breathe, swallow, sweat . . .

The power of co-focused reflectors did not escape buggers' notice. Somewhere out there—not necessarily on American soil—may still exist a curio of landscaping and architecture, probably considered quaint, arranged so that targets herd themselves into what is the focus of a disguised reflector. A co-focused companion reflector in the distance hears everything.

The inverse-square law applies to predicting range of a dish but blurs under reflection, refraction, diffraction, and atmospheric absorption. Big dishes also hit a limit in how small a spot they will focus. The bigger the dish, the hazier its sonic focus, a fact that creates a need for microphone apertures several inches across.

Horns

Horns match the high acoustic impedance at the throat to the low acoustic impedance where the mouth couples to air. Common examples include brass orchestral instruments and public-address speakers. Horn microphones work in reverse, coupling open air at the mouth to a microphone at the throat. The type offers a side benefit in that diameter of the mouth determines the low-frequency cutoff.

Horns commonly occur as miniature folded types meant for alarms or small PA systems. Converting a PA horn to a mic is often easier than building a horn from scratch, and it gives a piece that exists in disguise. The lower limit of frequency response depends on area of the mouth.

Small PA horns can be had on the surplus market for less than a fin. In stock configuration, they can serve as extremely low-impedance microphones whose sensitivity equals that of a stock-biased electret. They're easily disassembled by ripping out the dynamic driver and replacing it with an electret. Casual

tests of electrets so mounted showed >20 dB of gain over a bare electret. More, horn effects limit frequency response and make response directional. The modified horn is usable as is, or it can be placed at the focus of a large reflector.

Corner Boundary Mics

Due to physical laws that make sense after a couple of Coronas, a small microphone capsule placed close to and facing a flat surface gains 6 dB over the same mic in free air. Placed at the juncture of three boundaries, gain jumps to 18 dB, eight times the output of the bare capsule. Three boundaries make what's known as a sonic corner, which has a modified supercardioid polar plot.

In the world of corner boundaries, 'small' microphone capsule means 1 cm³ or less. Electret condenser mics default as the only common type this small.

Eighteen dB looks puny next to the gain of a big dish. Yet the corner achieves it without alignment woes, in an unassuming package that ignores low-frequency noise and has a strong directional preference, giving the closest thing in bugging to free lunch.

Construction is intuitive. Sides should measure at least 5″; bigger sides widen the capture zone, but bass response rises as well.

The principle applies to shapes other than flat sides, such as progressively deeper dishes, morphing into cones; and to bugs and their mounting, such that a bug can gain close to 18 dB by being mounted in a naturally occurring corner.

Resonant Cavity Microphones

Resonant cavity microphones (RCMs) had been buggers' faves for decades when they finally crashed out of stir in '91. The sound of a conch shell dramatizes the effect, for it echoes not the sea, but resonance excited by ambient noise.

The microphone trade has always fixed on flat response and means to squelch resonance. This may explain why the open literature ignores tools that promote resonance and points up cavity mics as a wide-open field for the experimenter.

A resonant cavity is a hollow object that rings in the bug band. Resonance amplifies and equalizes sound at the mic. Boost ranges from a few dB to more than 25 dB. The most common axial cavity type is a hemi-closed cylinder with a microphone mounted at the closed end. The mic can face forward or backward, but its diaphragm should be parallel to the closure. Closed cylinders exhibit one peak; irregular cavities can give multiple peaks that tend to be weaker than the single cylinder peak.

Variations on the basic cylinder alter its behavior. Those that taper open toward the mouth show a smaller peak than a regular cylinder but exhibit a wider capture zone. A lip on the cavity shrinks the acquisition aperture but enhances resonance.

One or more smaller "daughter" cavities ported on the main cavity resonate at higher frequencies and give multiple peaks. Cavities can combine into an array.

Recently, membrane cavity mics broke cover. They cap the aperture of an RCM with a very thin, compliant membrane. This harnesses the fact that pressure at the surface of a diaphragm rises as wavelength of on-axis sound approaches twice the diameter of the diaphragm. In plain terms, that means a bump of 6-9 dB in the response curve for on-axis sound. This peak occurs at 1,600 Hz for a 4″ diaphragm. Diameter scales by simple ratio for other frequencies.

To work up an axial cavity microphone, get the following items:

- a sinewave tone generator covering 300–7,000 Hz
- an audio power amplifier, such as a consumer stereo system
- an oscilloscope
- an electret mic soldered to the end of 3′ of shielded cable
- a wide-range loudspeaker

Ideally, the process takes place in an anechoic chamber. Short of that, choose the best-damped room available, preferably carpeted and draped.

Feed the sinewave signal to the AUX input of the power amplifier, connect the speaker to the amp, and connect the microphone feed to the oscilloscope. Place the speaker on a stand at least 2′ off the floor. With the mic facing the speaker from at least 10′ away, run a tone sweep of the bare element over 300–6,000 Hz; plot this curve to show obvious peaks due to speaker or room modes.

To screen individual cavities, push the mic fully to the back of the cavity. The felt cap on the mic keeps it from getting too close to the closure. With the cavity opening facing the speaker, repeat the tone sweep while watching the scope display. Note the frequency of the major peak. (Take care to distinguish wall resonance from cavity resonance. Sound can cause the wall of the cavity, rather than the air in the cavity, to vibrate. The two phenomena are different. Only resonance of air in the cavity pays off in the field.)

Experienced ears can screen without the scope by holding the cavity mouth about half an inch from the ear while running the tone sweep.

Any cylinder has a resonant peak. The trick comes in choosing peaks that coincide with useful formants in the bug band. Take the most promising cavities on field trials.

RCM feeds naturally sound unnatural, but, focused on the right formants, their output is highly intelligible. An RCM feed should receive the benefit of bug EQ and high-gain, low-noise amplification.

The foregoing describes the bare bones of the principle. The field is virgin turf for adventurous experimenters.

Combinations

Individual ADMs can combine to remedy defects or sum advantages. Dishes bigger than a few feet across focus, at best, on an area many times the size of a single mic. Other ADMs' ability to gather sound over an area of a few inches to several feet encourages combinations, for example:

- reflector feeding horn
- reflector feeding corner boundary
- reflector feeding resonant cavity
- horn feeding resonant cavity

- horn constructed with integral resonance (meaning many off-the-shelf PA horns)
- mic mounted boundary-style inside horn

Range

ADM range hinges on so many variables that predictions based on the inverse square law usually miss the mark. The ideal intercept occurs on a cold, quiet night. The right system working under optimum conditions can pull in signals from more than one mile away.

Applying ADMs

- Indoor testing is futile and, due to the essence of the tool, pointless.
- Wait until dark. Civilians have been conditioned to attend directional mics used anywhere but football sidelines. Dark also means cooler temperature and less traffic noise.
- Mount the ADM on a tripod or other support to get it up off the ground and isolate it from tendons squeaking in the user's hand.
- Use ADMs in quiet surroundings. Practical gain rises as ambient noise falls. No directional mic exists that will let the user aim across Sunset Strip and hear as though target and ADM were at opposite ends of the Louvre.
- Explore the option of using the directional mic as a stand-off piece. Not only does the ADM stand away from the target, but the operator monitors some distance from the ADM. The distance should be enough to allow escape in the event the ADM is detected.
- ADMs work surprisingly well through cover, such as an average forest or tall grass.
- ADMs can even work "around corners," using sonic reflections off natural and man-made structures.

PARABOLIC REFLECTORS

- big and obvious; conspicuous unless disguised
- map the area of the focus

Dish sources: Edmund Scientific sells 12", 18", and 24" aluminum pieces that should be blackened or grayed for covert work. Information Unlimited offers a 2' clear plastic reflector. At 3' and up, Fiberglas dishes salvaged from C-band satellite systems have begun to flood the surplus market. Those dishes are surprisingly light. One man can wrangle an eight-footer pretty easily, in four bolt-together sections.

A) Diagram of reflector operating principle; focuses energy from wide area on small area.

B) Taking a cue from astronomy, some designers have altered the package to include a second reflector that focuses on a mic behind the dish.

C) Operating principle of co-focused reflectors. Reflector does not have to be parabolic, but parabola selects parallel-incoming energy, giving it superior directivity.

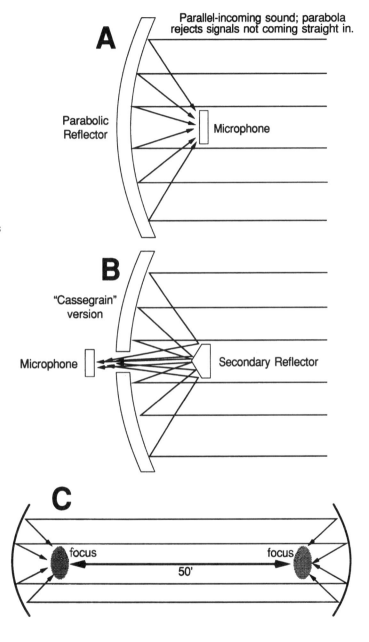

A
Parallel-incoming sound; parabola rejects signals not coming straight in.
Parabolic Reflector
Microphone

B
"Cassegrain" version
Microphone
Secondary Reflector

C
focus
focus
50'

HORN MICROPHONES

- *off-the-shelf horn speakers, 4–7"*
- *cheap, easy to use*
- *possible gain: >25 dB*
- *response is not flat; choose resonance in the bug band*

Horns are defined by many variables, key among which is taper.

A) Linear taper, typified by megaphone; response rolls off fastest of all types.

B) Elliptical taper has slower low-frequency roll-off.

C) Hyperbolic taper gives flattest response down to cutoff. Area of mouth of horn determines low-frequency response limit. Thus, small horns are useful in bugging because they naturally attenuate low frequencies.

D) Cutaway side view of small PA horn shows folded design, readily adapted to bugging.

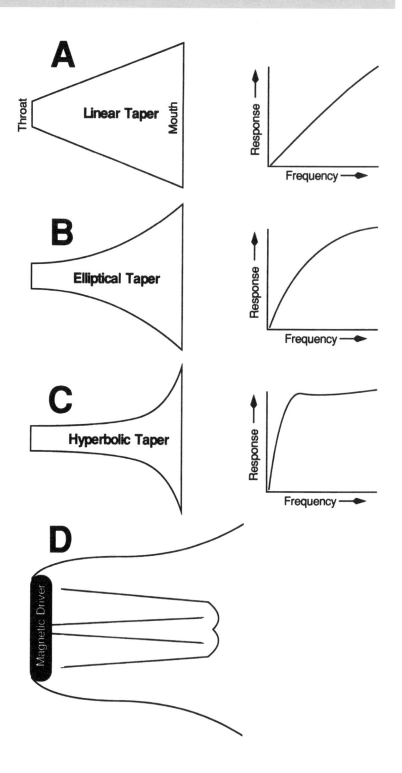

CORNER BOUNDARIES

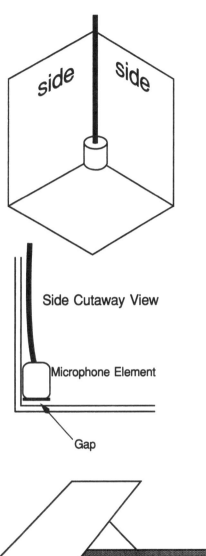

Side Cutaway View

Microphone Element

Gap

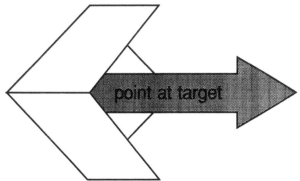

point at target

- *maximum gain just under 8 (18 dB)*
- *US Patent #4,361,736*
- *low-frequency cutoff determined by size of boundaries; use sides 5"–10" for bugging*

To make a corner boundary mic, cut three squares of thin, rigid material: acrylic, Masonite, circuit board stock, etc. Glue them together as a corner with airtight joints. Mount the electret condenser microphone with its aperture facing DOWN. Leave a gap of about 1/16" between mic aperture and boundary. Run cable up groove and secure with masking tape, or route cable through small hole in one side. CBM aims as if it were an optical corner, with the interior apex facing the target.

RESONANT CAVITIES

- *gain can exceed 25 dB*
- *although an infinite number of shapes are possible, cylinders and semicylinders are readily available*
- *easy to manipulate and reproduce*

RCMs exist in a variety of standard diameters and lengths, including common containers shown in photo.

The experimenter will find that each cylinder exhibits a characteristic peak that relates loosely to its volume (3.14 x r² x length). Experimentation will also show that utility of cylinders that resonate at the same pitch varies greatly. In "D," all cylinders hold the same 63.6 in³ volume. Yet of these, only #3 and #4 proved useful as resonant cavity mics. The systematic experimenter will find that, for each frequency, an optimum length vs. diameter exists where a sharp peak coincides with an adequate aperture. Cavities can combine into parallel arrays, or port one into another as a daughter cavity.

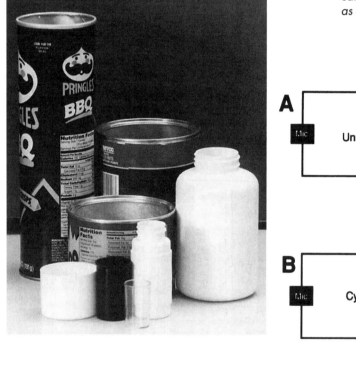

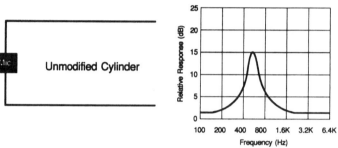

A Unmodified Cylinder

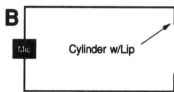

B Cylinder w/Lip

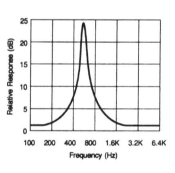

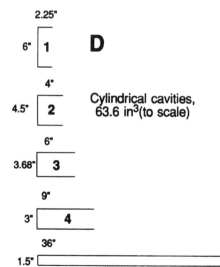

D Cylindrical cavities, 63.6 in³(to scale)

2.25"
6" **1**

4"
4.5" **2**

6"
3.68" **3**

9"
3" **4**

36"
1.5" **5**

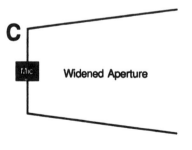

C Widened Aperture

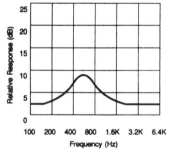

RESONANT CAVITIES

A) Simple dual-chamber device; main cavity resonates at frequency y, daughter cavity at frequency x. Change size of either chamber to tune peaks. Considerably more complex resonators are possible.

B) Response curves of bare microphone element and that same element mounted in device shown in "B."

C) Speculative rendering. Dual-cavity resonant mic has been modified with lips on each cavity to enhance resonance; the whole thing has been ported to a horn, one of many types of combination ADMs. Fertile field for experimentation.

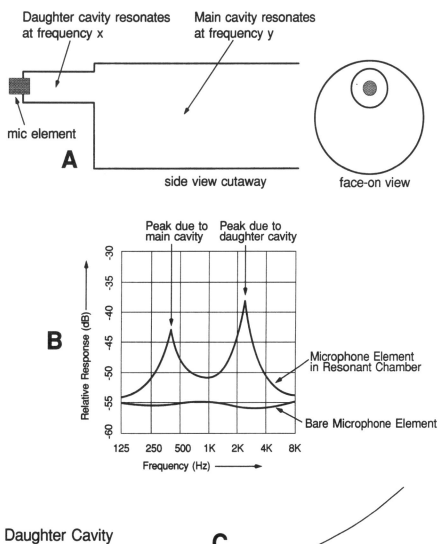

Daughter cavity resonates at frequency x

Main cavity resonates at frequency y

mic element

A

side view cutaway

face-on view

Peak due to main cavity

Peak due to daughter cavity

B

Relative Response (dB)

Microphone Element in Resonant Chamber

Bare Microphone Element

Frequency (Hz)

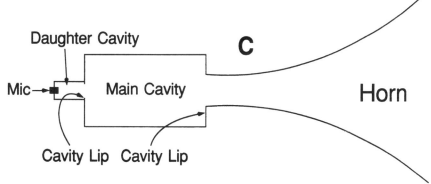

Daughter Cavity

C

Mic→

Main Cavity

Horn

Cavity Lip   Cavity Lip

RESONANT CAVITY ADJUNCT

Tunable audio-band sinewave generator for working up resonant cavity mics, based on XR2206 function generator, available for ~$5. Covers 150–5,000 Hz by tuning 100K pot on pin 7; use an audio-taper pot wired for minimum resistance in full CCW position; this confers fine control at high frequencies. Trim 50K and 500-ohm pots for minimum distortion; if no scope is available, put 50K

pot in center of range, and set 500-ohm pot at 200 ohms. Output amplitude variable 0–5V$_{p-p}$ by 100K pot in op amp feedback loop. Feed sinewave output to line input of home stereo system. Device needs a 12–24V supply. If device will be used without an oscilloscope, label key frequency points in 500-Hz intervals on dial.

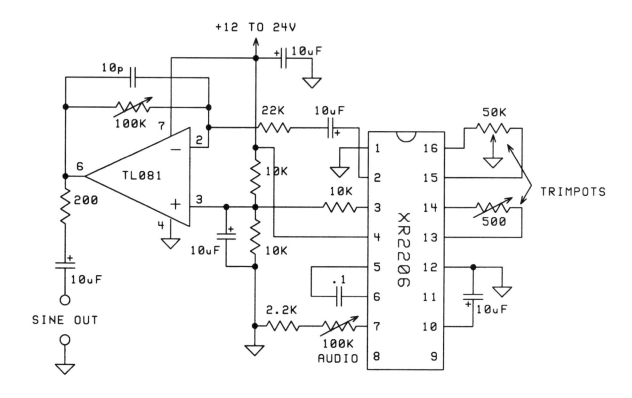

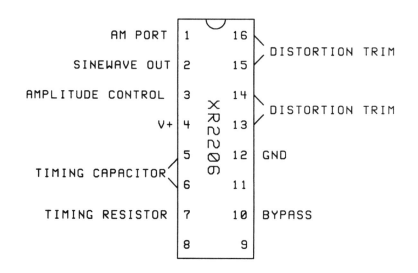

NONAMPLIFYING DIRECTIONAL MIC: THE SHOTGUN

Shotgun or "line" microphones are long, straight tubes built to quash resonance and exclude off-axis sound. They're directional but don't amplify. At best they give unity gain over the bare element. Shotguns enjoy limited use in bugging circles but can be handy at close range where the need to exclude off-axis sound outweighs the need for gain.

Half-closed cylinders resonate. Shotgun mics use proprietary patterns of slots and holes to break up standing waves and damping material to muffle them. They shroud the mic capsule in a thick, semi-soundproof chamber. The only tones it can hear are those that hug the tube.

The shotgun recalls what some deem the most egregious surveillance hoax of the postwar era, the infamous polytube device unveiled to the masses in *Popular Electronics* during the first run of *A Hard Day's Night*. Your author built one in '65, another in '67. Both stank.

Thirty-seven thin-walled aluminum tubes, 3/8″ diameter, 1-36″ long, were epoxied together in a spiral hex, feeding a crystal mic mounted in a funnel, boosted by the grizzled Lafayette Radio 5-transistor amp. The mic coupled to the amp through a step-down transformer, if memory serves, ditching a load of voltage at the point that could least afford a loss. The piece is worth dissecting for its object lesson in how not to rig an audio preamp.

Electronic signal coupling serves one of the following two aims:

(1) to transfer power
(2) to transfer voltage

RF gear dotes on power. Peak transfer happens when source impedance matches load impedance.

But audio preamps deal only with voltage. By Ohm's law, a 10K source feeding a 10K input loses 6 dB—half its amplitude—more than that if amp impedance is less than source impedance. The rule in audio gear dictates showing the source of a load impedance at least 10 times the source impedance. This preserves >90 percent of voltage. Stepping down voltage for the sake of impedance match defeats the point. The old Lafayette should have coupled straight to the mic.

The tube assembly reeked of optimism. Each tube was supposed to ring at a different pitch in the speech band. The sum should have avoided a monotone peak. The problem with that reasoning is that open tubes don't resonate nearly as sharply as half-closed tubes do; and coupling tubes into a common chamber actually dampened what resonance might have been.

The polytube shotgun suffered an inescapable flaw: it heard no better than the unaided ear. True, it had directional traits, but no better than a studio supercardioid that could have been used a lot more discreetly. An obvious and evil purpose made the shotgun a magnet for heat.

Weird vibes shrouded this supposedly potent tool. Some came to see it as a sick joke or a slick fraud, as though invisible hands had thrown out a sop to blunt the bent to court forbidden lore. The hoax may have peaked in an episode of *Slattery's People* that showed the shotgun protruding from the center of a dish, the silliest arrangement possible short of stuffing it in the ground. The saga dictates that buggers treat unverified lore as disinformation.

SHOTGUN MIC

Top photo shows the Cal-Rad 10-10, probably the least expensive shotgun mic sold in the past decade. Device uses hobby-grade electret similar to Radio Shack 270-090. Tube ~12" long, equipped with slots and internally padded to help quash resonance. Middle photo shows rear of unit; bias resistor can be accessed by inserting needle-nose pliers into holes, unscrewing the insert (bottom photo). Replace stock 1K resistor with 10K; use a pair of 6V PX28L batteries to power unit, and gain leaps more than 12 dB.

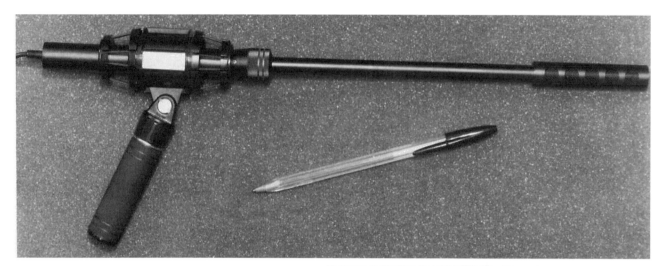

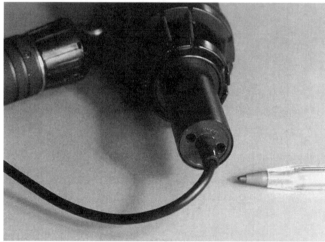

bias resistor

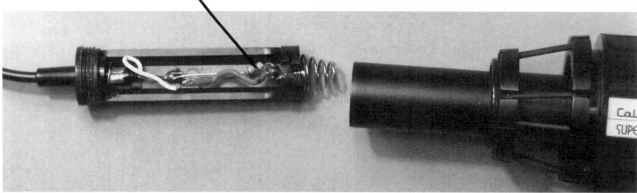

SHOTGUN MIC

Diagram shows side-view cutaway of microphone compartment. Top photo: disassembly of mic chamber *reveals hobby-grade electret. Bottom photo: Cutts compensator reduces muzzle climb.*

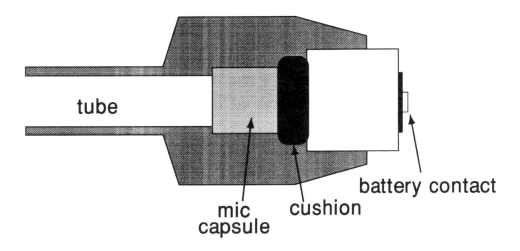

tube

mic capsule

cushion

battery contact

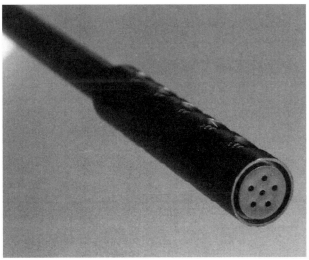

POLYTUBE SHOTGUN

Gross construction details of polytube shotgun mic. Biggest bugging hoax ever? Build one and see. Gaps between tubes, and in the funnel-to-tube coupling, should be sealed with caulk. "Then . . .": Lafayette Radio 5-transistor amp, circa 1965, redrawn after package insert. Transformer inside dotted line not part of amp, but recommended in original Popular Electronics construction article. Despite complex appearance, device is simple and consists of three capacitor-coupled common-emitter amplifiers. Collector load of final preamp transistor is a transformer winding; its secondary both drives and biases the bases of a differential pair, whose collector loads each consist of half the winding of another transformer that also carries one supply potential. PNP transistors require inverted supply polarity compared to NPN. If built with modern high-beta silicon transistors, this circuit would probably prove unstable, because each stage is configured for maximum gain; total looks to exceed 120 dB. Low beta of '65-era germanium transistors meant low gain per stage. All five germanium transistors can still be had as NTE102A. " . . . Now": One transistor and a 386? A mere 66 dB of gain, enough to leave the old Lafayette in the dust, and a lot quieter. Coupled to a high-output piezo mic like the Mouser model specified, this demure piece will give anyone wishing to try the polytube shotgun a fighting chance. In fact, bypassing the emitter resistor with 10µF and placing a 10µF cap on 386 pins 1 and 8 will boost gain beyond 90 dB—and the device is fully stable if built on a neat, spacious circuit board. . . .

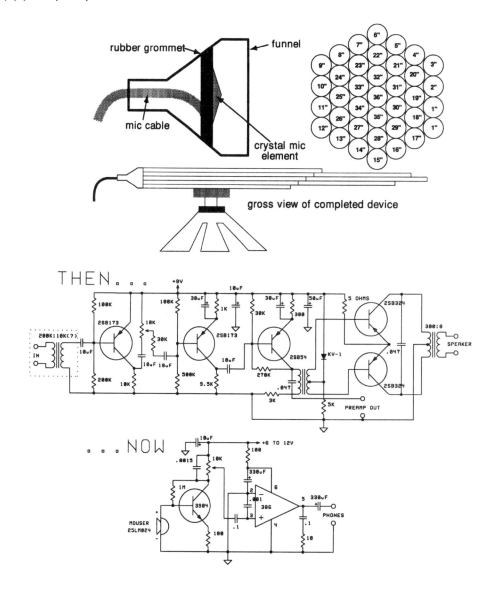

CHAPTER 10

Contact Mics, Etc.

Some sort of barrier often separates the bugger from his objective. That fact spurred the evolution of probes to penetrate sonic barriers.

CONTACT MICS

Contact microphones apply directly to the sonic barrier, such as a wall, window, or ceiling. They come ready-to-use as musical instrument contact mics, or as conventional mics adapted to the task. The ideal contact mic responds to vibration but not sound, to allow high gain without feedback.

A ceramic mic becomes a contact mic when the agent pries off the aluminum grille and tapes the mic to the target surface. This preserves the mic for return to vocal duty, with some sacrifice in contact performance. A better contact piece can be had by cutting away the aluminum foil diaphragm and gluing an extension to the yoke. This enables a direct link between the target surface and the piezo element, improving sensitivity to vibration while largely eliminating pickup through air. The extension should be made of light but rigid material, such as 1/32″ circuit board.

An electret, too, makes a good contact mic once freed of its felt dust cap. A simple fixture can make an electret the most sensitive contact mic the author has encountered. Insert a straight pin into the target wall, leaving about 1/4″ protruding. Glue or tie two 6-inch lengths of thread to the body of the electret, and suspend the electret from a pair of pushpins placed so that the head of the straight pin rests against the electret membrane. The fixture is delicate; perforated membranes happen often, but contact sensitivity is outstanding.

Dynamic mics can adapt to contact use but suit the task less than ceramic and electret mics. Certain piezo buzzers have wide enough response to make good contact mics.

One of the most effective contact mics-in-waiting, now a dying breed, is a phonograph cartridge. New samples sell for $50 and up, and old ones can be had for a song at yard sales. Ceramic cartridges are preferred for contact work because of their high output. Magnetic cartridges require greater boost and tend to pick up hum. Stereo cartridges have two outputs that correspond to vertical and lateral movement of the stylus. These outputs can usually be wired in parallel without loss of sensitivity. A phono cartridge should mount on the end of a light, rigid arm 6–10″ long, whose other end should rest in a hinge to keep the arm from canting. This pivot can mount on the floor and allow the cartridge to lean against the target surface, or mount on the target surface so that the cartridge hangs suspended against the target. A pressure of 1–5 grams is adequate.

In addition to voice intercepts, contact mics play a key role in safecracking, which differs from vocal work in that tones of interest lie at and below 1 KHz, some of them below 20 Hz. A cheap electret becomes a fantastic low-frequency contact mic when the mouth is sealed with a disk cut from 1/32″ circuit board.

ATTACHING CONTACT MICS

Technique depends on the type of mic. Tape attaches most contact mics. A very thin magnet glued to the mic works well with ferrous surfaces. A pair of magnets, pushpins, or thumbtacks can support a rubber band to hold the piece in place. Suction cups make great attachments for smooth, nonporous surfaces. The fixture is prepared from a suction cup salvaged from a toy bow and arrow set. Bore a 1/4″ hole into the cup, and glue in an electret with rubber contact cement. The fixture must be airtight. Lightly moisten the cup if necessary (use water; the lab boys will have a DNA field day if you lick the cup). Or simply glue the mic to the target surface. Whatever attachment technique, the agent should leave as little evidence as possible.

SPIKE MICS

A spike mic is a contact mic that uses an extension to bridge a gap between, say, sides of a wall. The extension is typically a steel spike but can be any rigid material, such as thin acrylic rod. The spike contacts, and often penetrates, the far wall used as a sounding board. Ideally, the spike passes through a hole big enough that the shaft does not rest on the interior wall.

HOSE MICS

As the name implies, a hose mic confines the sonic entry port to the end of 1/8″–1/4″ diameter tubing. Hose mics once entailed the hassle of keeping an airtight seal between the hose and a mic of larger diameter. Potting was a common resort that made for a clumsy tool. These days a 6-mm electret slips inside the tubing, stays put by friction, gives a perfect seal, and needs no potting. The assembly can be built in the time needed to solder leads to the mic.

Suitable tubing is available from lab supply companies, or in the aquarium department of discount stores.

The open end of the hose can be treated as a microphone and coupled to a corner bound-

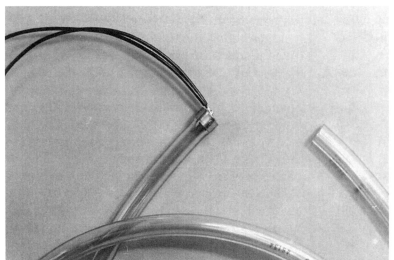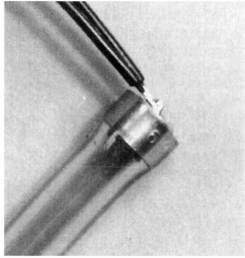

Super-simple hose mic can be built in the time needed to insert a 6-mm electret into the hose and solder leads to mic. Fold leads back onto side of tube and wrap with tape to provide strain relief. This type does not need potting.

ary, horn, resonant cavity, or air bladder. Hose mics make a quasi-repeater, the first stage being air coupled over 10–30′.

AIR BLADDER MICS

A balloon with a mic inside, placed between walls and inflated. The mic is usually an electret.

FUNNEL MICS

A funnel mic seals the element in the stem of a funnel. In use, the wide end of the funnel applies to a surface, such as a room wall or the interior wall of a briefcase. Caulking compound, modeling clay, or rubber cement makes an airtight seal. Rubber cement dries quickly and rubs off easily but should not be used on surfaces that react with acetone.

CONFORMAL CONTACT MICS

The piezoplastic PVDF can be applied to any flat surface. One of its best-known uses is the large conformal sonar arrays on submarine hulls.

Plastic piezo strips shown earlier in the book make poor contact mics because the type of stress that generates good output from them is not produced when they are simply taped or glued to a wall. They need to exist in some

arrangement that causes vibration to deform them, or one that focuses pressure on them.

NONCONTACT CONTACT MICS

In essence, these are nonlaser laser listeners that work an inch or less from the target. Short distance obviates a collimated beam. Type requires mounting on enough mass to keep it from moving; 30–50 pounds is usually adequate.

GAIN BLOCKS FOR CONTACT MICS

Because sonic barriers attenuate treble a lot more than bass, voice intercepts need extreme bass attenuation combined with sharp midrange/treble boost. Amps built for safecracking need sharp treble cut and deep bass extension, usually below 20 Hz.

DRILL A HOLE: PINHOLE MICS

The agent should not let potent contact mics cloud the point that contact mics suit cases that prevent drilling a hole. The best contact mic hearing through a half-inch of drywall cannot equal the audio available through a small hole in the same barrier. A "pinhole mic" is made by mating an electret to a very thin, rigid tube salvaged from certain aerosol products. A hole just over 1/16″ in diameter will pass this tube. The audio level jumps ~40 dB and needs no EQ.

CONTACT MICS

A) Common ceramic mic becomes contact mic by prying off cover and carefully cutting away aluminum foil diaphragm. Glue extension, made from 1/32" circuit board material, to yoke.

B) Some of the ways to attach contact mic to surface.

C) Basic spike mic setup.

D) Pinhole mic.

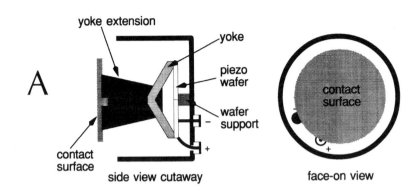

A

side view cutaway

face-on view

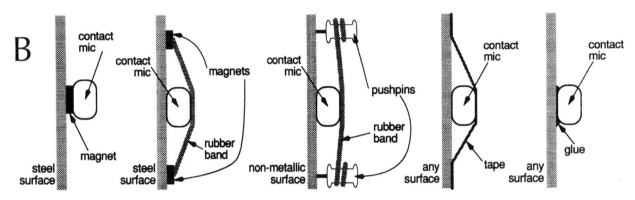

B

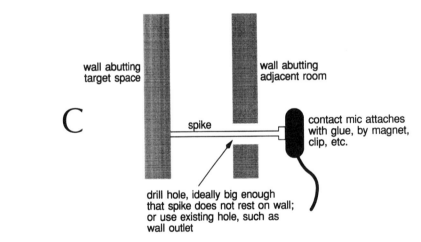

C

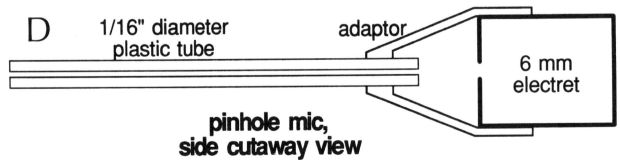

D

1/16" diameter plastic tube

adaptor

6 mm electret

pinhole mic, side cutaway view

CONTACT MICS, ETC.

A) Side cutaway view of funnel mic.

B) Side cutaway view of air bladder mic.

C) Two ways to mount phono cartridge used as contact mic.

D) A noncontact contact mic.

E) A means to put electret diaphragm in physical contact with target surface.

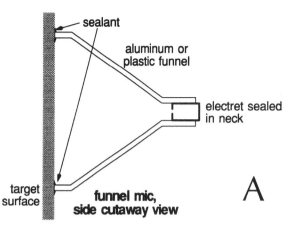

funnel mic, side cutaway view

sealant
aluminum or plastic funnel
electret sealed in neck
target surface

A

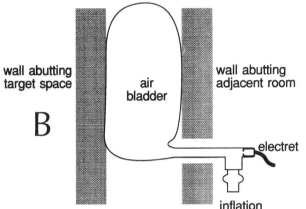

wall abutting target space
air bladder
wall abutting adjacent room
electret
inflation valve

B

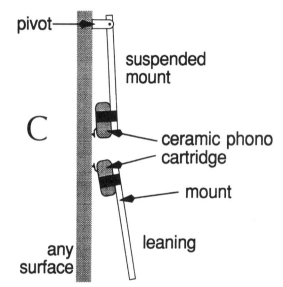

pivot
suspended mount
ceramic phono cartridge
mount
leaning
any surface

C

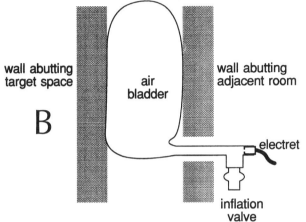

unitary reflective optical sensor
IR LED
ultrasonic transceiver
IR phototransistor
5–25 mm
any surface

D

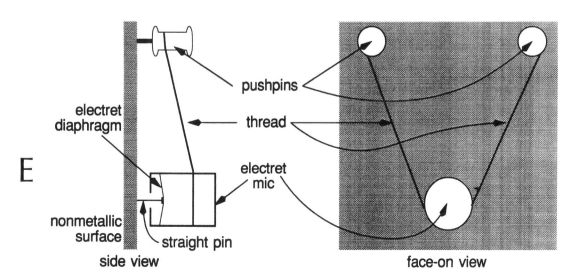

electret diaphragm
pushpins
thread
electret mic
nonmetallic surface
straight pin
side view
face-on view

E

CHAPTER 11

Optical Bugging

Optical bugging involves the following four steps:

- collecting and amplifying audio
- impressing audio onto light
- transmitting and receiving light
- recovering audio from light

Collecting audio uses all methods told so far. The process of impressing sound on light is known as modulation; recovery of audio is known as demodulation. Optical bugs use intensity modulation (IM), amplitude modulation (AM), frequency modulation (FM), and pulse-width modulation (PWM). Transmission happens through open air or fiberoptic cable.

INTENSITY MODULATION AND DEMODULATION

The most basic modulation scheme is called intensity modulation, which also describes the process. An optical emitter brightens and dims in response to audio. IM is extremely simple to implement and suits both open-air and fiberoptic transmission.

Intensity modulators use a technique called constant current. The emitter stays active all the time. Current flowing through it and, thus, its

brightness hold steady. The audio feed alternately increases and decreases this current, but the positive and negative peaks average to 0, leaving mean current unchanged. The mechanism is readily appreciated by using a visible LED in the system.

An IM receiver consists of an audio amp with a photosensor in place of a mic. This simplicity incurs a weakness, for it contains no means by which an optical receiver can reject the huge 60-Hz pulses produced by incandescent lamps.

AMPLITUDE MODULATION AND DEMODULATION

The amplitude modulation system impresses audio on a carrier. This carrier, rather than raw audio, is transmitted optically. Demodulation requires passing the carrier through a rectifier and a lowpass filter. The point of using a carrier is to give the optical receiver a means to reject optical interference.

AM is realized in analog multipliers, in discrete-transistor circuits, and in amplitude modulator integrated circuits. Optical carriers typically fall in the range 50–500 KHz. The carrier should be at least 10 times the highest frequency to be recovered.

OPTICAL TRANSMISSION

- *impress audio on light, with or without carrier*
- *audio impressed directly onto light is intensity modulation (IM)*
- *audio is impressed onto carrier, which modulates light in carrier-based systems:*
  - *frequency modulation (FM)*
  - *amplitude modulation (AM)*
  - *pulse-width modulation (PWM)*

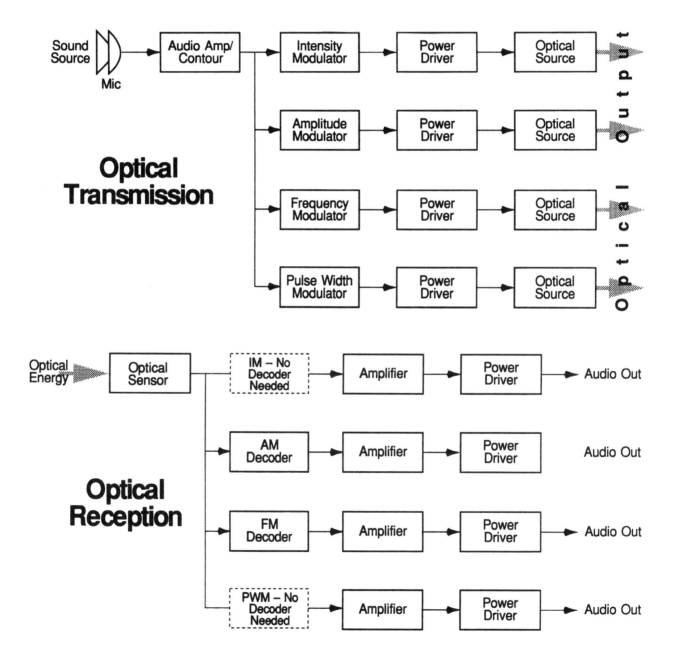

INTENSITY MODULATION/DEMODULATION

Graph illustrates the concept of constant current. With no audio input, a steady current flows through the optical emitter. When audio is applied, positive-going peak increases current; negative-going peak decreases current. The average current does not change. Constancy holds only so long as modulation stays in driver's linear operating range. IM is simple to implement and highly efficient in that modulation can approach 100 percent.

Schematic A shows an emitter follower driving LED in series with current-limiting resistor. Has voltage gain of ~1. R1 varies bias applied to base through R2, allowing trim of resting current.

B puts LED in series with collector load of common-emitter amplifier. In this case, voltage and current gain can be attained by manipulating relative values of R3 and R4, and by bypassing emitter resistor with C3. In both cases Q1 must be biased in its linear mode to accept audio modulation through base. Several LEDs can run in series if supply voltage is high enough to drive them.

C) Q2 is configured as a standard audio amp; input source is a phototransistor biased off R1.

D) Photodiode IM receiver feeding op amp. Note that D1 is reverse-biased. If R1 >10K, use an FET-input op amp for lowest total noise.

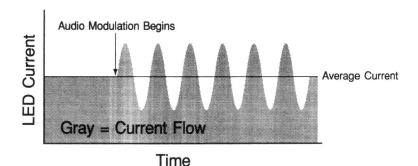

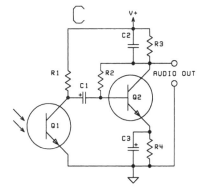

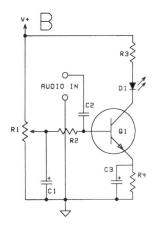

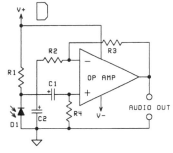

AMPLITUDE MODULATION/DEMODULATION

Diagram shows basics of amplitude modulation/demodulation. Audio modulates carrier, which is transmitted optically. Upon reception, carrier is rectified and lowpass filtered to recover audio. Schematic A shows a simple AM generator. CMOS 555 timer runs at ~60 KHz. Carrier mixes with audio in Q1; "hemi" AM converted to true AM by tank on collector. Important to note that this type exhibits nonlinear modulation; percentage modulation falls as audio frequency rises. Requires treble pre-emphasis to keep flat response.

B) Amplitude modulator based on LM3080 transconductance amp. This type accepts audio modulation more readily at high frequencies, a practical design. Photo shows audio modulating a 70-KHz carrier, the output of schematic "B."

C) AM demodulator suitable for demonstrating the principle in the lab. Carrier is buffered by AC emitter follower Q1; fed through halfwave rectifier D1–D2, integrated by C4 and active lowpass filter consisting of Q2 and surrounding components. If carrier is above 300 KHz, active filter might not be needed.

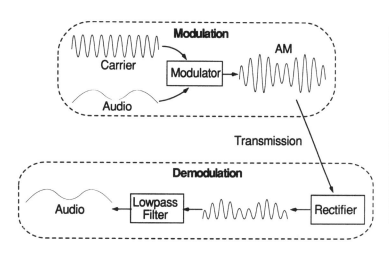

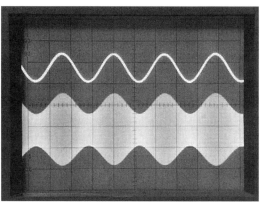

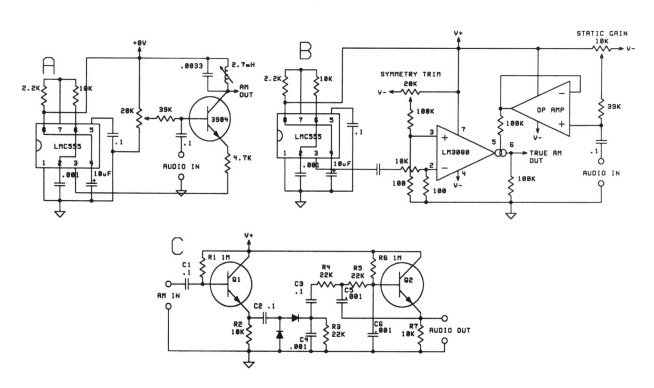

FREQUENCY MODULATION/DEMODULATION

Slight difference in nomenclature depending on whether the carrier exists as a sinewave or a pulse train. In both cases the amplitude remains constant but frequency of a sinewave (or the position of pulses in the case of a squarewave train) shifts with audio frequency, as diagram shows. The text refers to both modulation types as "FM." FM is readily implemented in common integrated circuits. A) LM567 PLL/tone decoder configured as a 120-KHz pulse position modulator. Pin 5 is a sensitive node requiring a buffer, such as 4069.

B) XR2206 function generator configured as a true frequency modulator. Output is a low-distortion sinewave. Trim both pots for lowest distortion. Chip functions above 500 KHz. Photos show unmodulated squarewave train (top) and jitter exhibited by frequency-modulated squarewave train (bottom).

C) 4046 phase locked loop FM demodulator; component values shown suitable for ~300–450 KHz. Trim 50K pot for best audio; raw output requires lowpass filter to strip carrier.

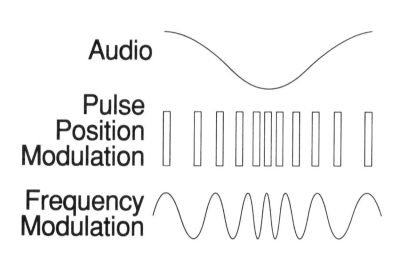

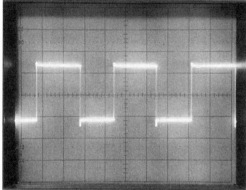

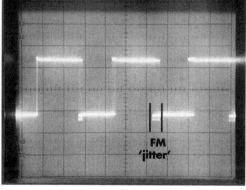

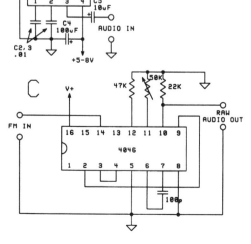

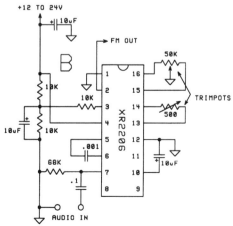

FREQUENCY MODULATION AND DEMODULATION

FM uses a carrier whose amplitude remains constant but whose frequency changes in response to audio. As with AM, carriers fall in the 50–500 KHz range.

FM generators are voltage-controlled oscillators (VCOs). The oscillator runs at the carrier frequency, but that frequency shifts up or down slightly in response to audio. Chip VCOs include the NE555 series; function generators, such as NE566, XR2206, and ICL8038; phase-locked loops, such as LM567 and LM565; and single-transistor oscillators of the type used in RF bugs but tuned down to the ultrasonic range.

Chip-based ultrasonic FM generators impart enormous frequency deviation compared to RF systems. They use phase-locked loop demodulators to track this wide deviation.

PULSE-WIDTH MODULATION AND DEMODULATION

This system uses an ultrasonic carrier whose frequency remains constant but whose individual pulse widths vary according to the audio level; in essence, it's an intensity modulator that gives the receiver a means to reject interference. Because it offers no particular edge over FM or AM, PWM is seldom used.

OPTICAL EMITTERS

Light-emitting diodes can generate red, yellow, green, and, lately, blue light. Infrared (IR) LEDs are preferred for bugging because they emit invisible energy, because common optical sensors work in the infrared, and because IR "holes" exist in the atmosphere and in fiberoptic cable.

Each LED has a minimum forward voltage necessary to get it to light. This figure is necessary to predict current that will flow through the LED and for calculating the number of LEDs that can run in series at a given voltage.

The amount of current an LED will tolerate is limited by the risk of thermal destruction. An LED rated 50 ma continuous forward current should be able to take 100 ma in squarewave pulses with a 50-percent duty cycle, or 200 ma in pulses having a 25-percent duty cycle, and so on.

Optical emitters include laser diodes, whose coherent beam can focus to a tiny spot at long range. They're used for tight-beam transmission and in the practice of laser-bounce bugging. Unlike LEDs, which can often tolerate several times their maximum rated current for short periods, laser diodes can be destroyed by a few percent more than their rated current.

A laser beam can cause permanent eye damage. Accordingly, experimenters should follow these precautions:

- Never look directly at a beam of laser light.
- Never look at reflected laser light.
- Never look at laser light through optics; magnification increases the risk of eye damage.
- Never aim a laser beam at persons, animals, vehicles, or aircraft.
- Unless you are a qualified, professional laser scientist, experiment only with visible, low-power, "eyesafe" lasers. Lasers labeled "eyesafe" are weak enough not to cause eye damage, even if accidentally viewed. However, when viewed through magnifying optics they are not eyesafe and should be handled with the same respect as noneyesafe lasers.

OPTICAL SENSORS

Optical sensors generate voltage or current in response to light. They include the following:

- phototransistors
- photodiodes (regular, PIN, avalanche)
- light-variable resistors (e.g., selenium sulfide photocells)
- solar cells
- photomultiplier tubes

Light-variable resistors respond too slowly for use above 100 Hz. Solar cells respond fast enough for audio but too slowly for an ultrasonic carrier. Photomultiplier tubes are very sensitive and extremely fast but are fragile and require a high-voltage power supply. Avalanche photodiodes require a bias of several hundred volts and an operating environment whose temperature is tightly controlled.

By default, then, phototransistors and photodiodes dominate optical bugging. Besides lacking drawbacks of the other sensors, they're widely available and cheap. The choice of phototransistor or photodiode depends on modulation scheme. Phototransistors are usually chosen for IM and carrier systems operating below 80 KHz; PIN diodes for any carrier-based system.

Phototransistors behave as transistors whose base current responds to light. They conduct current that drops a voltage across a resistor in series with the collector or the emitter. Photodiodes behave as reverse-biased diodes whose reverse current responds to light, dropping a voltage across an external resistor.

Phototransistors and PIN diodes exhibit good sensitivity in daylight, in part because ambient light excites them into a partly ON state. Their sensitivity falls in total darkness, a fact that led to the practice of dithering. Dithering is accomplished by providing a local source of infrared energy, such as an LED, oriented facing the rear or side of the photosensor. Dithering does artificially what ambient light does naturally.

At the other extreme, photosensors saturate in bright light. Saturation is a blocked state in which the sensor ceases to respond to low-level signals.

Photosensors exhibit a frequency-dependent response peak. Emitter wavelength should match this peak for greatest system efficiency. Using a 670-nm emitter with an 820-nm sensor retains >70 percent of full sensitivity; that same emitter with a 940-nm sensor keeps only ~40 percent of full sensitivity.

Besides selectivity of the sensor itself, many IR sensors come in cases that act as optical bandpass filters, further narrowing response enough to make use with off-band emitters impractical. These sensors are identified by a dark plastic case.

Photosensors "sound" quiet in complete darkness, not much noisier than an electret mic. In daylight they generate wideband hiss due to the random nature of natural light.

OPTICAL AMPLIFIERS

Design of an optical amplifier depends on whether it will amplify audio or an ultrasonic carrier. Optical audio amps follow the same design principles as microphone preamps. They differ in that sensor impedance is among the highest encountered in bugging, often in excess of 25K. FET-input op amps minimize $I_n \times R_s$ noise at this impedance; discrete-transistor amps should run at reduced collector current for the same reason.

IM receivers work with FM, AM, and PWM transmitters, because they perceive the several carrier-based signals as changes in brightness. They cannot reject interference as a true carrier demodulator can, however.

High-frequency carrier transmitters present no particular design obstacle; but a strong 100-KHz optical amplifier is a lot easier to build than an equally strong 10-MHz amp. A happy medium falls in the 50–150 KHz range.

OPTICS

Most optical emitters and sensors come with an integral lens that concentrates the beam of an emitter and provides optical gain for a sensor. Typical emitter angles fall in the range of 8–40 degrees. Emitters that lack a lens can show an emission angle in excess of 100 degrees. Integral optics improve efficiency enough to let some systems function at ranges up to 100′ without external optics.

External optics consist of common terrestrial telescopes used to amplify light falling on optical sensors. Less frequently, LEDs use a collimator, such as a planoconvex lens. Laser diodes nearly always use a collimator, which is mandatory to get a tight beam.

Special precautions attend the use of magnifying optics with lasers. Magnification of an invisible infrared beam is a recipe for permanent

PULSE-WIDTH MODULATION/DEMODULATION

Diagram illustrates concept.

A) A true pulse-width modulator (PWM). U1 is a 555 timer (bipolar or CMOS) which generates squarewaves at ~60 KHz and with a duty cycle of ~50 percent. These trigger U2, another 555 (bipolar only) configured as a pulse-width modulator. R3 biases the PWM input port to keep the resting duty cycle close to 50 percent. PWMs that use a single 555 are possible; this two-chip design facilitates experimentation. The 555 can drive optical

emitter directly, through current-limiting resistor. This type of transmitter works with IM receivers, which see the change in pulse width only as a change in brightness.

B) PWM receiver acquires some ability to reject interference through use of tank L1–C1 for phototransistor load. Tune tank to carrier. Q2 and surrounding components comprise an active lowpass filter; Q3 is an audio amp.

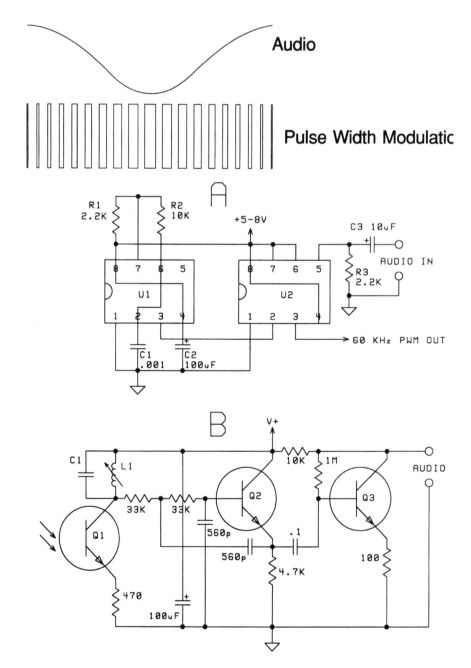

INFRARED LEDs

- wavelength: commonly 880–950 nm
- radiation angle: 8–115 degrees
- power: up to 25 mw from small types; several watts from arrays in TO-3 cases
- cost: $0.50 and up

LEDs can be destroyed by excessive current, so they're rarely driven without a series resistor to limit current. For a single LED, measure the forward voltage drop using circuit "A." Make V+ and R1 convenient values, say, 5V and 1K. LED will light. Voltage present at point "x" is LED's forward drop. For a string of LEDs, which need not be identical, use circuit "B" to measure forward drop. This value is the minimum voltage needed to turn the LED on. A 3V battery will power one LED with a forward drop of 1.3V. Three of those LEDs in series will not light @ 3V, because the supply voltage is too low to overcome the sum of their forward drops. To determine the maximum number of LEDs a given

supply can drive, divide the available drive voltage by the forward drop per LED. The integer is the maximum number of LEDs that supply can drive in series. If the drive voltage exactly equals the total drop, reduce the string by one LED. Forward drop changes slightly with LED temperature. Do not wire LEDs in parallel. Slight differences in forward drop cause most of the current to flow through one LED, sometimes destroying it. Photo shows typical LEDs. F5D1 comes in a metal case with an integral lens and a beam angle of 10 degrees; ideal emitter for bugs aimed in a specific direction, because it concentrates the energy; LN175PA has a broad, 115-degree beam angle, better suited to gigs in which reception angle is not known in advance. Both diodes have maximum optical output of 12 mw. The Radio Shack 276-143 typifies inexpensive IR emitters. Its 20-ma continuous current rating implies a safe pulse current of 40 ma, with a 50 percent duty cycle.

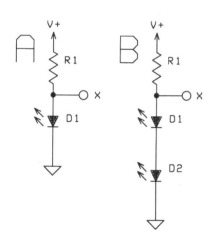

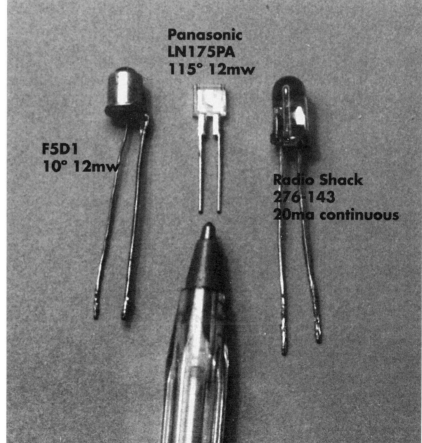

Panasonic
LN175PA
115° 12mw

F5D1
10° 12mw

Radio Shack
276-143
20ma continuous

INFRARED SENSORS

* *phototransistors and PIN photodiodes*

A) Common phototransistor bias scheme; R1 typically 10K–220K.

B) Output can also be taken off the emitter.

C) Typical photodiode biasing scheme.

D) Use of LC tank in place of resistor to reject interference; tune tank to carrier frequency.

E) Scheme useful in the event a photosensor is needed in a very bright environment. At low to medium light levels, photodiode D1 is biased through R2; at very high light levels, the voltage at juncture of D1–R2 exceeds voltage at juncture of R1–R3, plus the forward drop of D2, so D1 bias becomes the parallel value of R1–R3.

F) One example of an "active load"; Q1 and associated components function as the load for D1.

Graph illustrates why emitter wavelength should match

sensor peak. Common 670-nm visible laser diode could be used with 820-nm sensor, because doing so hits about 72 percent of sensor's maximum sensitivity. A 780-nm laser would be the better choice. Both emitters make poor choices with a sensor that peaks at 940 nm. In that case a 920–980-nm emitter would be ideal. Silicon IR sensors follow this general curve.

Photo shows common photosensors. L14G3 phototransistor typical of average performer—a 3-lead device, base clipped off this sample. QSC112 clear-case 2-lead phototransistor, also average. PN334PA PIN photodiode exhibits 2 ns rise time, but only when biased off ~50 ohms. Useful sensitivity demands much larger bias resistor, which decreases sensor speed. PN323BPA is also a PIN photodiode, somewhat slower; case is made of an IR filter that severely limits this sensor's ability to respond to off-band radiation.

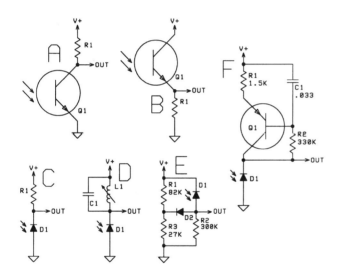

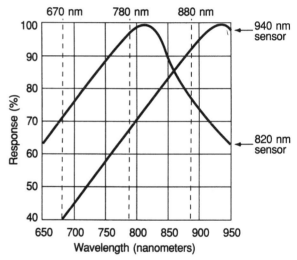

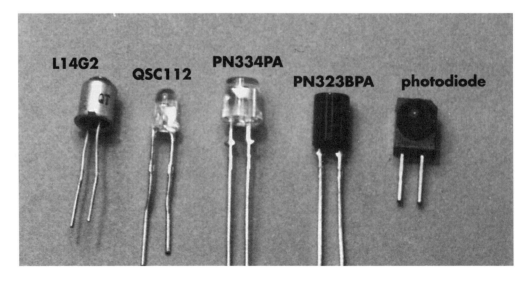

LASER DIODES

- wavelength: 635–1,300 nm
- cost: $5 (surplus) to >$1,000
- easily destroyed by excessive current
- power output: 1–100 mw
- efficiency: high, compared to gas lasers
- current consumption: 20 ma and up
- size: 9.6 mm and 5.6 mm
- raw diode output quasi-random; requires focusing (collimation) to be useful
- collimated beam is rectangular unless rounded by special optics

Most laser diodes come in a three-lead case that also contains a photodiode to facilitate current regulation. The laser diode shares a lead with the photodiode. Two wiring styles, one in which the laser anode connects to the case, the other in which the laser cathode ties to the case. Grounding and shielding are greatly eased with a laser diode whose cathode is the case. To power a laser diode, get laser threshold current and peak current from manufacturer's data sheet. Threshold current defines the point at which lasing commences; maximum current should be considered an absolute maximum that the diode will tolerate without destruction; a few milliamps above that value usually destroys the diode. Experimenters should work only with low-power, visible, "eyesafe" lasers.

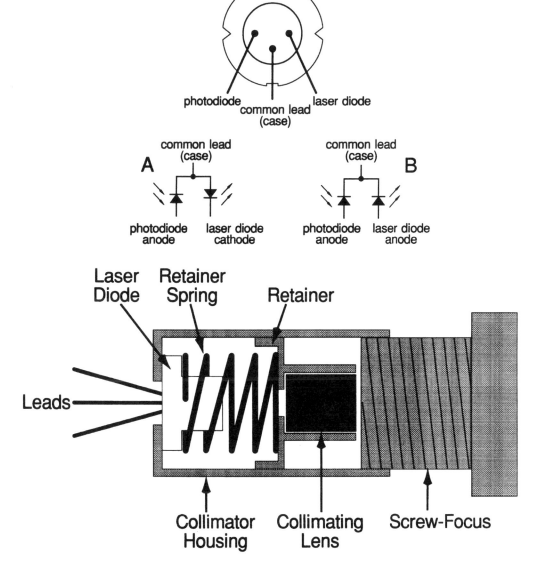

eye damage. Accordingly, the text repeats the warning: never view a laser beam directly, nor its reflection, nor view the beam through optics. This goes double for an infrared laser beam.

FIBEROPTICS

Fiberoptic systems exist in two tiers. The first can send digital data many miles with trivial loss. Cable, connectors, and transducers are expensive. A start-up system currently costs $500 to $1,000.

The second type predominates in bugging. Emitters and sensors cost less than $5 each. Cable costs less than 60 cents per foot, and it has a bandwidth that tops out around 1 MHz maximum and a practical range of some hundreds of feet. Stripping a cable for connection requires only a hobby knife or single-edged razor blade.

Fiberoptic bugging systems involve using fiberoptically coupled emitters and sensors in place of their open-air counterparts.

LASER-BOUNCE BUGGING

Laser-bounce bugging ("laserbugging") describes the act of bouncing a beam off a target, usually a window, whose vibration bears useful intelligence in the form of sound. The reflected beam acquires intelligence; an optical receiver can recover the intelligence in at least four modes: IM, AM, FM, and interferometry.

An IM laserbug uses a constant beam reflecting to an IM receiver. Vibration of the window modulates intensity by moving the reflection on and off the sensor. Basic trigonometry shows how distance magnifies linear displacement of a given angular displacement. Like conventional IM optical bugs, IM laserbugs possess no means to reject 60 Hz interference.

AM and FM laserbugs impress a carrier on the beam, usually ultrasonic but sometimes RF. Intensity modulation of the bounce becomes true AM by virtue of the presence of the carrier, which the receiver keys on to reject optical interference. Reflection off a vibrating surface also imparts a Doppler shift to the beam, mani-

fest as frequency modulation of the carrier. The relative portion of AM and FM depends on the angle between laser-target-sensor, as well as the vibration mode of the target.

Doppler shift also modulates the base light frequency. Intelligence can be recovered from the reflection by mixing it with a sample of light from the laser; phase cancellation recovers intelligence. This procedure is known as interferometry. Since the base light frequency measures on the order of 1,012 Hz, the wavelength is measured in millionths of a millimeter, enough resolution to detect the sag in a steel girder produced by the weight of a dime or vibration of a window produced by a whisper.

Despite dazzling bench performance, laser-bounce bugging suits situations so rare that the average bugger regards it more curio than marvel. A strong reflection demands a split system in which laser and sensor are placed far apart. Windows, the favored laser target, abut a noisy outside world. Useful intercepts often require extensive digital post-processing. If the targets move to another room the bugger cannot simply pan the beam to another window because doing so takes the beam off the receiver. Use of a visible laser heightens the risk of detection; use of an invisible beam heightens the risk that the bugger will sustain eye damage. The hardware is clumsy; possession is culpable.

DIRECT LASER TRANSMISSION

Sending audio on a laser beam gives an optical bug whose range is limited mainly by power and stability of the receiver optics. Drawback is that discovery of the laser shows the counterbugger the location of the receiver. This drawback means less if the beam is aimed at a spy satellite.

DESIGNING OPTICAL BUGS

Despite dozens of options, design of an optical bug is dictated by the answers to a few questions:

- *Will the intercept be subject to optical interference, as from incandescent light?* If so, this argues strongly for a carrier-based system.

- *When will the system have to operate?* Night is preferred for the lower ambient light level. Prevention of blocking in daylight demands use of an optical bandpass filter in the receiver optics.

- *How close can the monitoring station get without risking detection?* The answer to this question largely dictates power of the emitter and/or the sophistication of external optics.

- *Is fiberoptic linkage practical?* If so, and if it can be properly installed, a fiberoptic system is extremely difficult to find. Fiberoptic and open-air systems mix by using the bare end of the fiberoptic cable as if it were an LED.

- *How long will the bug have to remain active?* The bug itself can be built not much bigger than a stamp. Required operating life dictates size of the battery.

LASERBUGGING IN THE LAB

Practically impossible to go straight from newly built hardware to the field. Interaction of multiple variables dictates familiarization under controlled conditions. "A" shows small mirror fragment glued near center of speaker cone. Simulates mainly piston type of movement. Bounce is expected to exhibit predominantly Doppler shift, which manifests as frequency modulation. "B" simulates bowing type of movement by gluing reflective material to flexible cap of a small cylinder. Bounce is expected to exhibit mainly intensity modulation. These adjuncts help test split and coaxial laserbugs.

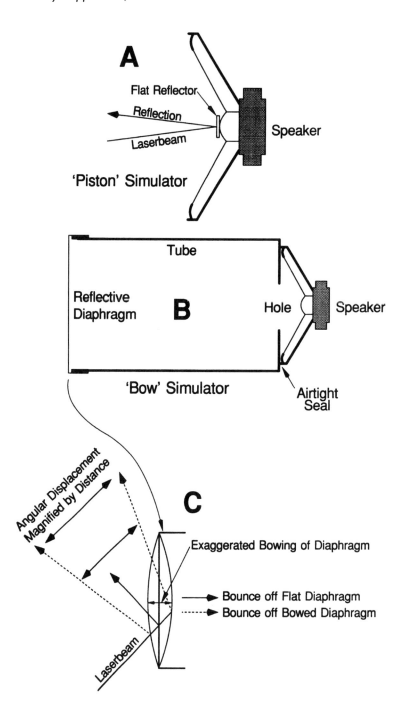

FIBEROPTICS

Schematic shows IM fiberoptic sender on left, IM fiberoptic receiver on right. Fiberoptic systems are a bit tricky in the sense that changing a variable at one end alters behavior at the other. R1 controls the resting brightness of MFOE71 emitter, in turn controlling resting base current of MFOD72 phototransistor at other end of cable. Value of bias resistance R5 that gives optimum output depends on resting base current, so changing optical transmitter bias requires retuning optical receiver

load. Gain occurs in transmitter and receiver (they're both common-emitter amplifiers), such that total gain of this type of system can exceed 60 dB. Photo shows MFOE71 fiberoptic IR LED and MFOD72 fiberoptic IR phototransistor. To prepare cable for connection, strip off ~1/8" of jacket, taking care to avoid nicking central fiber. Place screw collar on cable, insert stripped end into receptacle, screw on collar, finger-tight.

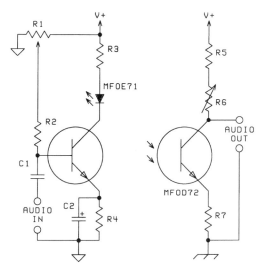

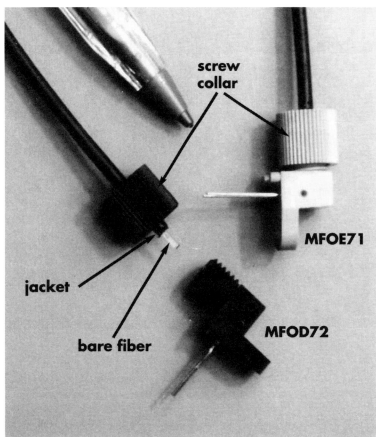

CHAPTER 12

Ultrasonics

By '67, the search for transmission media that resist debugging sweeps had come to ultrasonics. Three decades later the medium remains one of the most secure. The fact that ultrasonic audio is not something for which many counterbuggers scan helps compensate for limited range and acid-trip audio.

Common ultrasonic transducers work at 40 KHz, a few surplus ones at 25 KHz. As piezo-ceramics, they do not present a DC path and can couple directly to drivers and receivers. The transducers tend to be interchangeable, despite separate part numbers for senders and sensors. These transducers readily tolerate $60V_{p-p}$.

Sender and receiver resonate at the same frequency. Response curve of the pair shows a sharp resonant peak. Tech buffs will recognize this as an FM decoder known as a slope detector. So, ultrasonic receivers need no decoder per se; merely tune the transmitter to a point slightly above or below resonance, rectify, and lowpass filter the carrier to recover audio.

True AM transmission is possible, but not as clear—in the author's hands—as FM, apparently due to hangover at resonance.

Ultrasonic audio can turn corners and slip under doors; occasionally it can follow ductwork. It shines in line-of-sight applications. Range possible using bare transducers over an unobstructed path approaches 100 yards. That range extends to "surprising distances" (meaning a trade secret) by using a sonic dish antenna at the receiver. An effective dish can be as small as a silver dollar. In one case an agent doubled the range in extreme circumstances by using one lens of a pair of clip-on shades as a sonic antenna. Shallow dishes work much better than deep dishes in this application. Good ultrasonic reflectors tend to be small (the sensor is only 1/4″, despite a case closer to an inch) and shallow, such as a petri dish or a small curved plate. The Edmund Scientific "solar cigarette lighter" looks about perfect for this application.

Audio recovered from ultrasonic transmission sounds waterlogged. The audio feed is rich with low-frequency spuriae that demand highpass filtering. Using an ultrasonic bug gives an intuitive understanding of why early ultrasonic alarm systems were so finicky.

Resonant transducers resist audio modulation above ~1,200 Hz in both AM and FM modes. Anything approaching flat response must apply a sharp treble preemphasis. In practice it is pointless to try to impress frequencies above 3 KHz on these transducers.

Alternatives to the 40-KHz resonant transducers exist, working in the 75–220 KHz range, but at $50–$75 apiece have limited application.

Electrostatic transducers are not resonant, work over the range 40–100 KHz, and can be salvaged from sonic tape measures and

Polaroid® auto-ranging cameras. These transducers will take a drive voltage of up to $100V_{p-p}$. They will accept frequency modulation the same as resonant types, but the receiver requires a true slope detector or a phase locked loop decoder.

For the wealth of literature on radio transmitters in general, bugs command a distressingly thin segment. What has leaked has come roundabout from professional ranks, often pirated and bastardized; perhaps corrupted, as some believe, to suit dark motives.

ULTRASONIC TRANSDUCERS

- common cylindrical transducers measure ~5/8"
- the majority resonate at 40 KHz
- transducer availability: Digi-Key, Mouser, Hosfelt
- cost: $3.50/pr. to >$50/pr.

A) Shows relative acoustic output of emitter transducer; applies as well to receiver transducer; peak occurs at resonance.

B) Assuming FM generator is centered just below resonance at 39.2 KHz, this curve shows raw detector output. As carrier frequency moves toward resonance, output rises; as it moves further away from resonance, output falls. This describes the behavior of a slope detector. All that's needed to recover the audio is to rectify the carrier, then strip it with a lowpass filter. These principles apply only to resonant transducers. Wideband transducers require an alternative demodulation scheme. Photo shows 40-KHz transducers.

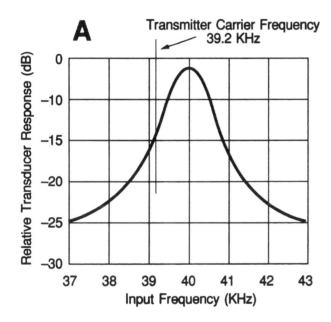

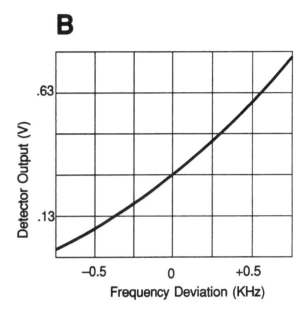

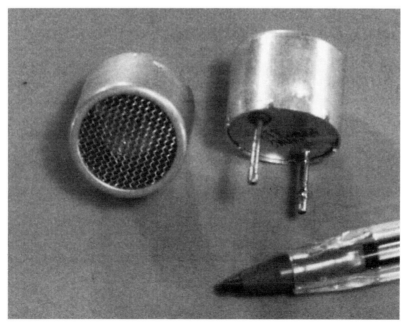

ULTRASONIC TRANSMISSION

By the sampling theorem, a 40-KHz carrier will support frequencies up to 20 KHz; in practice, the resonant nature of the transducers resists modulation above ~1,200 Hz. Will accept frequency or amplitude modulation, but FM transmission gives greater clarity.

A) Simple FM ultrasonic transmitter can be built from 555 oscillator, driving the transducer directly.

B) One way to boost output voltage—feed 555 output into 8:1K step-up transformer. Depending on supply voltage, transformer output can approach $100V_{p-p}$; requires appropriate precautions.

C) Basic receiver suitable for experimentation. Op amp amplifies 40 KHz; output couples to halfwave rectifier made from a couple of diodes; carrier stripped by passive lowpass filter C3. Recovered audio feeds 386 power driver. Ultrasonic systems work best over an unobstructed path. Limited capacity to turn corners inside dwellings. Receivers benefit from ultrasonic antennas; shallow dishes are much more effective than deep ones.

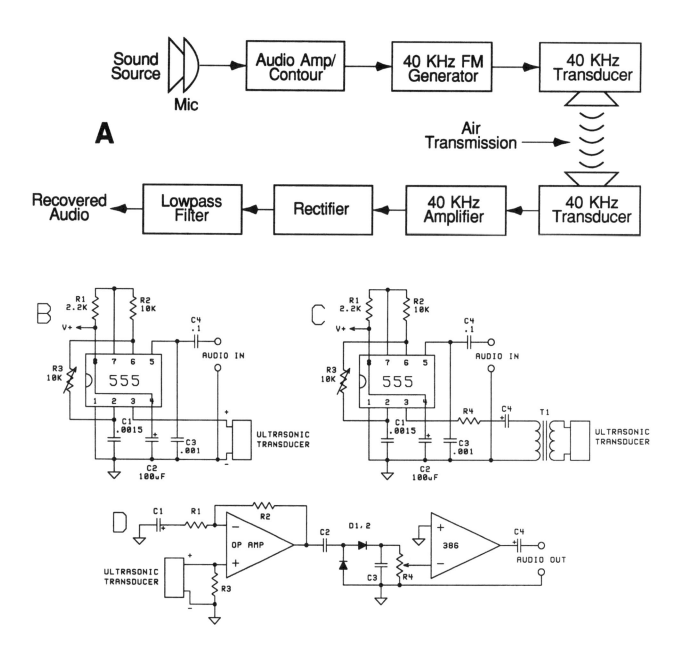

CHAPTER 13

Radio-Frequency Bugs

"Radio-Frequency (RF) bug" could be called pleonastic, "bug" being slang for a concealable radio transmitter. Nine in ten transmitters that hold themselves out as bugs share an RF core consisting of a tank-tuned transistor oscillator. Audio feeding the transistor base shifts junction capacitance enough to modulate the carrier frequency, making most bugs FM transmitters.

Bugs owe their vogue to simple construction, low cost, and ease of use, the latter due to a glut of submicrovolt scanning receivers available for less than two bills. Bugs plant and recover quickly, and they conceal readily in sundry objects. Properly constructed bugs bear no trace evidence.

Bugs range in size from several square inches down to surface-mount parts wired point-to-point. The resultant transmitter occupies less space than an electret mic. RF power available from one transistor spans several watts down to a few nanowatts. Bugs operate from any battery that can muster 0.9V, including hearing-aid types that could pass for saccharine pills.

DESIGNING BUGS

Most bugs consist of an audio stage, which amplifies and conditions sound, and an "RF core," the radio-frequency oscillator that

generates the signal. The audio stage can consist of a microphone, and the RF core can consist of one transistor, making the result a miracle of thrift.

But molding a workable bug involves more than getting the RF core to oscillate. A practical transmitter must do the following:

- oscillate at the desired frequency
- achieve modulation in the desired mode
- generate the correct amount of power in keeping with supply voltage and allowable current consumption
- deliver the necessary audio sensitivity
- exist in a package that will fit the gig
- resist betraying the builder by containing generic parts free of trace evidence

OSCILLATION AT THE DESIRED FREQUENCY

Most bugs tune by means of a tank on the collector. Resonant frequency (f_R) of an inductor and a capacitor is given by:

$$f_R = 1 / 6.28 \, (LC)^{0.5}$$

where:
L is inductance in henries
C is capacitance in farads

At radio frequencies, applying the equation to parts based on their labeled values gives a loose result at best, for the equation ignores stray capacitance. A better projection can be had by assuming 10–20 pF more than the value of the tank capacitor.

Commercial coils come canned (shielded) or uncanned; slug-tuned or fixed. Unlike hand-wound coils, they're consistent from sample to sample. Canned coils also retain partial prints and enough trace evidence to nail the builder; their purchase leaves a glaring trail. Hand-wound coils cost less than a penny apiece and are impossible to trace. They're smaller than commercial coils but impractical to shield. Winding them reproducibly takes practice. Cylindrical ("solenoidal") coils are specified as x turns of #y wire wound on a core z'' in diameter, usually the smooth shank of a standard drill bit. Inexpensive software is plentiful to predict inductance from these variables, but the results are vague enough to demand fine tuning in hardware.

Toroidal coils wound on fiber washers give a third option. The nature of the toroid confines the field and resists interference. Toroids correspond even less predictably to formulas than do solenoids and are often worked up empirically.

The transmitter is tuned by trimming a variable cap with a fixed coil, trimming a variable inductor with a fixed cap, or altering the spread of a fixed coil working with a fixed cap.

Although each bug has a main frequency, most bugs luxuriate in harmonics, each as receivable as the carrier. Their "dirty" signal stands out on a spectrum analyzer because purity is the first test of a legal transmission. Government contracts, beyond cookbook-bug level, usually call for harmonic suppression. These bugs are riddled with LC networks tuned to pass the carrier or shunt harmonics, and they are housed in metal cases to staunch radiation from any source but the antenna.

CRYSTAL CONTROL

Tank-tuned transmitters suffer drift due to changes in temperature and local capacitance.

Applications demanding stability—especially narrowband transmitters working with a scanner—call for crystal control. Crystal transmitters are not terribly more complex than LC types but seem much less well understood, at least outside amateur radio ranks.

A tank circuit shows a Q of 50–300. A crystal's Q can exceed 10,000. This, coupled with a low thermal coefficient, explains crystals' stability. Tuning a tank is iffy enough that the agent counts on his receiver to tune to the signal. A crystal can be "cut" to a frequency with enough accuracy to program that frequency into a scanner, confident that the signal will be there and will not drift.

Crystal-controlled bugs operate in overtone mode. The crystal oscillates at its fundamental frequency but generates an output rich in multiples of the fundamental, known as overtones. One or more LC networks select the desired overtone, while attenuating the fundamental and the unused overtones. By this method a 17-MHz crystal cut to "3rd-overtone mode" can stabilize a 51-MHz bug.

Crystal control above 200 MHz often involves frequency doubling and tripling, whose details lie beyond the scope of the text.

Crystal oscillators found in bugs lean to the unconventional, at least by ham radio stock that dotes on Colpitts & Hartley. Where ham circuits reek of redundancy, bugs eliminate all non-essentials. The crystal might show up wired between base and ground or between the collector of one stage and the base of the next. The system is biased almost as if it were a tank-tuned bug; the crystal is inserted at a point that lets it control frequency.

Several mail order firms sell custom-cut crystals. The part will arrive with its own quality control sheet and will perform to spec. It will also leave an acquisition trail as singular as a fingerprint. Buggers put custom-cut crystals in legitimate contract bugs. "Black-bag" bugs use crystals salvaged from computers, scanners, and pre-synthesis CB radios, all plentiful on the yard-sale scene.

Surface acoustic wave (SAW) resonators make a recent alternative to crystals. They cost about

$6 each and oscillate in fundamental mode, at discrete frequencies in the 180-450 MHz range. The number of frequencies available is limited; purchase leaves a blatant trail.

MODULATION MODES

An RF core can generate AM, wideband FM, narrowband FM, or some combination of modes.

Wideband and narrowband have specific connotations for RF systems. FM radio stations transmit in wideband mode, limited by FCC regs to ±75 KHz frequency deviation. In the center of the band this corresponds to 0.15 percent. Narrowband FM used in VHF and UHF public service radios deviates only ±3 KHz, or about 0.004 percent at 150 MHz, 1/37th as much as wideband FM. By comparison, 555-based ultrasonic frequency modulators can produce deviation in excess of 20 percent.

An RF core's modulation mode depends on several factors. A very weak audio feed generates narrowband modulation; stronger audio generates wideband modulation. The Q of the tank affects how hard it resists movement away from the carrier frequency. The lower the Q, the greater the deviation to a given level of audio. The Q can be altered subtly by changing the ratio of inductance to capacitance while keeping the same resonance (the greater the L/C ratio, the higher the Q), or altered radically by placing a resistor in series with the tank. Crystal-controlled transmitters tend to be narrowband devices because the crystal's high Q resists frequency modulation. Transistor bias determines whether audio modulates amplitude as well as frequency. Most bugs try to minimize the AM component.

Modulation mode dictates choice of receiver. Narrowband FM detectors distort wideband signals; wideband detectors give feeble audio from narrowband signals. The distinction is readily demonstrated using a modern scanner. Tune to a commercial FM radio station; toggle mode between wide and narrow and note the change in audio.

Modulation has implications for stealth of the bug. The greater the deviation, the "wider"

the signal looks on a spectrum analyzer and the easier it is to spot.

Other modulation schemes include upper sideband, lower sideband, and double sideband. Though many scanners can now demodulate these signals, complexity of the modulator rules them out for most bugs.

RF OUTPUT POWER

"Correct" bug power is hard to specify, for it rests on interdependent variables:

- allowable bug size (including battery)
- allowable antenna size
- required operating life
- required range
- risk that the target will detect the signal
- risk that third parties will detect the signal

The bugger wants just enough power to let him receive the signal at a specific range. Any more power shortens battery life and raises risk of detection.

RF power is measured using a standard dipole antenna feeding a calibrated RF wattmeter, with the bug 1 meter from the antenna. This reading allows prediction of range of the bug under test based upon the known range of bugs having known power, and working at the same frequency. The builder can also estimate power using a calibrated sniffer.

Mating the bug to the gig demands that the builder control the amount of RF power the bug generates. The simplest way is to change the supply voltage. Other things being equal, the higher the voltage, the greater the RF power.

Working at a fixed voltage, power can be altered by placing a resistor in series with the tank (bypassed with 0.001µF where it connects to the tank, to keep tank Q from changing). This limits current available to the RF core. Changing the emitter resistance has a similar effect but can shift frequency or quench oscillation.

The antenna has a tremendous bearing on RF power output. A typical, low-power bug might exhibit the following performance:

CONFIGURATION	RANGE
no antenna	30′
2″ antenna	120′
12″ antenna	1 block
pruned, quarter-wave antenna	2–3 blocks
center-loaded resonant antenna	3–4 blocks

Bugs resign themselves to inefficiencies because few gigs demand, or necessarily allow, configuration for maximum power. A bug destined for the underside of a desk cannot bring with it a center-loaded resonator. Even 2″ of wire may be too much for some gigs. For that no-antenna bug to be practical, the builder will have to raise power generated in the RF core by increasing the current, in turn shortening the bug's life.

The typical "optimized" bug settles for a pruned, quarter-wave antenna. Length of a quarter-wave straight vertical wire is given by:

$$l \text{ (inches)} = 2{,}951 \text{ / frequency (MHz)}$$

To prune a wire antenna, plug frequency into the formula and calculate quarter-wave length, cut the wire 10 percent longer, and solder it to the bug. Mount the bug on a light wooden or other noninductive surface with the wire hanging straight down. Power up the bug and a bug sniffer and establish a reading. Snip off a quarter-inch of wire and note sniffer response. The reading will rise as antenna length approaches quarter-wave. Once the rise begins, reduce bite size to 1/8″. At the peak, an additional snip will not change the reading, or it will cause a slight decline in power. If you overshoot the peak, replace the wire and repeat the procedure.

Once the antenna is pruned, any change in frequency will "deprune" it.

A plot of optimum antenna length vs. frequency shows commercial FM bugs needing 2–3′; 165-MHz bugs, 1.5′; 450-MHz bugs, half a foot; 920-MHz bugs, 3″; and so forth.

ALTERNATIVES TO DISCRETE-TRANSISTOR RF OSCILLATORS

Chipwise evolution has put transmitters covering 27 MHz to 2.4 GHz in integrated circuits. They find use in cordless and cellular telephones, pagers, video transmitters, and walkie-talkies. Chips take the guesswork out of construction because the accompanying data sheet specifies every detail, often including a printed-circuit layout for microwave chips. While these benefits eliminate unknowns, they come at the cost of an acquisition trail that glares too brightly for bugging.

THE AUDIO STAGE

Bug audio stages include nothing not previously discussed, but the designer should be aware that coupling the audio feed to an RF oscillator can quench oscillation. Insertion of a series resistance in this path usually corrects the problem; the resistance value is found empirically. Audio exceeding a certain level may shift the RF core into undesired modulation modes. Limit the audio to the proper level using dynamic control techniques discussed in a prior chapter.

RF sometimes feeds back through the audio stage, resulting in instability. If the audio stage and the RF core work great when tested separately, and if mating the two causes instability not due to oscillator quenching, try placing a ferrite bead on the mic feed and on the base of each transistor in the audio stage. A bead turns each lead into an RF choke.

CHOOSING A FREQUENCY

The bugger today faces quandaries undreamt of at the peak of puce polyester. Half the world seems to own a scanner equipped with frequency search, and half those radios seem to be seeking new signals at a given time. The advent of computer-controlled scanners tweaked to log new frequencies has made detection of many bugs a serious risk. The problem is compounded by a confluence of factors that steer bug design into the scanner's peak range of 100–500 MHz, where cheap, generic parts meet robust power and practical size.

A few buggers have resorted to spread-spectrum: frequency hopping, or signals so weak and so wide that they vanish in the noise floor. Scanners rarely detect these signals and can't despread them, but their use raises cost and complexity an order of magnitude over a plain vanilla bug.

Bugs built in anticipation of skilled counter-measures often hide where most RF counterbugging gear doesn't look or has trouble seeing: below the AM radio band, above the microwave oven band, and "inside" TV and FM radio carriers. The literature has danced for decades around this ploy of hiding the bug signal in a commercial transmission. FM radio gives 75 KHz on either side of the carrier; not exactly a prairie of bandwidth, but sometimes enough. Television channels occupy 6 MHz apiece. A lot can hide in that.

A bug whose signal deviates ±1 KHz occupies only 0.03 percent of a 6 MHz TV carrier. Power is relative and governed by the inverse square law. At some distance from the TV tower, the bug's signal will equal that of the 50-kilowatt transmitter. A practical bug must not work too close to the transmitter to avoid being swamped, yet not work so far from the trans-mitter that its own signal stands out against the TV carrier.

Propounding the stowaway ploy always raised the never-answered question of how one recovered this dainty signal from the vast overlapping one, a feat akin to finding a fart in a sewer. One answer is to use a synchronous receiver, whose first oscillator syncs perfectly to the transmitter oscillator. Coupled with directional antennas for transmitter and receiver, oriented such that the system operates at right angles to the interfering source, well, that's enough information to build a system.

BREADBOARDING RF TRANSMITTERS

Rat's-nest wiring typical of audio spells doom at RF. Jumpers and resistors should lie flat on the board; other parts should have their leads cut to the minimum length necessary to seat in the socket.

Bypass becomes critical at RF. Perfectly good RF cores refuse to oscillate without correct bypass. Most cores need a 0.001µF ceramic disc. Bypass with electrolytic caps can quench oscillation. If the audio stage needs electrolytic bypass for stability, isolate the audio stage from the RF stage with an RC network.

Switching from one brand of breadboard to another can shift local capacitance enough that the value of the tank cap has to be changed to stay on frequency. Even the surface on which the breadboard rests can shift frequency.

While RF behavior will change upon transfer to a printed circuit board, neat breadboard technique can keep this below 10 percent.

CONSTRUCTION

The higher the operating frequency, the more flux acts as a shunt. RF circuit boards benefit from removal of flux. Rosin requires an organic solvent, such as absolute isopropanol. Some buggers build their bugs using solder containing water-soluble flux. Washing must take place before soldering nonwaterproof parts.

If the transmitter uses more than one un-shielded coil, separate the coils as far as practical, and orient them at right angles to each other.

Bear in mind that tool marks on the bug (from hacksaw, wire clippers, etc.) are distinctive. Means to avoid leaving trace evidence are some of bugging's biggest trade secrets.

"KIT" BUGS

The novice may weigh the hassle of working up a bug against the cost of buying one of the many commercial pieces advertised in hobby magazines and patently suited to bugging, despite disclaimers. Unfortunately, heavy traffic in contraband punctuates how deeply purchase incriminates the buyer. Financial, proprietary, and shipping records are computerized, kept forever, and available without subpoena. These units' high power means great sound, long range—and everybody with scanner-search tuning in. Most will peg the meter on a sniffer. They drop out first in a sweep. The breed bears so many shaky traits that mail order "bug" vendors are rumored to operate at official pleasure.

RF CORE

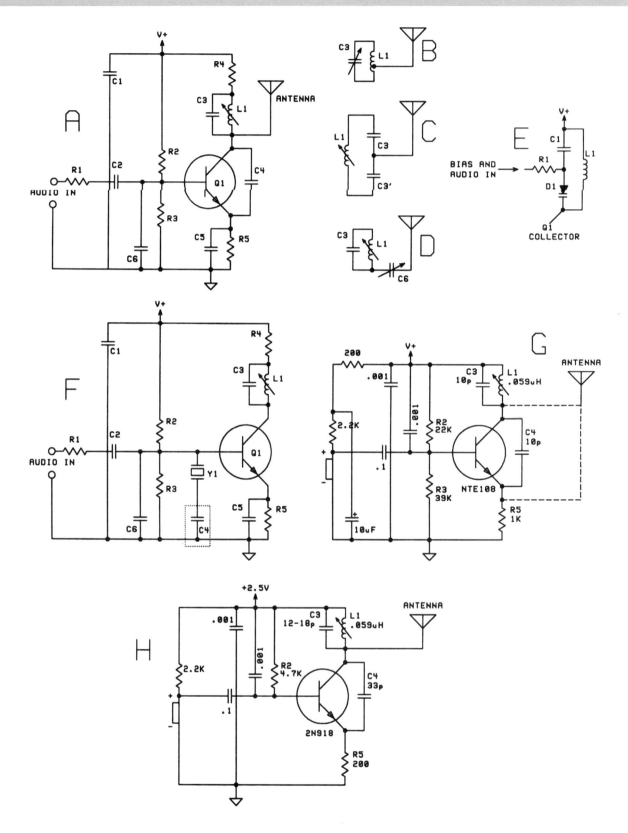

RF CORE

RF bugs covering 100 KHz to ~200 MHz can be worked up empirically; fastidious breadboard technique facilitates transfer to printed circuit.

A) Generic example of the elements that make up an "RF core." Many different transistors will work, but the novice will have the best luck using types listed in catalogs as "RF oscillator" or "VHF/UHF amp." Common examples include 2N918, 2N5179, MPSH10, and MPSH11. RF oscillation is effected by biasing the transistor in an ON state, giving it frequency-selective gain, and providing a feedback path between collector and emitter. R2 and R3 are the bias resistors in this example; their values are found empirically; R3 may not be needed in circuits working below 3V. Tank L1–C3 gives the transistor selective gain; resonant frequency comes from inductor L1 in parallel with C3 and the associated stray capacitance, which is often substantial at radio frequencies. C4 provides a feedback path between emitter and collector; typical values fall in the range 0–100pF; the higher the frequency, the less feedback capacitance is required, because stray capacitance acts as feedback capacitance. C1 is a coupling capacitor for the audio feed; R1 may or may not be necessary, depending upon whether coupling the audio stage to the RF core quenches oscillation. If quenching occurs, insert R1; find the proper value empirically. C1 is an RF bypass cap, often critical to oscillator function; C6 is a shunt to keep RF out of the audio path; it can tie from transistor base to V+, or from base to ground. R4 lowers the Q of the tank to increase deviation; value 1–22 ohms; omitted in many circuits. R5 is the emitter resistor; in general, the lower its value, the higher the RF power generated; emitter bypass C5 might or might not be needed to effect oscillation; determine need for C5

empirically. Antenna feed is shown being taken off collector, but many other options exist.

B–D illustrate alternative means to couple the tank to the antenna, with improved power transfer resulting from better impedance match. Antenna feed may also be taken off emitter, so long as oscillator uses no emitter bypass cap.

E) An alternative to base modulation; audio changes capacitance of varactor diode, which is part of tank, in turn modulating frequency.

F) Generic example of a crystal-controlled RF core. Collector tank is usually tuned to 2^X or 3^X crystal fundamental frequency; stage may be followed by additional bandpass elements to purify the signal or a frequency multiplier to work in UHF. C4 might or might not be needed.

G) The "bench bug," a simple RF transmitter suitable for testing various concepts on the breadboard. Device tunes just above 108 MHz using component values shown. Many manually tuned FM radios will reach this high without having to alter the tuner. The bug's antenna is ~1' of solid, insulated, 24-ga. wire. Connect antenna to emitter, then connect to collector; note that frequency shifts, requiring retuning the inductor. Device supplies semi-narrowband modulation. Once tuned, note that volume is very low. Power down, place a 10-ohm resistor in series with the tank, power up, and note increase in volume due to increased modulation resulting from a lower tank Q. Circuit also works with 2N918, but frequency will shift. Run circuit at 2.5V; higher supply voltage results in substantial RF output that invites detection.

H) Another bench bug, proper RF breadboard configuration shown in photo #1. Tunes ~87 MHz using components shown. Illustrates how low supply voltage allows base bias with single resistor.

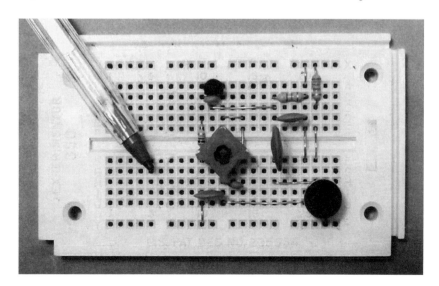

1

RF CORE

Photos #2 and #3 show how base bias affects modulation mode. In photo #2, practically no amplitude modulation is visible despite a 2V audio input to base; in photo #3, base bias has been altered; device still functions as a frequency modulator, but now a substantial AM component has been introduced. Photo #4 shows: a) canned RF coil, in the can; b) what's inside canned coil; c) typical handwound soldenoidal RF coil; d) small toroidal RF coil wound on fiber washer; e) noninductive hex tool for tuning canned RF coils.

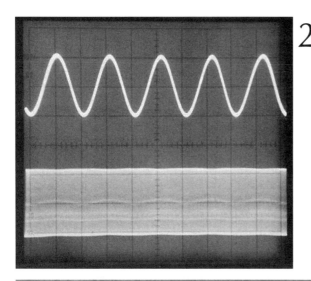

2

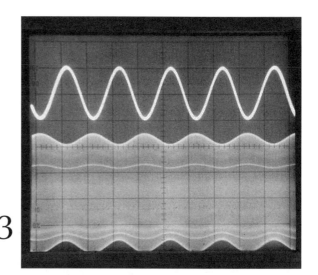

3

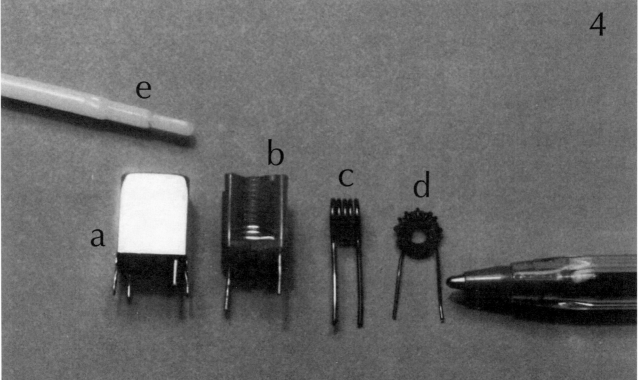

4

e

a

b

c

d

CHIP TRANSMITTERS

A) Schematic shows manufacturer's recommended circuit for 49.7 MHz transmitter; 16.5667-MHz crystal oscillates in primary mode, 3rd harmonic selected by several LC networks. All four coils are small cans. Photo shows this type of circuit used in a commercial product—too large for covert use; note ferrite loop antenna. Benefits of this type of transmitter include stable, predictable behavior and attenuation of harmonics by 50 dB or more.

B) Oscillator contained in the NE602 can function as an FM transmitter; in this case frequency modulation is achieved by varactor diode part of tank circuit. Internal oscillator workable to ~200 MHz; can use crystal control, in overtone mode.

C) Schematic representative of surface acoustic wave oscillator. Circuit values shown suitable for Digi-Key p/n PX315S1, 315 MHz.

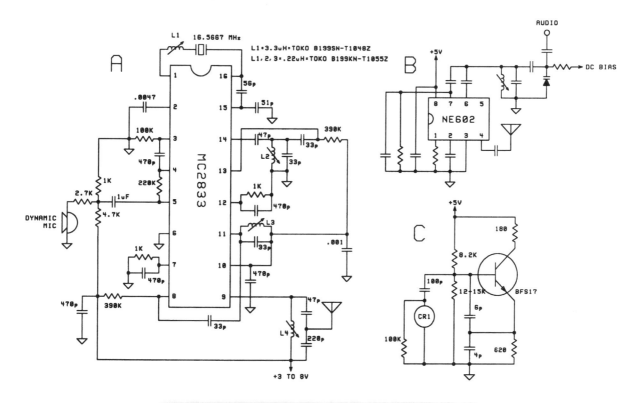

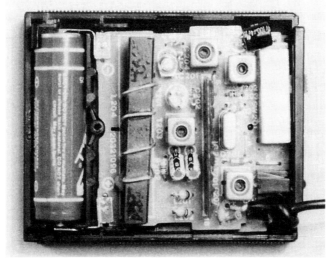

SUBCARRIER BUGS

Ordinary bugs impress audio directly onto the RF carrier. The receiver recovers audio through techniques that eliminate tones above ~15 KHz.

An alternative mode uses audio to modulate an ultrasonic FM carrier, which in turn modulates RF. Recovery of audio demands recovery of the ultrasonic carrier, from which audio is then derived. Impressing one carrier on another is known as subcarrier transmission. FM radio has been doing it for decades, for FM stereo is a subcarrier system. Monophonic FM— left channel + right channel—modulates the RF carrier. Left channel minus right channel modulates a 38-KHz subcarrier. Recovery of stereo at the receiver is achieved by recovering (L+R) from the RF carrier, and (L-R) from the 38-KHz subcarrier. The signals are then added and subtracted: (L+R) + (L-R) = 2L; (L+R) - (L-R) = 2R. Muzak® and other background music suppliers lease 67-KHz and 92-KHz subcarriers that ride on commercial broadcasts.

Buggers adopted subcarrier transmission in partial response to *scanneristas*, who can detect the RF carrier but cannot decode the subcarrier, because scanners quash the world above 20 KHz. Subcarrier modulation is visible on a spectrum analyzer. The counterbugger not already equipped with a subcarrier decoder may have to do some fiddling with the analyzer's IF but will find demodulation no big deal if he cares to pursue it. A subcarrier transmission outside the commercial FM band is practically diagnostic of a bug.

RADIO RECEIVERS
SUITABLE FOR BUGGING

The key options include the following:
- scanner
- communications receiver
- stock/modified FM radio
- a receiver built from scratch

Scanners offer a great price/performance ratio that keeps getting better: microvolt sensitivity for less than $100; programmable frequencies accurate enough for crystal transmitters; and the ability to demodulate AM, wide FM, and narrow FM. Even hand-held models can cover the range 100 KHz to the low gigahertz. Most come with a BNC jack suitable for external antennas and RF amps. Scanners have become mass-market enough to be anonymous, if the user takes precautions in their purchase. On the downside, some scanners tune in bites too big to let them lock on tank-tuned narrowband FM bugs. The scanner's memory can incriminate the bugger in the event the scanner is seized and found tuned to the bug frequency. The scanner's memory backup battery should be removed prior to a gig. If the scanner uses nonvolatile memory, program an innocent frequency over the bug frequency immediately after the gig ends.

The line between scanner and general communications receiver (GCR) has blurred. GCR implies a table-model piece with bells and whistles that range from selectable intermediate frequencies to a built-in spectrum analyzer. Ownership of a GCR implies more than a passing interest in RF.

Commercial FM radios reek of innocence. Practically everybody owns one. They look natural in the dash, or as a portable lounging in the back seat, or clipped to a belt while jogging. This innocence led many buggers to transmit in the FM band, or a few MHz above or below commercial broadcast limits.

Building a receiver from scratch hasn't been a big deal since *Less than Zero*, when receivers on a chip hit the scene. The top of the line costs less than $10. One chip and a relative handful of support parts gives ~200 nv sensitivity over the range 30–200 MHz. Tuning can be crystal-controlled or capacitor-controlled. Receivers on a chip include MC3362, MC3363, and TDA7000. Scratch-built receivers see use in repeaters and in custom subcarrier receivers awkward to realize by modifying stock radios.

Buggers working the mobile scene should view their setup through skittish eyes. The only radios that belong in a vehicle are FM, CB, and cell phones. Scanners look suspicious enough to trigger extra scrutiny if noted on a chance traffic stop. A full-featured communications receiver up and running demands an explanation, as do exotic antennas. Mounting an odd antenna on a car is tantamount to broadcasting one's trade; doubly so on a van.

WALKING THE TUNER

Bugging's best-known secret involves finessing an FM radio to receive a few MHz above or below the broadcast band. The radio remains stock to all but expert inspection, yet receives a signal beyond the reach of FM band-surfers.

This trick, called "walking the tuner," is enabled by the way manually tuned FM radios work. The first step in reception mixes the broadcast signal with another radio signal generated inside the receiver. The two signals are spaced exactly 10.7 MHz apart, so that the radio's oscillator runs at (station frequency) -10.7 MHz or (station frequency) +10.7 MHz. Sum or difference doesn't matter for this discussion; assume that the oscillator frequency is 10.7 MHz above the station frequency.

Top: inside a capacitor-tuned AM/FM radio. The tuning capacitor is inside the black oval; the 4 trimmer caps are inside the white rectangle.

Bottom left: close-up of trimmer caps. One of these is the FM oscillator trimmer.

Bottom right: the tuning capacitor of an AM/FM portable; the four screws are the four trimmer caps.

In stock configuration, the radio can receive 88.1 to 107.9 MHz. Therefore, the oscillator inside the radio tunes over the range (88.1 + 10.7) = 98.8 MHz, to (107.9 + 10.7) = 118.6 MHz. If the oscillator ran slower, the radio could receive signals below 88.1 MHz; if the oscillator ran faster, the radio could receive signals above 107.9 MHz.

Both feats are enabled by the fact that the oscillator tuning capacitor is wired in parallel with a trimmer capacitor. Adjusting the trimmer capacitor shifts the oscillator range.

Perhaps 98 percent of manually-tuned AM/FM radios—table-model and portable—use a main tuning capacitor equipped with four trimmers: the FM oscillator trimmer, the AM oscillator trimmer, the FM antenna trimmer, and the AM antenna trimmer. To change the tuning range, adjust the FM oscillator trimmer.

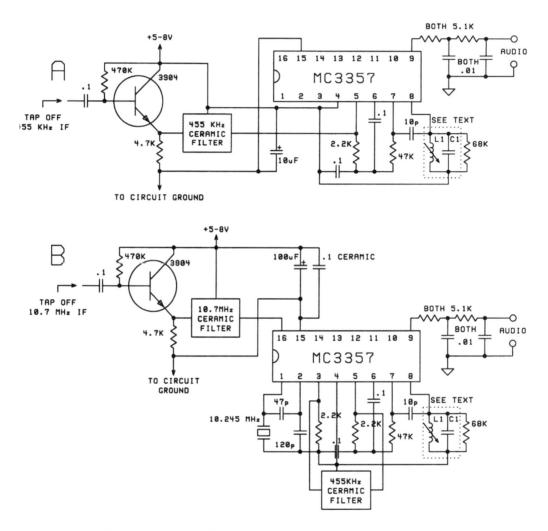

Schematic "A" shows simple add-on board to allow commercial (wideband) FM radio to generate robust audio from a narrowband signal. Stock radio can lock on signal, but volume is more than 30 dB less than that of broadcast station. Narrowband demodulator recovers full volume. Circuit takes feed off output of final IF. Transistor is configured as an AC emitter follower, to serve as buffer to 455 KHz FM ceramic filter, such as Murata CFU455D. Schematic "B" suits radios that use 10.7 MHz as final IF.

Chip contains 10.245 MHz oscillator/mixer to convert 10.7 MHz to 455 KHz. The tank on pin 8 is known as the "quad coil" and consists of a 1 mH inductor and a 100pF cap, tuned to give peak audio. Quad coils can be had with integral capacitor, tunable to 455 KHz. Parallel 68K resistor lowers Q of tank. Audio is taken off pin 9; carrier is stripped by lowpass network. Both circuits can be built using standard-size parts on boards not much bigger than priority mail postage.

To identify the FM oscillator trimmer, tune the radio to a strong FM station. Using an insulated screwdriver, pick a trimmer screw and turn it 1/8 to 1/4 turn. If turning has no effect, return the screw to its original position and try the next screw. One of the screws will detune the radio and will probably tune to an adjacent station. Return that screw to its original position, and mark it as the FM oscillator trimmer.

To extend tuner range above 108 MHz by a specific amount, tune to a station near the upper end of the band, say, 107.5 MHz. Wait for a recognizable song or a news broadcast, then move the station indicator to a point 2 MHz lower on the dial. Trim the oscillator cap until you can hear the 107.5 MHz station. Now, when the pointer reads 108 MHz, the radio will be receiving 110 MHz.

To extend tuner range below 88 MHz by a specific amount, identify a strong station around 90 MHz; put the dial on 92 MHz; tune the trimmer to hear the 90-MHz station at 92 MHz. Now, when the dial reads 88 MHz, the radio will be receiving 86 MHz.

The FM antenna trimmer might or might not affect reception. On radios equipped with a signal strength meter, get the bug up and running but place it at a distance that gives a weak reading on the signal meter. Adjust the antenna trimmer to peak the signal strength meter.

To return to stock configuration, put the tuner dial on the known frequency of a strong station and tune the oscillator trimmer to receive that station. Then tune to a weak station near the center of the band, and peak the antenna trimmer while watching the signal strength meter.

This procedure applies only to manual, capacitor-based tuners. Digital synthesis tuners can be walked but require a different technique.

The preceding instructions assume the operator to be a competent adult, 21 years or

Left: 10.7-MHz ceramic filters as they look installed.
Bottom center: Filter in the raw.
Bottom right: Ferrite beads.

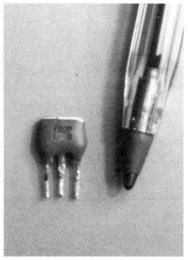

older, familiar with risks and proper safety precautions for AC-powered devices. Lethal voltage is present inside AC-powered radios. Do not attempt this procedure unless you are a competent adult who is absolutely certain that he or she can conduct the procedure safely. Safety aside, the procedure carries the risk of permanently damaging the radio. If you are unwilling to sacrifice the radio, do not attempt to modify it.

Fiddling with the radio is not illegal. Transmitting RF is—this by way of noting that "experimenting" with bugs brings the risk of discovery. The signals associated with working up a bug are distinctive. Mere possession of a buglike transmitter could, at bureaucratic whim, be used as evidence of intent to commit a crime. Do not speak during tests. Exactly 0.9 seconds of speech is enough to create an evidential voiceprint. Never stay on the air longer than necessary. For serious work, consider building a Faraday cage for the lab.

THE NARROWBAND CONVERSION

FM radios demodulate wideband FM. They can receive narrowband signals, but because narrowband deviation is a fraction of wideband, recovered audio is vestigial at best. Buggers who work FM and para-FM often build the bug for narrowband modulation. A rube who locks on the carrier won't hear much, even with the volume all the way up. Buggers trick out their own receivers to demodulate narrowband FM.

Unlike walking the tuner, this is no screwdriver mod. It involves adding a narrowband demodulator to the receiver. The new circuit takes the 10.7-MHz IF and mixes it with 10.245 MHz to yield another IF, 455 KHz, which feeds a narrowband demodulator known as a quadrature detector. A passive lowpass network removes the carrier, leaving line-level audio.

FM radios use ceramic filters to refine the 10.7-MHz IF, often two filters in series. Their appearance is characteristic. Most have "10.7" or "107" printed on them. Take the tap off the output of the ceramic filter, feed it to the narrowband demodulator, tune the quad coil for best audio.

(Depending on the radio, the narrowband conversion might entail little more than a screwdriver mod. Some FM receivers use a quadrature demodulator. If the quad coil naturally has a low Q, the user can replace it with a high-Q coil [10.7 MHz or 455 KHz, depending on the frequency at which demodulation occurs]. If the quad coil is a high-Q narrowband type that has been shunted with a resistor to lower the Q for wideband reception, narrowband demodulation can be as easy as desoldering the shunt resistor; or placing a switch in series with the resistor, to enable toggling between wide and narrow.)

CHAPTER 14

Carrier Current

Carrier current refers to a (usually FM) carrier of 40–1,000 KHz that rides either on a dedicated pair or on wiring used for some other purpose, AC house wiring being the most common. The "current" tag derives from the fact that the AC power grid has a very low impedance at ultrasonic frequencies. Current travels better than voltage in such lines.

Given an FM modulation/demodulation scheme, the obstacles to implementing carrier current are (1) coupling the high-impedance carrier signal to a low-impedance line, and (2) isolating the system from AC line voltage that could destroy it and electrocute the operator.

Ohm's law to the rescue. Pick a carrier frequency, say, 300 KHz. At that frequency, a 0.1µF cap has a reactance of 5.3 ohms. At the 60-Hz line frequency, the cap's reactance exceeds 26,000 ohms.

The answer, then, is to couple the carrier to the line through capacitors that have low impedance at the carrier frequency but exhibit very high impedance at 60 Hz. Such coupling capacitors must be rated to withstand the AC line voltage without breakdown. A rating of 200 volts AC or 630 volts DC is usually adequate.

Coupling through a resonant circuit keeps >99 percent of the line voltage out of the modulator circuit.

Carrier current systems have been common in consumer electronics since Thank God It's Friday. They can be found in "anywhere" phone extensions and remote power-control systems. The latter use a protocol known as X10, which sends 120-KHz pulses at precise points in the power cycle. Thus, 120 KHz makes a poor carrier choice for bugs.

Carrier current signals can usually be received at any point off the same side of the power step-down transformer, an area that extends, depending on local power wiring, to several houses on a block, or to whole wings of apartments. While the carrier will not penetrate the power transformer's huge inductance, the agent can extend the range of the system by bridging the power transformer with a pair of 0.1µF 20KV capacitors—obviously, a rare resort.

Carrier current systems escape detection unless the counterbugger specifically screens the line for a carrier. Screening involves viewing the line on a scope connected through an appropriate highpass filter.

Despite FM's theoretical ability to reject interference, AC lines carry switching transients and hash that intrude on the carrier and do cause interference, usually not at a level that defeats the point of the bug. Also, the high voltage actually modulates the impedance of the line, making complete suppression of 60-Hz interference difficult.

Carrier current bugs are often secreted in something that connects to the AC line: lamps, consumer audio gear, appliances, or wall sockets. Preferred host articles contain a DC supply that can drive the audio amp/modulator.

The experimenter need not connect anything to the AC power line to test a carrier current system. Build an inert line simulator from 200′ of 18-gauge AC line cord with a 4.7-ohm resistor and a 0.1µF capacitor wired across the line for good measure. This shows the carrier close to a dead short, just as the power line does. The simulator enables testing and debugging most systems without the risks of handling lethal voltage.

Note: Coupling a system to the AC power line (or to any energized line, such as the phone line) is the proper business only of experienced, qualified professionals who understand the risks (death by electrocution, fire, etc.) and the correct safety procedures. This text warns everyone other than experienced, qualified professionals not to experiment with house current or any other hazards.

CARRIER CURRENT

- *Systems that tie to the AC power line pose a lethal shock hazard and are strictly for qualified professionals*

A) One technique used to couple an ultrasonic carrier to the AC power line while isolating system from AC voltage. Capacitor values chosen to give low impedance at carrier frequency and very high impedance at 60 Hz AC line frequency. Capacitors must have rated working voltage of at least 200 volts AC (630 volts DC). Self-contained systems leach power from the AC line through a transformer; direct AC-to-DC converters can be built but are extremely hazardous and are not recommended. Devices secreted in AC-powered consumer electronics can tap DC directly off the system power bus.

B) If a dedicated, neutral pair is available, units can couple directly. At ranges exceeding half a mile, this type may benefit from loading the line (i.e., shunting it with resistors), resulting in a cleaner signal.

C) Unshielded, twisted pair cable can conduct 10 MHz baseband video over one mile; range is several miles at lower frequencies. Trimmer pot and capacitor for video contrast and brightness. Impedance placed on pins 3 and 5 allows user to tailor response. Will even accept crystal as frequency determining element; extremely useful for narrowband applications. Essentially the Maxim databook circuits. Signal travels as current, rather than voltage. Such systems prove useful when they may be subject to monitoring by audio-band equipment.

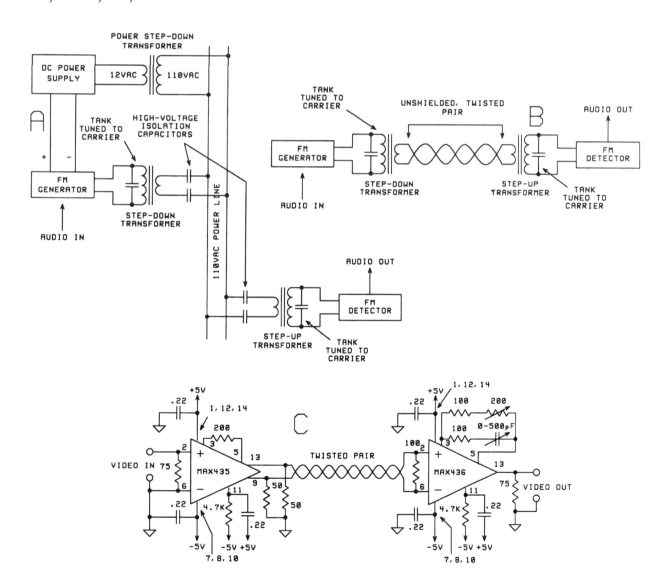

131

CHAPTER 15

Hardwire

Nothing sees more use in professional setups, and nothing gets less press than hardwire. Fabled D.C. townhouses aren't strewn with radio bugs. No pro risks the fruit of his labor in America's most feverishly scanned tract. Armies of dilettantes are out there running computer-controlled AOR-3000s that spot a strange frequency in seconds. No, regal bungalows are hardwired.

"Hardwire," without modifiers, denotes systems linked through unshielded, twisted-pair copper wire. Advantages include simplicity, fidelity, and stealth, for hardwire leaks nothing to excite a bug sniffer.

Twisted pair implies low impedance and balanced transmission. Low impedance minimizes noise voltage induced by stray current, as from omnipresent AC power fields. The wires' twisted state tends to equalize the amplitude and phase of an induced voltage, making it a common-mode signal rejected by a differential receiver. If this description sounds familiar, pick up the phone. Telephone cable is a balanced low-impedance line that can pipe clean audio over more than 10 miles. Hardwire bugs enjoy at least the same range.

The simplest hardwire system is a sound-powered headset of the type that swamped America in the war-surplus '50s. Once used extensively aboard warships to ensure communications in the event of power failure, the system consists of dynamic transducers connected by a twisted pair.

An amplified receiver turns that arrangement into a useful bug. The microphone could be a loudspeaker, say, one in the ceiling used for background music or paging.

Hardwire's true potential manifests in systems that make the sensor an active device with a power supply and a preamplifier. Performance rises exponentially. Stable systems with 100 dB of gain can be built from a handful of parts, and draw so little power that a lithium 9V battery can run them for weeks.

Unshielded, twisted-pair wiring is available through most electronic suppliers. Gauge is not critical; get the thinnest wire possible down to 30 ga. Thinner wires are effectively invisible but break easily.

The twisted pair has surprising bandwidth. Simple circuitry can send 10-MHz baseband video over one mile on a twisted pair.

Special apps let the agent use studio microphone cable, a shielded, twisted pair whose third conductor allows studio-style phantom power. That, in turn, enables remotely powered tools whose potential is limited only by the imagination.

Hardwire installation can be tricky and extremely difficult to explain. As to how one installs hardwire, well, not every termite inspector actually works for Orkin®.

For all its pluses, hardwire lives knee-deep in quicksand. The wire ties the agent to a felony bust as surely as the Devil's umbilical. Once the cable is found, debugging is easier than following the yellow brick road. Buried or hidden cable can be traced using a cable tracer (ultrasonic signal injector and companion receiver) of the type now in plentiful supply, and which works through walls and at a distance of several feet. This vulnerability explains why hardwire looms large in the vista of repeaters.

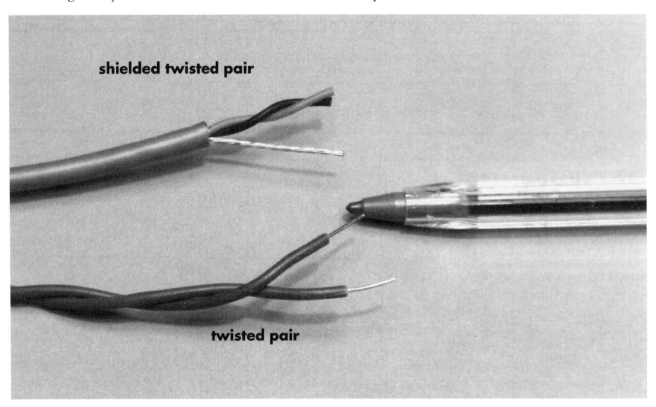

shielded twisted pair

twisted pair

HARDWIRE

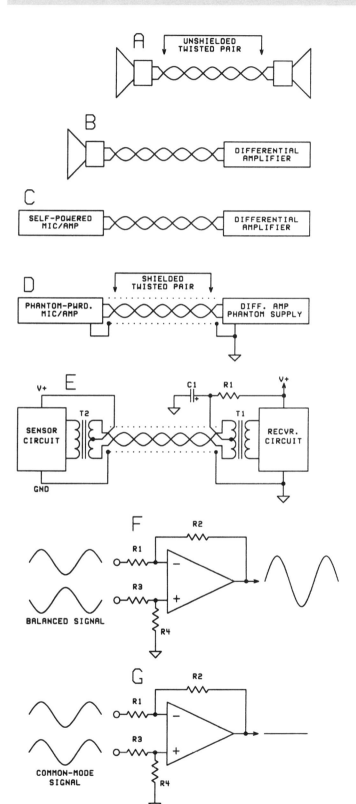

- *cheap, simple*
- *superb fidelity*

A) Sound-powered headset; two dynamic transducers linked by twisted pair cable.

B) Transducer, usually dynamic, feeds remote differential amplifier through twisted pair.

C) Remote, self-powered sensor feeds differential amp. In this incarnation hardwire starts to show its power. Stable system gain in excess of 100 dB is possible with such a setup.

D) The shielded, twisted pair that is studio microphone cable enables phantom powering of extremely sophisticated gear.

E) Circuit details of phantom power. Lowpass network R1–C1 ties to center tap of T1; remote device takes power off center tap of T2. Transformers isolate the systems.

F and G) Differential amplifier, also known as op amp subtractor. In "F," true differential input signal is equal amplitude but opposite polarity between channels. In "G," common-mode signals are equal in phase and amplitude in both channels; differential amp ignores them. In both F and G, R1 = R2 = R3 = R4. Many other means exist to achieve differential amp, but all share the ability to ignore common-mode signals.

H) Breadboard this circuit to dramatize common-mode rejection. Differential amplifier inputs are tied together such that each sees the same thing. Whatever signal is applied will be common-mode. Feed in high-amplitude sinewave, say, $4V_{p-p}$ @ 60 Hz. Connect output to oscilloscope. Trim R1 to output null. In this case, despite huge signal present at input, output shows virtually nothing because signals are common mode. Op amp type not critical.

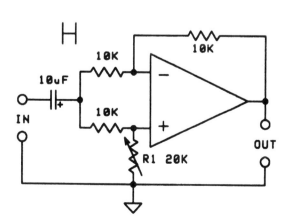

CHAPTER 16

Repeaters

If not the final frontier, repeaters are still a topic that dim cabals dread seeing in print. The problem with all unitary bugs is that they lead back to the bugger. Say the sweep uncovers a low-power transmitter at 295 MHz. Weak signal equals proximate receiver, often within a radius of a block or two. Simply touring the neighborhood locates the blatant Surveillance Van: mirrored windows, roof turret, scanner antenna, bumper plastered with P.A.L. stickers. The first oscillator of the receiver in that van will be running at—and radiating—one of a limited number of predictable frequencies. This radiation can guide the knowledgeable counterbugger straight to the target.

More, by tuning to an intermediate frequency standard in modern receivers, the counterbugger can actually hear what the bugger hears.

Once the receiver is confirmed an old scene plays out: "You have the right . . ." A felony bust, welcome another snitch to the fold. Not infrequently, the perp is already owned. He merely has to spill juicy details about the gig, maybe provide copies of his intercepts, and he remains on line, another tireless minion in America's war on, uh, crime.

Consider an alternative scenario. Same bug, but this time the patrol turns up nothing. When the RF directional gear is brought in, it leads to a clump of brush in a vacant lot one block away. Physical surveillance of the lot is set up, but by next afternoon no one has approached.

The counterbugging team descends on the lot. Search uncovers a cheap scanner tuned to the bug. The scanner's headphone jack connects to a tiny twisted pair that leads toward a hill behind the lot.

Agents trace the brown wire, practically invisible in the underbrush. It leads over the hill, around a crop of rocks, and finally runs up a power pole a quarter-mile away. A brown camo case is bolted to the pole, leaching power from the line, driving an array of light-emitting diodes. The chief counterbugger leans back in his climbing belt and surveys the landscape from a perch 20 feet off the ground. The box is visible for miles, from an angle of 150 degrees.

The boys shake their heads sadly, then pack up and leave.

The team has uncovered a trimode repeater: RF to hardwire to optical. Their search gave the monitoring agent ample time to decamp from his post half a mile from the pole. (He took dandy snaps of the counterbuggers before he split.)

Of course, had the first sequence been hardwire to RF, the bug might have escaped detection.

A repeater is a combination receiver/transmitter. It might or might not demodulate the signal before retransmission; might or might not change the transmission medium. Repeating breaks the link that always exists between transmitter and receiver, and which will eventually betray the careless bugger.

Repeaters happen through concatenation of elements. Time and money limit the number of stages, but certain configurations have survived vicious Darwinian selection. The short list follows:

- RF to hardwire
- RF to IR/laser
- RF to fiberoptic
- hardwire to RF
- hardwire to ultrasonic
- hardwire to IR
- fiberoptic to RF
- fiberoptic to hardwire
- ultrasonic to hardwire
- ultrasonic to RF
- carrier current to IR

The key principle in designing a repeater is to chain media so as to isolate the system from the target's best countermeasures. Because RF countermeasures are the most highly developed, many repeaters place at least one silent medium (fiberoptic, hardwire) between the primary bug and the radio transmitter.

Repeaters have surfaced as sophisticated decoys. Discovery of a repeater is enough to convince naive sweepers that they have found The Real Bug.

Repeaters multiply building costs and demand elaborate installation. The likelihood of breakdown seems to grow as the square of the number of media changes. Yet repeaters' power to immunize the agent from capture makes them worth the hassle in peace of mind.

CHAPTER 17

Intermittent Bugs

The point of intermittent operation is to reduce emissions that betray the bug, and to prolong the life of battery-powered bugs. Intermittent bugs confer less protection than a repeater but resist countermeasures better than constantly active bugs.

Intermittent bugs are classified by activation mode:

- command activation
- activation by pervasive environmental cues
- activation by contextual cues: voices, power drain, change in phone line voltage, etc.
- timer activation

COMMAND ACTIVATION

The command depends on the nature of the bug. Some hardwire bugs use the wire as the power feed. The bug lies dormant until remotely powered. Hardwired bugs with on-board power can activate by a remote electronic switch that, optionally, runs the bug at some fraction of full power.

For cases in which the activation path carries other traffic, the bug needs a discriminator to prevent false triggering. A passive bandpass filter will serve for most applications. Though less sophisticated than tone decoders, these systems remain viable because they leak no energy in reception mode.

Perhaps the best known command-activated bug was the infamous infinity transmitter. In salad days long past, the agent could dial a number, then, by sending a tone through the phone line, prevent the phone from ringing but activate the carbon mic in the handset, despite the phone being on the hook. Some models bypassed the handset and used their own mic/amp for greater sensitivity. Early models responded to a single tone and were readily flushed by sweeping a pure tone through the line. Infinity transmitters became a lightning rod for wiretap hysteria that swept America in the mid-'70s, but they have waned of late, due to the difficulty of placing a call without leaving an electronic trail.

TIMER ACTIVATION

Off-the-shelf digital timers will run for years on a coin cell and can be programmed to issue one or two trigger-signals per 24-hour period. They suit situations in which traffic is known to be available only in specific periods each day.

Simple timers such as the 555 and 322 can be rigged to run for weeks or months before triggering a bug. These long-duration timers let the agent plant a bug that will sleep for months before activating itself, or one that will run for a set period and then turn itself off in anticipation of countermeasures.

ACTIVATION BY PERVASIVE ENVIRONMENTAL CUES

The environmental cues are the onset of day and night, for cases in which traffic is a lot likelier during one than the other. Of dozens of possible designs, those based on small solar cells are among the simplest and most reliable. The load draws no current when the final switching transistor is in the OFF state. The circuit uses PNP transistors because a fraction of a negative volt turns the PNP device ON, while turning an NPN device ON requires several positive volts.

Light-cued switches also enable bugs to resist sweeping. For example, a bug hidden in a space whose inspection requires light can be equipped with a switch that turns the bug off in the presence of light.

ACTIVATION BY CONTEXTUAL CUES

These are discussed under wiretapping. They include voice-activated switches and voltage-sensitive switches. Other potential triggers include proximity sensors and switches that detect power drain of a specific item, such as a lamp; something as simple as a pressure switch under the bed; or something as sophisticated as an infrared movement sensor.

INTERMITTENT ACTIVATORS

A) Simplest hardwire remote activation uses wire to power device.

B) Devices having self-contained power activated by application of DC voltage through control feed; current flowing to load can be varied by the control voltage, running bug at some fraction of full power.

C) In some cases a DC control feed is not possible; here an AC tone is sent through the line, converted to DC in a charge pump; resultant control voltage turns transistor ON. Addition of L1 makes a simple bandpass filter to improve immunity to spurious activation. A key feature of B- and C-type circuits is that load draws no measurable current in absence of activation voltage; thus, battery life

can be extended indefinitely. Occasionally used in "sleeper" bugs planted years ahead of anticipated need.

D and E) Ultra-simple transistor-based electronic switches driven by solar cell about 3/8" diameter. In D, light falling on solar cell creates a negative potential at PNP transistor base, turning that transistor ON, making potential at emitter LOW, in turn turning second PNP transistor ON and applying power to load. Dual transistor action sharper than single and tends to snap OFF when light is removed. First transistor stage of "E" is identical to "D," but in this case, emitter goes HIGH when light is absent; positive voltage at NPN base turns transistor ON in darkness. In all examples, the load is the bug.

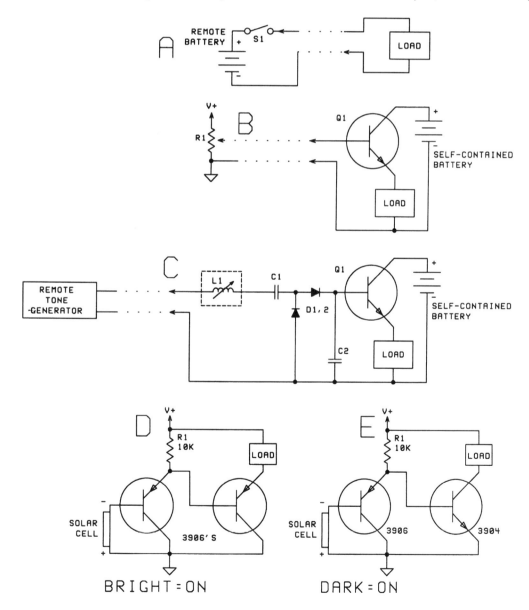

INTERMITTENT ACTIVATORS

A) Basic NE567 phase locked loop tone decoder. Pin 8 is tied to one end of an electronic switch inside the chip whose other end ties to ground. Switch goes LOW when loop locks, HIGH when loop loses lock. R2 can consist of a bug drawing up to 50 milliamps.

B) For controlling heavier loads, 567 switches relay. "A" and "B" respond to single tones only.

C) One type of dual-tone switch; 567 No. 1 provides the "ground" path for 567 No. 2; 567 No. 1 must trigger first; both tones must be present for power to flow through load.

D) Another dual-tone activator, in this case, both loops must lock before NOR gate goes high.

E) Simplified DTMF (dual tone multifrequency) decoder of the type used in the 1970s. Each rectangle represents one 567; 10 integrated circuits required to decode standard telephone signals. DTMF decoding has migrated to a single chip; circuit illustrates one way for bugger to make a custom multi-tone activation system.

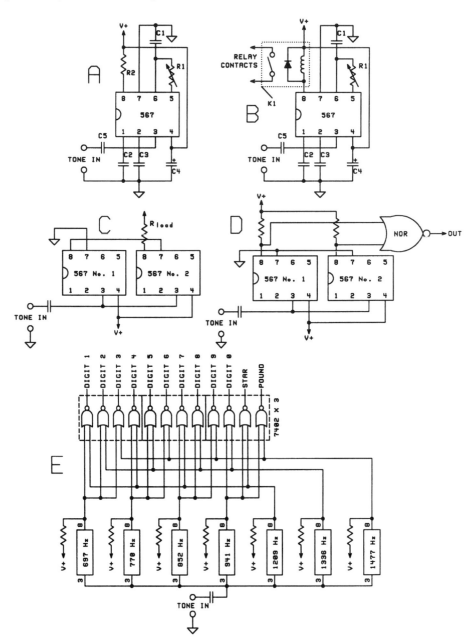

CHAPTER 18

Special Techniques

STEREOBUGGING

Consumer audio undertook an ill-fated excursion into quadraphonic sound in 1969. Though discrete four-channel recordings were issued on 8-track tapes, predominant formats encoded or "matrixed" four channels into two, to let quad material travel on stereo LPs and cassettes. These two matrixed channels fed through a decoder that extracted the original four.

. . . Or so they said. In fact, theory and performance parted company in hardware. Channel separation was lucky to get within 30 dB of a discrete quad tape. Because decoders used phase cues to separate one channel from another, they fell prey to phase shifts induced by improperly aligned tape heads and phono styli. The musical image shifted from one speaker to another with each turn of the record.

To make matters worse, matrixed quad existed in competing and incongruous formats, the predominant pair being SQ (CBS) and QS (Sansui). Each system would decode the other, after a fashion, but neither managed to excel with foreign feeds.

By the time quad died in '79 its taste lay bitter on many tongues. "Superdecoders" entered the market that year, finally making good on a decade-old promise. Their fantastic performance could be traced to custom integrated circuits, each more complex than a color television. The degree of channel isolation possible in wholly analog gear exceeded 50 dB. The quad wars also spun off several means to "decode" ordinary stereo as though it had been encoded.

Quad failed, but managed to launch the matrix process that cinema surround-sound used in the days before digital. Quad also left a legacy of circuits made to isolate one sound from another based on phase cues, along with a surplus decoder bonanza.

The business of phase discrimination was not lost on buggers. Decoding necessitates cancellation of some sounds while preserving others, raising at least the prospect that a stereo bug might capture traffic with sufficient phase cues to let a superdecoder separate speech from noise, or one voice from another.

The basic SQ decoder chip remains available through NTE (NTE799). Superdecoder chips have to be salvaged from superdecoders.

BINAURAL BUGGING

A dummy human head fitted with a mic at each ear becomes a binaural microphone. Recordings made with it sound dramatically flat when heard through speakers but erupt with ambience when heard through headphones. They show a peculiar power to transport the

RF STEREO BUGGING

- BA1404: one-chip FM stereo transmitter
- 18-pin DIP
- contains 38-KHz oscillator, multiplexer, RF generator
- single supply, 1-3V; >3.5V can damage chip
- meant for 88-108 MHz but can tune outside this range
- built-in oscillator tank-tuned; adapts to external crystal or frequency synthesis
- availability: DC Electronics
- cost: ~$3

Schematic shows basic 1404 stereo transmitter. Audio couples through pre-emphasis networks R1–C1 and R2–C2 to complement the deemphasis found in commercial FM radios. The 38-KHz multiplex carrier is provided by a crystal oscillator; crystal can be replaced with variable cap (10–60pF), but stereo quality suffers. Tank L2–C6 controls FM frequency; values shown act with stray capacitance to tune ~87-92 MHz. Tank L1–C5 reduces harmonic level. First, tune L2 to desired frequency, then tune L1 for best signal. Prune a quarter-wave antenna. Configuration shown is meant for line-level inputs that should not exceed 200 mv to avoid overloading the chip. Bugging application will need mic and preamp for each channel. RF output rises significantly with supply voltage, such that peak performance comes with a regulated 3V supply. Receiver needs automatic fine tuning. Photo shows a stereobug prototype equipped with the necessary extra circuitry.

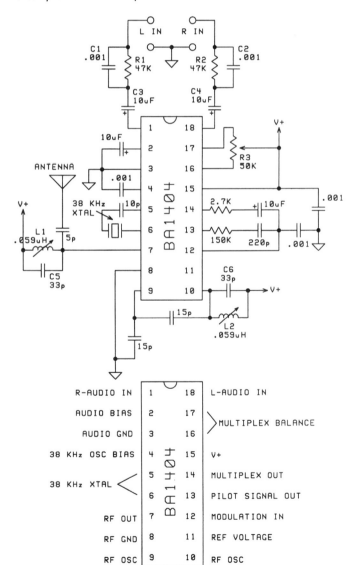

listener to the recording milieu. Binaural seems to accentuate the fantastic discrimination abilities of the human aural tract. For covert work, this gimmick offers a startling rise in perceived volume of speech. Talk sounds bigger than life, especially indoors. Whispers 50′ away sound five feet away. One binaural mic can hear pretty much anything that goes down in a four-bedroom brick ranch. If the windows happen to be open its reach can embrace a one-acre lot. Binaural is also great for pastoral venues that prevent panning a directional mic to track moving targets.

A proper binaural mic doesn't have to resemble a head. A cardboard box having roughly the same dimensions—4″ × 6″ × 8″—works great; a box 9″ × 11″ × 17″ has served with no dilution of the effect. This range implies a wealth of concealment options.

STEREO TRANSMISSION MODES

Stereobugging demands a dual feed. Hardwire adds a second pair. Fiberoptic systems usually multiplex the feeds at several hundred kilohertz. RF stereo posed a conundrum because it had to either accommodate the commercial FM stereo multiplex system or build a custom stereo transmitter and decoder. Buggers were filling contracts worth many thousands of dollars for custom RF stereo systems as late as 1988.

In '89 the commercial FM stereo encoding function was chipped out in the Rohm BA1404. This IC contains dual audio input stages, a 38-KHz oscillator for the stereo pilot, a mixer, and an RF oscillator. A potent stereobug built around the chip costs less than $20.

REGENERATION

Conventional op-amp gain blocks suffer two drawbacks: (1) negative feedback limits single-stage gain to a point inside the open-loop gain curve; (2) the bug band is still wideband in noise terms. The fact that noise varies as the root of bandwidth, and that the intelligence in speech resides in relatively narrow segments, suggests an alternative to wideband gain for systems already maxed.

Regeneration hearkens from the dawn of radio, a means to feed in-phase signals back from amplifier output to input, boosting sensitivity and selectivity of one-tube receivers. The same principle surfaced decades later in active audio filters.

Op amp theory has always doted on negative feedback. As a result, few designers considered that positive feedback could shatter the open-loop gain curve. For instance, the TL082 can give a maximum 60 dB of gain at 1 KHz. The same chip with regeneration has no trouble topping 75 dB.

The amp rings like a resonant circuit when tuned to the brink of oscillation. Ambient noise will trigger some ringing—the conch-shell effect—but tones close to center frequency tend to ring exponentially more than others.

Though harder to tune, regenerated amps give an edge over parametric EQ because the process happens during preamplification, where it allays a tremendous amount of input noise. Obviating post-preamp EQ also eliminates the noise of an equalizer's multiple, cascaded op amps; maximum boost of a regenerated amp far exceeds that of a parametric equalizer.

In one stylish twist regeneration delivers more gain than just about any other one-stage mode; it equalizes signal, minimizes noise, and yields outstanding results from cheap parts—which pretty well sums up the pro's prime directive to let physics do the work.

DELAY MIXING

Bucket-brigade delay lines convey an audio signal with a delay of a few milliseconds to several hundred milliseconds. This alters phase between delayed and straight feeds. If the channels are recombined, those signals 180 degrees out of phase cancel, those in phase add, and those between yield varying sums. Since the delay line affects the whole audio spectrum equally, phase becomes a matter of frequency. The sound produced by varying this continuously and rapidly can be

REGENERATION

To take a quick fling with regeneration, breadboard the circuit shown below. Omit Cx to start. The first stage is an inverting amp whose nominal gain, working with a 10K input impedance, is ~20 dB. Its output feeds the standard 386 headphone amp but also feeds unity-gain inverter U2-b, whose output is in phase with that of the mic. Regeneration control R3 varies the amount of signal fed back to the input of U1-a. Because 100 percent regeneration equals oscillation, R4 acting as a divider with R3 limits the amount of signal fed back.

As regeneration is increased, preamp gain increases and band of boost narrows. Tuned to the verge of oscillation, preamp gave 75 dB of gain at 7 KHz, beating the 082's open loop gain curve by more than 10 dB.

Now power down and insert Cx, a 0.001μF capacitor to start. This time as regeneration is increased, the boost frequency centers on 1,600 Hz but will not break over into

oscillation because oscillation threshold rises with value of Cx. The value of R4 can be lowered to ~90K to increase regeneration. Repeat the test with several caps; note different boost frequency with each.

Regeneration shifts with enough variables that op amps other than the 082 might give different center frequency and different oscillation threshold.

The experimenter will find that, the greater the regeneration, the narrower the band of boost. Narrowband amplification is inherently quiet because noise varies as the root of bandwidth. Regeneration lets noisy chips sound quieter in narrowband amps than quiet chips sound in wideband amps. This narrowed boost need not be a disadvantage. Heavily regenerated tones sound unnatural but intelligible. In practical gear, make Cx switchable to center boost on key formants.

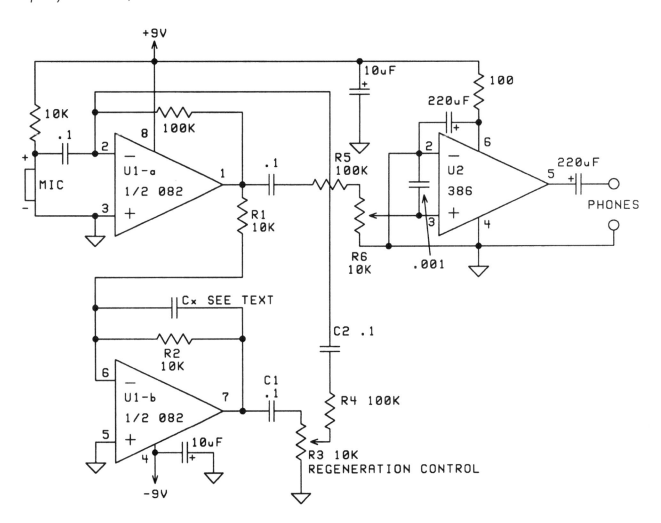

heard in "Itchykoo Park" or the second half of "Axis: Bold As Love."

Delay mixing is occasionally useful as an EQ technique distinct from classical EQ. A bench circuit is illustrated elsewhere in this chapter.

SYNCHRONOUS DETECTION

Synchronous detection is enabled by the fact that $1 + (-1) = 0$. A synchronous receiver alternately multiplies the input by +1 and -1. Noise, or an interfering signal unrelated to the rate of the multiplier, averages to zero. The signal of interest, which must exactly match the rate of multiplication, does not average to zero and can emerge from noise up to a million times greater, a signal-to-noise ratio of *minus* 120 dB.

Synchronous detection is the mode of choice when working at the limit of conventional detectors. Some professionals even hint, after a few Dos Equis, that the technique works at audio frequencies, applied to, say, the tape of a conspiratorial conversation drowned by the sound of faucets opened all the way.

DELAY MIXING

Block diagram illustrates concept; schematic shows a bare-bones bench demo circuit. Signal is split into identical feeds. Signal from U5-b goes through MN3204 delay line configured for fixed delay of ~2.5 ms. Signal from U5-a feeds a second MN3204, configured for variable delay, 2.5–25 ms. The two signals feed difference amp U3. When a time delay exists between the two, some frequencies will cancel, some will add. Frequencies affected depend on delay between the feeds. 50K pot controls balance of the difference amp. Signal could feed

to summing amp instead of difference amp. Circuit lets experimenter examine concept in the lab. Practical hardware should precede delay lines with sharp lowpass filter to minimize aliasing at low clock frequencies; another lowpass filter should follow the delay line to remove clock artifacts. Also, the 5.6K resistors that form the output network can be made a 10K pot used to null clock feedthrough. Panasonic delay lines available from Digi-Key. Op amp supply and bypass not shown.

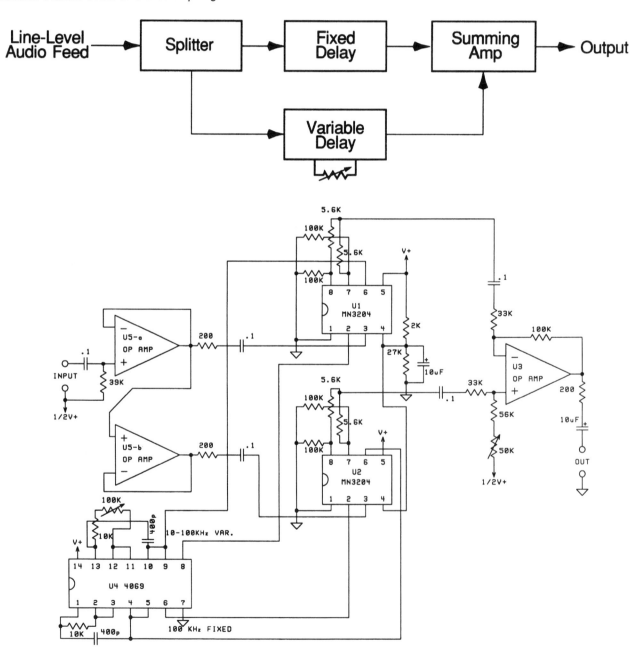

SYNCHRONOUS DETECTION

Block diagram illustrates concept: signal source impresses modulation on carrier, which should be at least 10 times upper frequency of interest. Carrier passing through transmission medium becomes buried in noise or interference. Synchronous detector multiplies the received signal alternately by +1 and -1 in perfect synch with carrier frequency. Because 1 + (-1) = 0, noise or interference averages to 0; carrier does not. Intelligence is recovered by stripping the carrier in a lowpass filter. Synchronous detection will demodulate FM and AM. Schematics show three ways to implement synchronous detection. Degree of rejection of noncarrier interference depends on how perfectly the amplifier's positive and negative gains match. This usually calls for trimming the resistors. S1 is an electronic switch, such as a 4066.

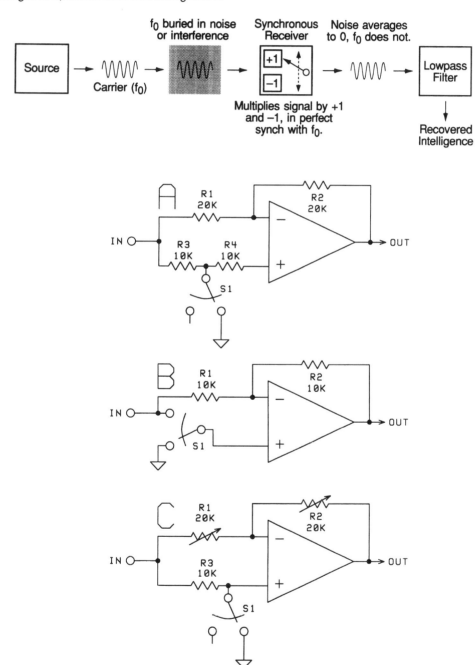

CHAPTER 19

Advanced Microphone Techniques

When tweaking an individual electret hits its limit, the bug builder can stretch the envelope by doing the following:

- summing outputs of several mics
- converting unbalanced feeds to balanced
- changing microphone impedance

Several mics whose outputs add make up a *microphone array*. Summing has several effects. First, transformer-based methods deliver a true algebraic signal sum. Each mic element still generates noise; but noise adds in quadrature, the root of the sum of the squares. The signal-to-noise ratio of a true summing array rises as the root of the number of mics in the array. Four mics not only give four times the output of a single, but deliver it at a S/N ratio 6 dB better than the single. Noise is further reduced by the fact that the preamp runs 12 dB cooler, amplifying its own noise 12 dB less.

Arraying mics increases their frontal area. This enables a properly sized array to gather close to 100 percent of the sound at the fuzzy focus of a large parabolic reflector. Arrays of up to 10 electrets are still small enough to harness the boundary effect.

Unbalanced, high-impedance feeds travel poorly enough that runs of more than a few feet lose amplitude and pick up interference. They take on a studio demeanor when properly shielded and converted to low-impedanced, balanced lines through a coupling transformer. The 5 percent transformer loss is negligible. Converting a high-impedance unbalanced feed to balanced low-impedance enables a hundred-yard cable run.

ADVANCED MIC TECHNIQUES

A) One way to sum the outputs of dynamic transducers, applicable mainly to speakers used as mics. Any number can be wired in series (note polarity) to generate an output usable as single-ended or pseudodifferential. Speakers used as mics don't need to be stepped down, because they exist in low-impedance form. Due to large size, phase cancellation can be a factor, mainly above 3 KHz. Best to use identical speakers in this type of array.

B) Speakers 1 and 2 are in series; speakers 3 and 4 are in series; and each pair is wired out of phase to generate a true differential output. (There is no advantage to wiring speaker-mics in parallel.) Each speaker impedance is only 8 ohms. So long as total impedance does not exceed 200 ohms, thermal noise is inconsequential.

C) Piezo transducers benefit from transformer coupling to convert to low impedance, balanced line. R1 is a loading resistor whose use is optional; generally equals ~4X the impedance of the transformer winding.

D) Occasionally, the need arises to get a differential output straight off an electret. This schematic shows one way. Let R1 = R2.

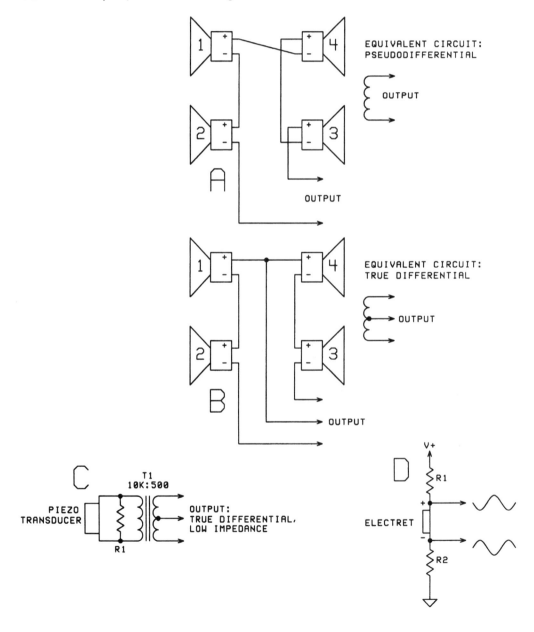

ADVANCED MIC TECHNIQUES

A) The drawbacks of a high-impedance mic coupled through unbalanced cable are instantly cured by biasing the electret, M1, off the 10K winding of T1. T1's secondary winding has low impedance and can be treated as unbalanced, pseudodifferential, or balanced (true differential). The voltage "loss" of this technique is illusory, for it is easily recovered. A cheap electret sounds clean and punchy over a long cable run using this technique.

B) The simplest electret array runs a string of mics off a common bias resistor. The technique does not add outputs in strict algebraic fashion, but arrays of 3–10 mics increase output by 6–12 dB over single mics. Moreover, the value of bias resistance that realizes peak output drops with the number of mics, lowering impedance-related noise factors. The optimum bias value varies among brands of electrets and should be determined empirically.

C) Transformer coupling opens up worlds of possibilities for cheap electrets. Here two electrets are stepped down to very low-impedance windings, which are wired in series, producing a true algebraic sum of the

outputs. Losses occur due to phase cancellation because two mics cannot occupy the same locus; these losses are insignificant in arrays up to several inches across. Just as important is what happens to microphone self noise. Noise adds in quadrature. Thus, series wiring of transformer secondaries has four effects: (1) steps down impedance to accommodate ultralow-noise preamps; (2) renders the summed signal in a way that the user can treat as single-ended or pseudodifferential; (3) adds signals algebraically; (4) adds noise in quadrature. The last two cause S/N ratio to rise as the square root of the number of mics in the array.

D) Illustrates another of many variations; M1 and M2 are wired in series, as are M3 and M4; their outputs are wired in series, but out of phase (note phase dots on transformers) to generate a true differential output with very low impedance. Note the possibilities of combining technique "B" with the others. Circuits on this and preceding page show a fraction of the possibilities. Mic manipulation is fertile ground for research and development.

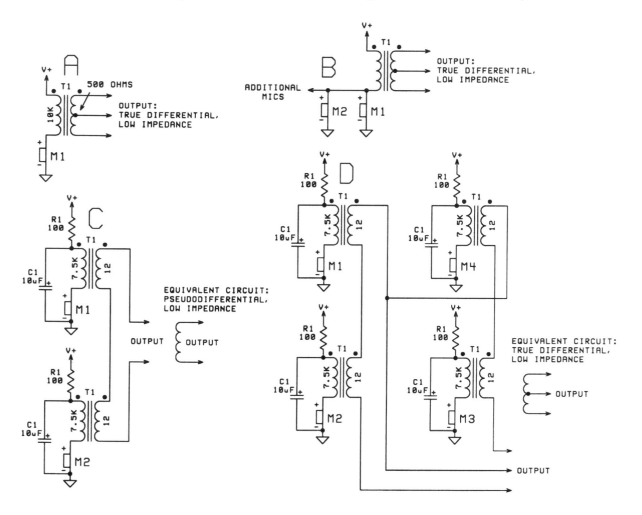

CHAPTER 20

Wiretapping

Strictly defined, wiretapping means covert interception of telephone traffic. The topic follows basic bugging because wiretapping can use all modes told so far.

Wiretapping continues to yield lavish intelligence despite an aphorismal predicament: "Don't use the phone if you don't want it known." The typical caller concedes the point, then proceeds to tell his phone secrets that would get him ejected from a confessional. Wiretapping captures both sides of a conversation or a fax transmission and can yield local audio while the phone is on the hook. It also gives digits entered through the DTMF keypad, which contain social-security and credit-card numbers, voice-mail and computer access codes.

This chapter deals with hardwired telephones and their link to the first exchange. Interstation loops and wireless phone traffic lie beyond the scope of this text.

BASIC TRAITS AND TERMINOLOGY

The ease of placing a call hides a manifold process. Telephone traffic moves between subscriber and local exchange on a wire pair known as the local loop. Buggers and telco personnel refer to a specific line as "the pair."

When a phone is on the hook, the line bears a DC potential that averages 48V. In this condition the phone's ringer is wired across the line through a DC-blocking capacitor. The rest of the phone circuit is isolated from the line by the hook switch, which is held open while the phone sits in the cradle. Lifting the phone off the cradle closes the hook switch; the phone draws current from the line. The local exchange senses this drain as an off-hook condition and connects the dial tone and dialer sensing circuitry to a phone ready to place a call. Also, the DC line voltage drops from 48V to ~5V by virtue of loading effects.

Dialing a number on a rotary phone, or keying in the number on a Touch-Tone phone, sends a series of digits to switching circuitry at the local exchange. Decoding and routing that follow do not pertain to this discussion. Once the called phone is identified, the telco network sends the ringback to the calling phone and initiates the ring cycle for the phone called. The ring cycle is a periodic pulse of 90VAC @ 20 Hz that averages 2 seconds on, 4 seconds off. This high voltage penetrates the blocking capacitor in the called phone to sound an audio transducer: "the phone rings."

Lifting the ringing phone off the hook closes the hook switch and loads the line, which the local exchange senses as an off-hook condition. The exchange stops the ring cycle and connects the calling party to the answering party. As with the calling phone, the DC line voltage seen by the answering phone drops to 5V.

When the call ends and both phones hang up, the hook switches open and unloads their respective lines. Each central station senses the on-hook condition; both lines return to 48V.

MORE DETAILS

The local loop is a balanced line with a nominal impedance of 600 ohms. Each mile of phone line exhibits parasitic capacitance of 0.07μF, series inductance of ~1 mH, and series resistance of 42 ohms. This line will conduct audio over a distance of 10 miles. Some rural lines run longer but require the phone to compensate for line losses. (Compensation circuitry consists of an amplifier whose gain depends on the amount of current flowing in the local loop. Design of this amp assumes line current to be a function of length of the local loop: the less current that flows, the longer the local loop is presumed to be and the more gain the amp applies to compensate.)

The ability of a single pair to carry both sides of a conversation is known as full duplex. The fact that each caller can hear his own voice in the receiver is due to deliberate mixing that occurs in every phone. The portion of the speaker's voice shunted to his own earpiece is called a sidetone and allows the speaker to modulate his speaking volume.

Audio travels at line level in the local loop, averaging $0.5V_{rms}$. The local loop in isolation has a bandwidth of 10 MHz over short runs, falling rapidly with distance due to parasitic inductance and capacitance. It can still conduct 100 KHz over more than a mile. Filters inside the local exchange limit frequency response to 4 KHz.

The phone line is charged because the system was designed more than a century ago for the line to power individual phones. Until federal antitrust action broke up American Telephone & Telegraph, virtually all phones contained a carbon microphone that ran off the 5V line bias present in the off-hook condition. Deregulation obviated antique circuitry in the design of new telephones, but those phones still had to run on 5V.

Telephone cable inside a dwelling, or between a dwelling and the pole, consists of 4-conductor 26-ga. insulated copper wire grouped as two color-coded pairs, one red/green, one yellow/black. Most single-phone hookups use the R/G pair, known in

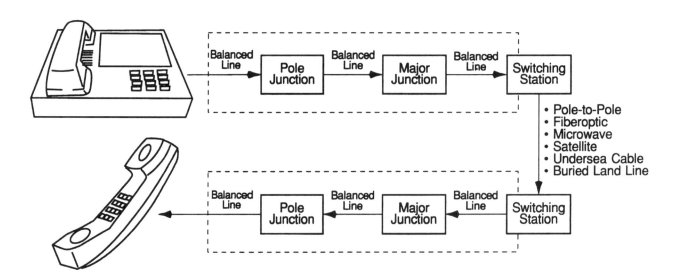

Diagram illustrates telco attack points. Telephone insecurity results from length of exposed line; the known, simple traits of the phone line; and a society thoroughly brainwashed regarding telephone privacy. Typical telco line characteristics found at all points inside dashed lines.

TELCO GLOSSARY

control signal—pure tone used by telco switching and control circuits; 2,600 Hz is the in-band tone, 3,700 Hz the out-of-band control tone

dial tone—an audible tone consisting of 350 Hz + 440 Hz, whose presence signals a caller that his line is connected to telco switching circuits

DTMF—dual tone multifrequency; a system of tone generators and tone decoders used to send number and letter codes over the phone line

full duplex—ability of a single pair to carry two conversations simultaneously

half duplex—ability of a single pair to carry two conversations, but not simultaneously

handset—in a two-piece phone, the part the caller holds to his ear; contains a microphone known as a transmitter, and an earphone known as a receiver

hook switch—a/k/a the cradle switch; connects DC phone circuitry to the phone line; open when phone is in the cradle; closes when handset is lifted off the cradle

hybrid—telco term for a complex transformer that resolves full duplex traffic into two pair, one send, one receive, for long-distance transmission

in-band—between 300 and 3,000 Hz, as in "in-band control signal"

infinity transmitter—a device usually installed inside a phone and which keeps the phone from ringing but activates a mic in the phone, allowing the caller to hear as though the phone were off the hook

induction coil—telco term for the complex audio transformer inside pre-1980 phones, which couples audio between phone and line and performs the sidetone function; induction coils have been replaced by integrated circuits in modern phones

local exchange—the first switching station encountered by the local loop

local loop—the two-wire "telephone line" that runs from a subscriber's residence or business to the local exchange; may include junction boxes, and length may exceed 10 miles

off-hook condition—state that results when the hook switch closes; resting DC line voltage drops to 5–10V due to Ohm's law; in this state the central exchange connects a calling phone to dialer sensing circuitry or connects a called phone to the calling party

on-hook condition—a state in which a nominal 48 volts DC is applied to the line by the local exchange; in this state the phone is connected to an off-hook-sensing relay

out-of-band—outside the speech band but below 4,000 Hz; e.g., 3,700 Hz is the out-of-band control tone

parasitic (inductance, capacitance, etc.)—capacitance produced by proximity of conductors; or, in the case of inductance, occurring as a native property of the wire

PBX—private branch exchange; any of countless private phone systems and intercoms

punch-down block—a junction built to tie pairs of 22–28-ga. solid copper wire; the universal commercial user-telco interface; telco lineman will bring the line as far as the punch-down block, at which point wiring responsibility passes to the subscriber

punch-down tool—a tool that punches 22–28-ga. wire into the clip, strips insulation, and cuts off the excess in a single stroke

ring—the negatively charged lead, usually red in four-conductor phone cable

ringback—the tone a calling party hears to indicate that the called phone is ringing

ringer—an audio transducer that makes a noise to signal that a call is coming through; formerly a mechanical bell, now usually a piezo transducer

ringing cadence—relative durations of the ring pulse and silence during the ring cycle; domestically, averages 2 seconds on, 4 seconds off

ring cycle—a burst of high-voltage alternating current; nominally 90VAC but up to 130VAC, at 16–60 Hz; purpose is to activate a ringer in the phone to indicate that a call is coming through

sidetone—the small amount of a telephone talker's voice fed to his own earpiece to allow proper volume modulation

spare pair—the yellow/black pair in 4-conductor telephone cable; not used in single-line hookups

speech band—in the phone system, 300–3,000 Hz

talking battery—the source of 48VDC at the local exchange; prior to 1980, powered the carbon mic in all phones; today powers an entire electronic phone

telco—generic term for a supplier of local phone service, as distinct from long-distance carriers who have nothing to do with the local loop

"the pair"—slang for a specific phone line under consideration

tip—the positively charged lead, usually green in four-conductor cable

VOX—voice-activated switch

telco slang as "tip" (green/positive) and "ring" (red/negative). These terms date from days when they told which wire connected to the tip and ring of plugs on the telephone operator's switchboard. The Y/B pair is known as the "spare pair." These four wires jacketed in gray or beige plastic make what's commonly called telephone cable. Single lines combine in telco junction boxes into cables consisting of multiple wire pairs, each bearing a color code that facilitates pair-identification. For example, a green wire having white stripes pairs with a white wire having green stripes.

The level of current at which the central station senses the phone to be off the hook ranges nominally from 6 to 25 ma. The exact trip level varies among local providers but rarely falls below 6 ma to allow for leakage current due to humidity and corrosion, and to tolerate the tiny current that some electronic phones draw to keep numbers in their memory. Trip level is rarely set above 25 ma because some phones draw scant current and/or reside at the end of a long local loop whose series resistance limits the flow of current. The local loop is dcsigncd to supply up to 120 ma to a phone. Series resistance at the local exchange limits current in the event the local loop shorts.

The preceding data is all that's needed to build dozens of wiretaps because the local loop keeps this electrical personality all the way from a subscriber's phone to the point the line enters the local exchange. Private (PBX) phone systems and intercoms resemble the phone line enough that telco tap techniques apply.

WIRETAPS

"Wiretap" denotes only a means to lift audio from the phone line. Once obtained it can be monitored, recorded, or sent to another location. Taps break down by how they couple to the line (series, parallel, induction); by how they get power (self-powered, line-powered); and by when they function (during calls, between calls, all the time).

It is apparent from the prior discussion that anything connected to the phone line must:

- Survive the ring cycle. This averages 90VAC but can peak at 130VAC, enough to wax many semiconductors. Taps guard themselves with series resistance to limit current and some type of shunt to limit peak voltage entering the circuit. Shunts include diode clippers, metal-oxide varistors, and neon lamps.

- Not draw excessive current. On-hook taps must draw less current than the off-hook threshold, or the line will remain in an off-hook condition, prompting telco action. Off-hook taps should draw no more current than an extension phone. Otherwise, they dampen the audio enough to tip the target that a tap is in place.

- Not load the line with an impedance that weakens the audio level. Parallel taps show the line a high impedance, usually 5K or more. Series taps show the line a low impedance, usually 100 ohms or less.

- Isolate itself from the 48V line potential. Parallel taps accomplish this with one or two DC blocking capacitors. Series taps do not require isolation.

- Account for the fact that the line voltage is polarized and that it falls from 48V to 5V when the phone is taken off the hook.

With these constraints noted, taps practically design themselves.

SERIES TAPS

Series taps interpose a circuit in a break in one or both sides of the subscriber loop. Any impedance added by the tap appears as a series impedance with the loop. Thus, series taps must provide a low-resistance DC path. The phone system readily tolerates up to 100 ohms' additional resistance. Series taps must also sustain the current drawn by the phone in operation.

A transformer best meets these requirements. It offers low series resistance, gives clean audio, and provides a feed in balanced or unbalanced form. It draws no power and isolates connected circuitry from up to several hundred volts in the line. Transformer output is usable raw to drive the spare pair or a dedicated hardwire line.

Series taps can draw power from the line, but only in the off-hook condition. Nontransformer series taps place a low-value resistor in series with one side of the line and use each end of the resistor as a power-supply terminal.

Series taps are the type most susceptible to counterbugging. A change in static loop resistance of a few ohms will register on a digital multimeter. A series tap has to break at least one side of the line. That means unscrewing one wire from a terminal, or cutting into the line. This explains why physical search finds many wiretaps.

PARALLEL TAPS

Parallel taps bridge the pair. They can couple to the line directly or through capacitors, but they must show the line a high impedance to avoid blunting the audio.

These taps can draw power from the line. The amount depends on whether they activate in an on- or off-hook condition. Drain in the on-hook condition must not exceed 3 ma to avoid triggering an off-hook condition. Off-hook taps should draw no more current than an extension phone.

Parallel taps can treat the line as balanced or unbalanced. They lend themselves to quick attack against targets of opportunity, such as an unattended junction box or modular outlet.

Properly designed parallel taps are essentially undetectable by remote means, including tone sweeps and time-domain reflectometry (TDR).

INDUCTIVE TAPS

Inductive taps use the fact that current flowing in a conductor generates an electromagnetic field. This field induces a current in another conductor placed in the field. One of the most common products to employ the principle is the telephone pickup coil, a dandy

inductive tap that's still sold for a couple bucks. A single turn of phone line wrapped around the coil gives mic-level audio. More turns raise the level, but the diameter of 4-conductor cable limits the number of turns. Tighter coupling can be achieved by breaking the line and wrapping multiple turns of a single strand of wire around the coil. Induction can provide a completely passive tap that sends balanced audio over a hardwired line.

Unshielded audio transformers of 600–10K ohms also make great inductive probes (the $2 Mouser transformers, not the $20 MagneTek pieces, whose toroidal design renders them insensitive to extraneous fields). An audio transformer used as an inductive probe should leave the unused winding open.

Inductive taps are sensitive to AC hum, making their use impractical near a power transformer.

While an inductive tap does not alter the line's DC or gross AC characteristics, it does alter inductance in a way that shows on TDR and could show on a tone sweep.

SELF-POWERED TAPS

Self-powered taps get power from some source other than the line. The practicality of battery power depends on required life of the tap, the amount of current it draws, and the available battery space. High-capacity lithium batteries can run a micropower bug for months. Intermittent taps on infrequently used lines can run off batteries for more than a year.

Taps whose projected life is gauged in years often cut into the AC power line because power lines tend to run near phone lines under a house. This mode gives the option to couple audio to the power line using a carrier current system.

LINE-POWERED DEVICES

Line-powered bugs leach current from the phone line. Those that operate in the off-hook condition can draw as much current as an extension phone; 10–20 ma is reasonable and will power a variety of bugs. Those that operate

PHONE LINE TAPS

- 48VDC nominal on-hook voltage (operating limits: 47–105VDC)
- 5VDC nominal off-hook voltage (operating range: 5–10VDC)
- 20–80 ma nominal off-hook operating current (operating limits: 20–120 ma)
- nominal local loop resistance 0–1,300 ohms (operating limits: 0–3,600 ohms)
- nominal allowable loop loss: 8 dB (operating limit: 17 dB)
- ring signal nominally 90V$_{rms}$ @ 20 Hz (operating limits: 40–130V$_{rms}$ at 16–60 Hz)

Phone line is modeled as a wire pair charged with 48VDC (5VDC in the off-hook condition), nominal audio impedance 600 ohms. Series tap breaks one or both sides of the line to interpose bug. Parallel tap bridges the line. Inductive tap consists of telephone pickup coil or miniature transformer, 600–10K ohms. Diagram shows one side of line coiled around inductive probe. Because signal travels in balanced form, radiation is minimized because local magnetic fields tend to cancel. In practice, wrapping the pair around the inductor results in a mic-level signal.

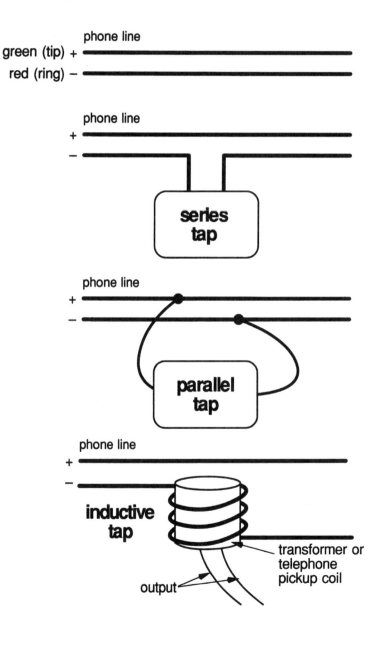

SERIES TAPS

Any circuit placed in series with the phone line must offer low resistance. Average phone resistance is 400 ohms; upper limit of loop function is ~3,600 ohms. Resistance of series tap should not exceed 100 ohms. Must also survive ring cycle, which can peak at 130VAC. A transformer meets these criteria compactly and economically. As "A" shows, the raw transformer output can drive a dedicated line or the spare pair. This makes a complete phone tap consisting of one component, and one that can send audio nearly as far as driven phone line.

Alternatively, transformer output can couple to other circuitry. Diodes protect circuit from ring cycle.

"B" shows something of a hybrid device. Two relay coils inside Teltone 949 placed in series with line; each has resistance of ~18 ohms. When phone is taken off hook, current flows, energizing coils and closing relay switch, connecting a parallel tap to line; tap can be line-powered or self-powered. Relay specifically designed for telephone interface devices; photo shows an M-949.

C) Line-powered series interface uses rectifier bridge.

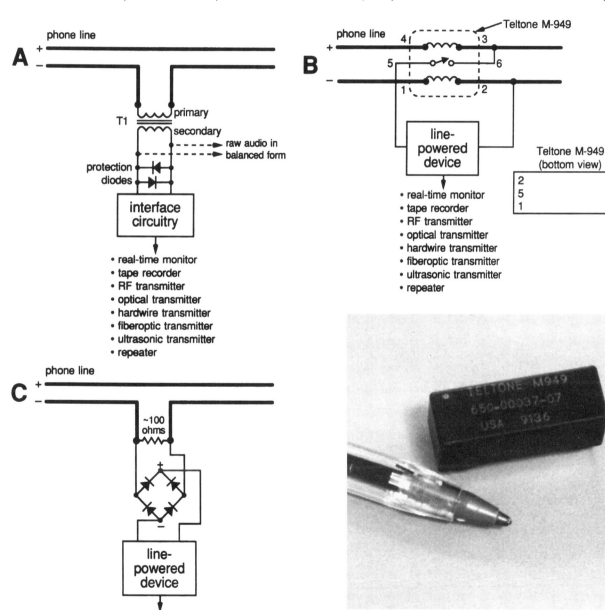

A

phone line

T1 — primary
secondary
→ raw audio in
→ balanced form

protection diodes

interface circuitry

- real-time monitor
- tape recorder
- RF transmitter
- optical transmitter
- hardwire transmitter
- fiberoptic transmitter
- ultrasonic transmitter
- repeater

B

phone line — Teltone M-949
4   3
5   6
1   2

line-powered device

- real-time monitor
- tape recorder
- RF transmitter
- optical transmitter
- hardwire transmitter
- fiberoptic transmitter
- ultrasonic transmitter
- repeater

Teltone M-949
(bottom view)

2	3
5	6
1	4

C

phone line

~100 ohms

line-powered device

- real-time monitor
- etc.

PARALLEL TAPS

Because phone-line audio is balanced, the most natural parallel tap is balanced, feeding differential amplifier, which rejects common-mode noise. Self-powered device "A" isolates itself from DC potential with blocking capacitors C1 and C2; limits peak current and shows line a high impedance through R1 and R2; shunts the ring cycle with D1 and D2, typically 1N4007 or similar. Components inside dotted line can be replaced with a short, converting balanced to unbalanced, but case ground should not contact line. "B" illustrates one type of line-powered bug. Device works in an on-hook condition. Rectifier bridge BR1 renders attachment insensitive to polarity; 48V nominal line voltage stepped down and regulated by R1 and zener D1; powers audio amp and electret mic. Audio couples to phone line through C1, which could just as easily tie to other side of line. Device could be made to function while on-hook but would defeat purpose of bug and might result in detection. Bug sends audio over the phone line while the phone is on the hook. "C" shows another option, line-powered tap driving RF transmitter; audio couples to transmitter in balanced from, through C1 and C2. "B" and "C" must run on 3 ma or less to avoid causing an off-hook condition.

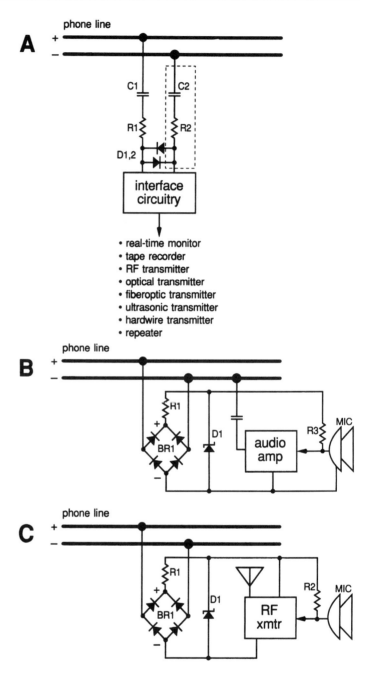

- real-time monitor
- tape recorder
- RF transmitter
- optical transmitter
- fiberoptic transmitter
- ultrasonic transmitter
- hardwire transmitter
- repeater

INDUCTIVE TAPS

A) The ancient and glorious telephone pickup coil, a staple of snoops and sneaks, here shown in action. Also makes a dynamite inductive tap; impedance ~10K, single-ended output; extremely sensitive to AC power fields.

B) Two turns of four-conductor telephone cable wrapped around pickup coil gives mic-level audio; girth of cable limits the number of turns.

C) An alternative inductive probe, a 10K:10K audio transformer used as an inductive tap. Multiple turns improve coupling and thus audio level. Leave the unused winding open.

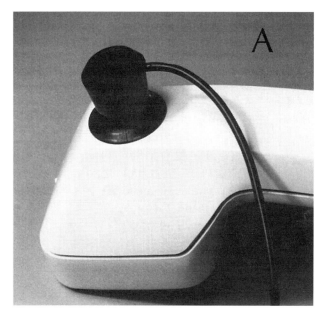

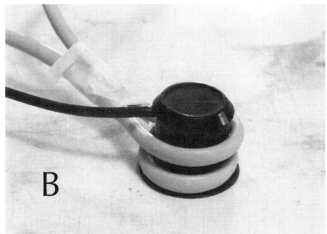

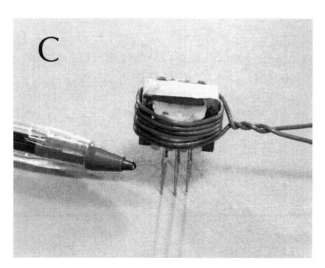

in the on-hook condition must draw less current than the off-hook trip threshold. A prudent safety margin limits them to <3 ma.

Despite line-powered taps' presumptive complexity, designing them is a no-brainer. Study the interface schematic for any modern electronic phone. Note the way it both powers itself from, and couples audio to, the line. Realize that, packaging aside, an electronic phone is a parallel line-powered tap that sends audio over the line in the off-hook condition.

The telephone power interface contains a diode bridge to render attachment to the line insensitive to polarity, because the output of the bridge is the same irrespective of how it connects to the line. The bridge is followed by a means to limit the DC voltage seen by the circuit and to protect the circuit from the ring cycle. A zener-diode regulator, consisting of a current-limiting resistor and a bypass capacitor, meets the requirement.

This circuit's output voltage depends on state of the line. In the on-hook condition, the 48V line voltage loses two diode drops in the bridge and is limited to the zener value. In the off-hook condition, line voltage does not approach the zener threshold and reflects the off-hook voltage, less two diode drops in the bridge, further reduced by divider action of the zener resistor and the circuit.

ATTACKING THE PAIR

The pair is accessible at many points:

- in the phone
- between the phone and the modular socket
- in the modular socket
- behind the modular socket
- under the house
- at the telco-subscriber interface on the exterior of the house
- at the punch-down block
- between the exterior of the dwelling and the telephone pole
- on the telephone pole
- at junctions and in trunks prior to entry to the local exchange

Some points make more practical targets than others. Meddling with the line on the pole or at a junction box, at least in daylight, is for professionals equipped to impersonate telco linemen. Climbing spikes, safety belt, and a lineman's handset make convincing props. A setup bolstered by a telco-colored van and orange traffic cones will fool most civilians. It will not fool a passing telco lineman, who will radio the sighting. Pros post lookouts, maintain radio communications, arrange multiple escape routes, and keep legal aid on tap in the event of a pinch. In practice, this limits the approach to the clandestine services.

Civilians can buy a lineman's handset for $100–$400—a waste of money because the handset is a glorified unitary phone equipped with alligator clips instead of a modular plug. Wrangling a lineman's handset is hard for anyone but a lineman or a phone-service installer to explain; it's not a prop the agent wants on the seat beside him in a chance traffic stop.

A pair of alligator clips turns a unitary phone into a tool that lets the agent make calls from anybody's line, which is as far as this text cares to take that topic.

Business phone taps often take place at an interface known as the punch-down block, whose name describes the contact mechanism. The block consists of horizontal rows of cloven metal clips that grasp wires "punched down" into them by a special tool. In one stroke this tool strips the wire, seats it in the clip, and trims the excess. Mail-order vendors sell the tool for ~$40.

Punch-down blocks come in different sizes, the most common being M66 (shown in the photos). A typical block contains 50 rows of four clips, which will accommodate up to 25 pairs of wire.

The block is held to a bracket by plastic clips easily opened with the fingers. The bracket screws to a metal backing that dismounts with a screwdriver. The bulk of unused space seems made to hide bugs. The serious wiretapping student should buy a punch-down block and explore the possibilities.

LINE MONITORS AND TARGETS OF OPPORTUNITY

Wiretapping includes the sudden chance intercept, which can be as easy as picking up an extension phone. The faint "click" and the shift in line ambience tend to alert the target. Knowledgeable targets might have armed themselves with a black box that signals an extension off the hook.

Given access to an unattended tap point, such as a punch-down block, external junction, or open line, the wiretapper needs a monitor that attaches quickly and stealthily with a pair of alligator clips. This type of line monitor also suits bugs that send audio over the phone line in the on-hook condition. A simple preamplifier will serve. Like fixed wiretaps, it needs high impedance, and protection against resting 48V and the ring cycle.

ATTACKING THE PHONE

Expanded options partly offset the risk of attacking the phone. Phone taps are stealthier than line taps because the phone offers tap points that do not affect static line traits, making them practically undetectable without disassembling the phone. Still, being picked up for skulking around a telephone pole is not quite the same as being pinched inside a house with a bugger's tool kit.

Outwardly, a telephone can vary as much as deregulation allows. All FCC-approved phones and accessories must meet requirements that specify what bandwidth they produce and accept, what impedance they show the line, what degree of voltage isolation they place between themselves and the line, and what audio level they feed the line. If a subscriber connects a device that is not approved, or that interferes with telco operations, the phone company has the right to disconnect that line from the system.

The telephone's outward simplicity hides a tangled heart. A phone is a hardwired transceiver that powers itself from the line. It amplifies, conditions, and couples audio to the line; performs the sidetone function to let the speaker modulate the volume of his voice; and generates dialing pulses or tones.

Pre-1980 phones with rotary dial and drop-in carbon mic are nearing extinction. Modern phones run on chipped-out electronics whose schematics look knottier than they are. By ignoring dialer circuitry, the phone simplifies to a hardwire bug. The agent needs to know enough telephone anatomy to access audio and power inside the phone; to identify pertinent ancillary circuitry; and to use the phone's electrical traits to hide the bug.

Attacks against a specific phone should start by procuring a phone identical to the target, then disassembling the phone and identifying the power bus and the audio path. A pinout of the chip helps but is not essential. Power up the phone, trace the signal path, build and test the tap.

AUTO-START DEVICES

Auto-start devices activate a tap or bug in response to a stimulus that means traffic is likely. They save power in battery-powered gear, save tape in recorder setups, and save RAM in digital storage banks. Auto-start devices exist as two main types: those that trip in the off-hook condition, and those that trigger on sound.

Line-status switches can work several ways. One uses loop current to operate a relay, such as the Teltone M-949. Loop current flowing through series-wired relay coils closes a switch tied to external circuitry. This operating principle is found in "single phone tape recorder controls," such as Radio Shack catalog number 43-228. They can be made to work for all phones if attached to the line before branching occurs.

Another type of switch triggers on the drop-in line voltage that occurs when any phone is taken off the hook. The circuit is a voltage-sensitive switch, such as Radio Shack catalog number 43-236.

Voice-activated switches (VOXs) trigger in response to sound. A VOX should trigger

THE PUNCH-DOWN BLOCK

- *commercial telco-subscriber interface*
- *also gives access to PBX phone lines*
- *block provides ample room to hide bugs*

Blocks are designated in terms of "columns × rows," e.g., a 4 × 50 block has 4 columns of clips, 50 rows. Typically, but not always, telco side is on the left, subscriber side on the right. Block in photos is a 4 × 50 model found in many proprietary phone systems; accommodates 25 pairs. Each two rows comprise one pair. Left two segments internally connected, right two segments internally connected, but left and right segments have to be bridged by a clip to connect the local loop to the subscriber's phone system. A punch-down tool of the correct blade type is practically mandatory for clean connections to the block. These tools are available through business tool suppliers. Purchase leaves a blatant trail.

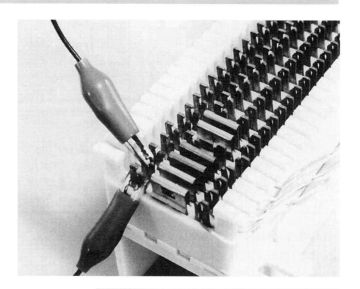

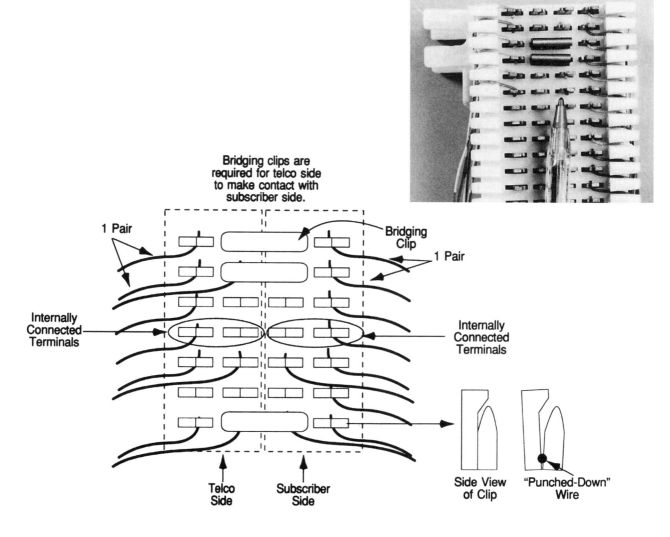

Bridging clips are required for telco side to make contact with subscriber side.

1 Pair

Bridging Clip

1 Pair

Internally Connected Terminals

Internally Connected Terminals

Telco Side

Subscriber Side

Side View of Clip

"Punched-Down" Wire

THE PUNCH-DOWN BLOCK

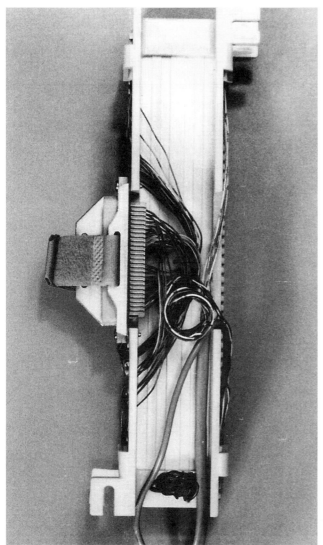

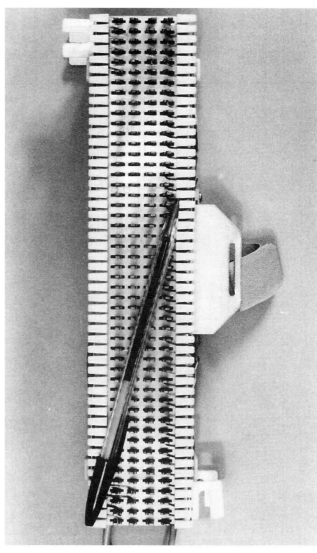

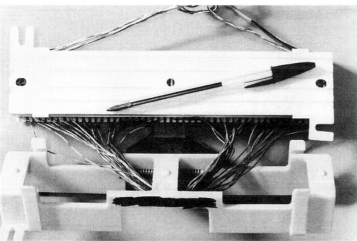

Much space exists behind block and behind metal bracket to which block is attached. Counterbugging a business telephone system always involves physical search of the punch-down block.

HOW "CARBON MIC" PHONES WORK

A) Simplified schematic of domestic telephone prior to breakup of AT&T. Ring pulse bridges DC blocking capacitor in series with ringer, phone rings. When handset is lifted from cradle, hook switch closes, connecting phone to 48V in phone line. Load, by Ohm's law, drops voltage to ~5V, powering carbon mic in handset. Complex transformer mixes a portion of the speaker's voice (the sidetone) into his own earpiece, to let him modulate speaking volume. Transformer and other components were potted in a K-500 module to simplify phone construction and repair.

B) Simplified depiction of what goes on at the local exchange. Each phone line is powered by a 48V "talking battery," which is actually a regulated DC supply. The 400 ohms of resistance in series with this voltage limits current to 120 ma in the event of a dead short. Loop resistance and phone resistance limit actual loop current. If this falls below 25 ma, current-sensing relay may return to on-hook condition. Telco circuits isolated from subscriber loop by transformer; protected by many surge-suppression devices not shown.

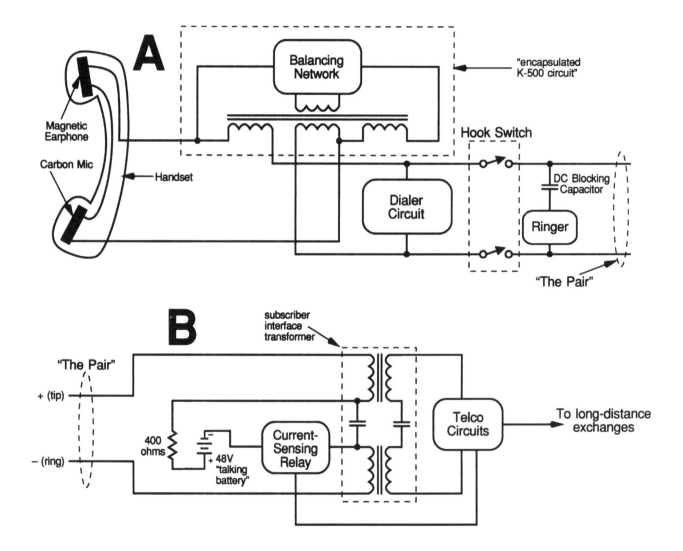

HOW ELECTRONIC PHONES WORK

A) When telephone receiver is cradled, S1 ties phone line to ringer. Lifting receiver off cradle makes DC contact with phone circuit. Line voltage is rectified in bridge BR1, regulated by R1–D1, powering TEA1067 integrated phone interface circuit. Chip amplifies, limits, and conditions audio to meet telco specs. It performs sidetone mixing, drives earpiece and electret mic, and conveys tone/pulse inputs from keypad or memory to the line. Knowledge of chip anatomy enables wiretapper to take a line-level feed from chip, without affecting electrical profile of the phone line.

B) One type of line-powered bug circuit. BR1 renders attachment insensitive to line polarity; R1 and D1 regulate supply voltage and protect the bug from the ring cycle; C1 bypasses the supply. In the on-hook condition, the circuit sees voltage equal to zener value (say, 15V); in the off-hook condition, voltage through bridge does not reach

zener value and circuit sees line voltage less two diode drops. Designer can render bug circuit such that this voltage will not drive the bug, making it an on-hook-only bug; or, in the case of a line-powered RF bug, one that will work in on- and off-hook state. Bug audio output couples to line through C2 in single-ended mode, or through optional inverting buffer and C3 in balanced mode.

C) Bridge eliminated, bug ties directly to the line, does not suffer two diode drops from bridge; however, in this case line polarity matters; circuit must be connected correctly to function. Note addition of R2, to avoid shunting effect of C1. In Circuit B, forward drop of bridge prevented first 1.2V of audio from being shunted. Note that B and C are not phone-line taps but bugs with built-in mics that power themselves from, and transmit audio over, the phone line.

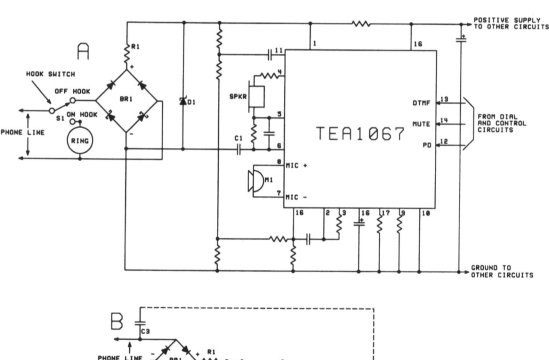

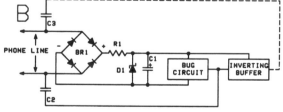

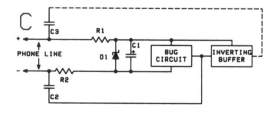

ATTACKING THE PHONE

Open the phone, identify the pair and the diode bridge; trace the signal path. Consult chip pinout if available; if not, power the phone from battery and trace signal path. This model is an early-eighties-vintage pulse-only cheapo. The pair and the diode bridge are readily identified; single chip.

the pair

diode bridge

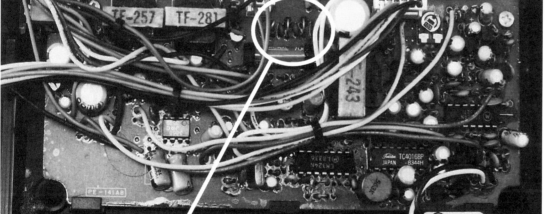

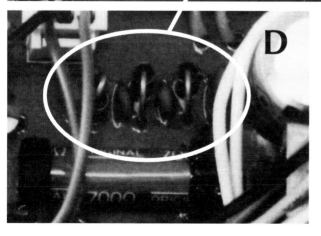

Attacking a full-featured, table-model, AC-powered electronic phone. Top photo shows most of interior; needlessly imposing, for memory and dialer circuits (A) are irrelevant. The smaller board on bottom (B) is where the action is. Three audio transformers; dead giveaway to speech circuits. Further enlargements C and D. Diode bridge connects directly to the pair.

A piece of cake . . .

PHONE LINE MONITORS

- *because phone-line audio is line level, any simple amp will do*
- *single-ended or differential*
- *must protect itself and user from ring cycle and resting DC voltage*

A) Block diagram of a single-ended line monitor. C1 blocks DC, R1 limits current, voltage shunt stops the ring cycle; simple audio amp, typically a power driver.

B) Embodiment. C2 has been added to enhance isolation of monitor circuit ground from phone line. Voltage shunt consists of heavy-duty rectifier pair. Remainder of

circuit common-emitter amp feeding 386 audio power driver.

C) Block diagram of differential-input line monitor. C1 and C2 isolate circuit from 48VDC, R1 and R2 limit maximum current.

D) Embodiment of concept. Voltage shunt is again a diode pair. The op amp is configured as a differential amplifier. R1= R2, R3 = R4; gain = R3 / R1. In all cases, line-coupling capacitors C1 and C2 should be rated 200VAC or 630VDC. These devices let the agent attack targets of opportunity; can be built into case the size of a pack of Camels.

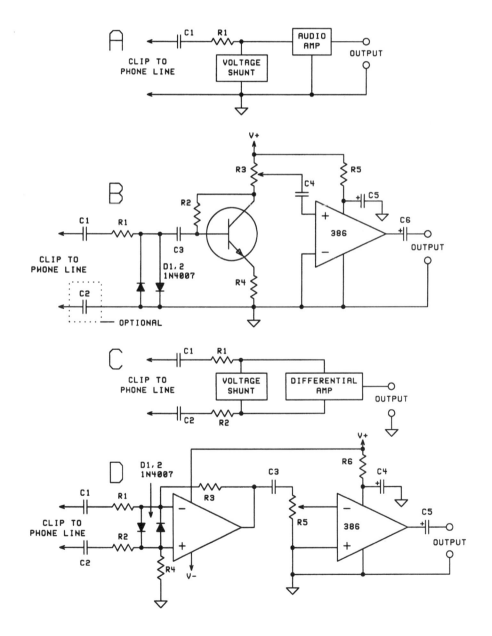

instantly but stay on several seconds after triggering to avoid missing bits of conversation. One type of VOX uses a charge pump to generate a DC voltage that activates an electronic switch. Another uses audio to trigger a comparator, in turn activating a delay consisting of a peak detector, or an adjustable one-shot made from a 555.

FINDING THE LINE

The agent can tap the line miles from the phone, but at that point the line might have joined a trunk, making the target pair indistinguishable from others. The agent needs a means to identify the pair. The most popular method is to inject a tone into the line near the phone and detect this tone with an audio monitor or tone decoder at the tap point.

A proper tone lies near the edge of hearing and outside the passband of filters at the local exchange. Ten to 30 KHz makes a good choice. The companion tone decoder is usually a 567 but could also be a meter preceded by a bandpass filter. Commercial line-locator systems inject an audible tone detected by a high-impedance inductive probe feeding a speaker for audible, rather than visual, signaling.

USING THE SPARE PAIR

Economics mandated the spare pair to avoid having to rewire every house that put in a second line. The fact that most spare pairs are unused makes them an option to feed audio to some remote point.

The spare pair can be counted on to travel only as far as the first junction. Four-conductor cable sheds the extra pair when the active line combines with other feeds into the first trunk.

TAPPING PAY PHONES

Pay-phone lines differ from residential lines only in that the line is armored for some feet after it leaves the phone. But pay-phones are such popular tap targets that the agent may find that several parties have gotten there ahead of him. And tapping a pay phone is not a light venture, for discovery of a pay-phone tap will draw federal notice.

GENERAL OBSERVATIONS ON TELEPHONE SECURITY

Beyond weaknesses implied by tap lore, all telephone calls generate an evidential record that includes date, time, duration, number calling, and number called.

Some security experts treat long-distance calls as though they were being monitored by parties who, if not overtly hostile, might not hold the agent's interests dear. Pros assume also that voiceprint ID and voice-stress analysis are being applied, and that overseas calls undergo automated scanning for specific terms, such as "explosive" or "cocaine." Calls from global hot spots draw powerful scrutiny. In addition, parties close to the trade feel the several telephone companies to be riddled with snitches. The text can neither confirm nor dispute these opinions.

PHONE LINE LOCATOR

Simple theory: inject tone into line, detect tone at a distance using tone decoder. Tone should travel many miles, yet lie outside range of telco bandpass filters and human hearing; 10–30 KHz ideal. Both pieces should run off batteries and use common parts.

A) 20 KHz readily generated by 555 bipolar timer, boosted by transformer. If R3 = 10 ohms, T1 unloaded output measures ~38$V_{p\text{-}p}$. Current consumption on the order of 20 ma. Raise or lower value of R3 to balance signal amplitude against current drain. This configuration offers advantages of true balanced injection into line.

B) Companion receiver uses transformer input to reject

common-mode noise in the line. C7 and C8 have an impedance of ~72,000 ohms at the 20 Hz ring frequency, only 80 ohms at the 20-KHz tone frequency. D1 and D2 clip level at 1.2$V_{p\text{-}p}$. T1 secondary couples to input of comparator U1-a in a way that makes a sensitive zero-crossing detector; triggers reliably on 20 mv$_{p\text{-}p}$. U1-a constant amplitude output divided by ~10 to avoid overloading input of 567 tone decoder. LED lights when tone is detected. Both tone generator and tone detector are insensitive to line polarity. Transmitter transformer is Mouser 42TL001; receiver transformer is Mouser 42TL218.

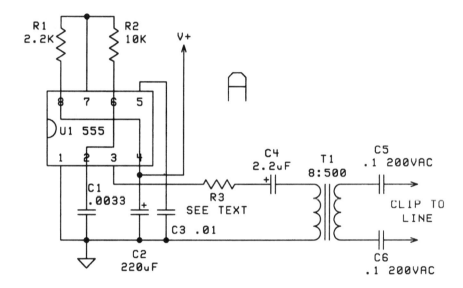

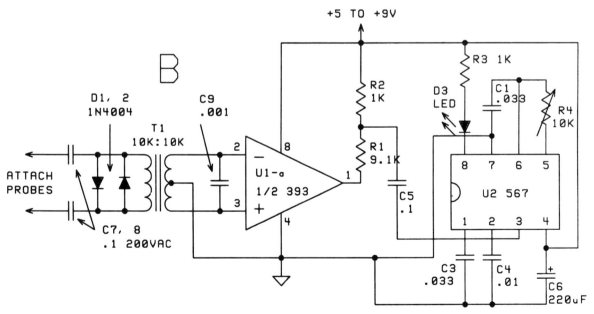

DTMF

- *dual-tone multifrequency*
- *Touch-Tone phones*
- *tones easily generated and decoded using integrated circuits*
- *DTMF digits can be decoded from tape recording*

Much juicy information (Social Security numbers, bank account codes, etc.) is recoverable from tapes of DTMF tones. Bare-bones decoder schematic simplified from ARRL version. American telephones do not contain extended keypad A–D tones; used in Europe, or can be accessed for clandestine use. Input to decoder should stay between 20 and 600 millivolts. The two ICs can be had for ~$7. Connect each 4514 output to 1K resistor to anode of LED whose cathode is grounded, or to a single-transistor LED driver. LED corresponding to number will light when decoder chip hears the tone. Commercial DTMF decoders and kits w/alphanumeric readout and number storage currently sell for >$100.

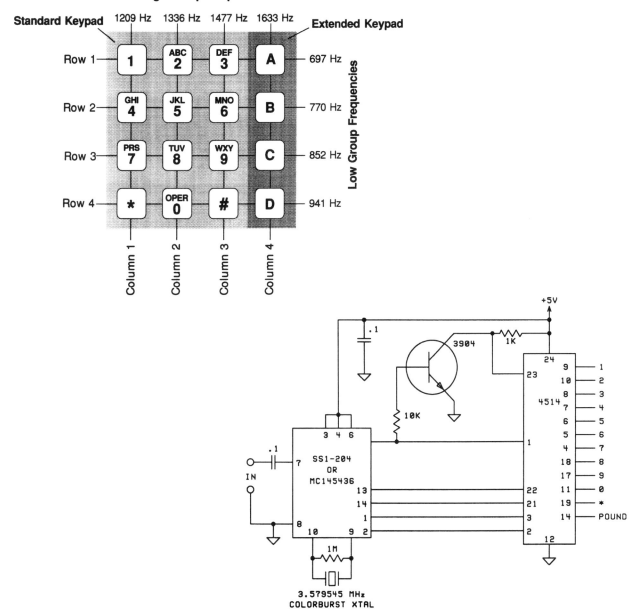

CHAPTER 21

Counterbugging

Countermeasures flow from knowing what bugging methods are possible, practical, and likely; what traces planting the bug will have left; and what leakage accompanies various bugs in operation. Buggers make good debuggers.

Debugging has worth not because it can secure premises so parties may speak freely, but because discovery of a bug tells the target to change his behavior. The nature of the bug also gives a derivative view of the adversary and what price he has put on the insights, in turn shrinking the pool of likely culprits.

Counterbugging involves a lot more than a search for bugs. Like all crimes, bugging bears a statistical signature that tells the counterbugger what types of bugs to anticipate in a given venue. Industrial spies who target couturiers tend to work an MO different from those rampant in the icy skyscraper canyons of Music City, USA. Datasorts can show who within a specified radius knows how to build bugs; who recently has bought the parts that comprise the bug; and who, based on postal scans, financial transactions, magazine subscriptions, and catalog requests has evinced Excessive Interest in bugging. (Only the tactless wonder how seemingly private data comes to be pooled on the populace.)

Despite this chapter's hardware emphasis, the serious counterbugger tempers his reliance on tools, because tools alone can't do the job.

TELEPHONE COUNTERBUGGING

These instructions presume the reader to be a skilled operator, conversant with safety precautions vital to high-voltage circuits. Unqualified persons, and persons under the age of 21, are warned not attempt these measures.

First, examine the line on an oscilloscope. Start with the phone on the hook. Resting DC voltage should read within specified limits. Switch to AC coupling; crank up scope sensitivity. Place a radio near the phone (each phone in turn, if more than one). The scope will show audio from an on-hook tap, as well as an ultrasonic carrier going out over the line.

Take the handset off the hook, dial "1" to kill the dial tone, and continue to monitor the line on the scope. Only the resting DC voltage should change; the only audio present should come from the mic in the handset.

Examine the spare pair on the scope. It should be accessible behind the modular jack. Unless a second line is connected, the spare pair should act inert, either an open circuit or a short, depending on whether the pair is open or shorted at termination. The spare pair should not react when the phone is taken off the hook.

Unplug the phone, remove the jack from the wall, open and inspect the jack; all of them, in fact, because each contains enough room to hide a bug. Any wires other than telco cable must be accounted for.

Next, go under the house, visually trace all phone cables from the point they penetrate the floor to the point they feed through the wall to the telco interface mounted on the exterior of the house. Note whether the line appears to have been cut, stretched, or coiled at any point.

Inspect the subscriber interface on the outside of the house. A screwdriver opens the subscriber interface; a special tool is necessary to access the telco terminals behind it. The interface box contains at least one modular jack. Removing the modular plug from this jack disconnects household phone wiring from the central station.

Visually inspect the phone line leading away from the house as far as possible until it ties to a pole junction. Use binoculars if necessary, or a video camera equipped with a strong zoom lens. Professionals have been known to don climbing belt and spikes and run up the pole for a lineman's look, but this practice holds too many risks to commend.

Counterbugging commercial systems demands disassembly of the punch-down block. Inspection is the only way to confirm that no bug hides behind it. Account for every wire present on both sides of the block. Telco practice limits each clip to one wire, so any extras merit special attention.

Prepare the line for a tone sweep by unplugging all phones and disconnecting the line from the telco interface (in dwellings, open the interface box and unplug the modular plug; commercial users can remove the appropriate bridging clips from the punch-down block). On an ohmmeter, the line in isolation should read as an open circuit. Connect an oscilloscope and a sinewave generator across the line. The generator should be capable of sweeping 10 Hz to 500 KHz, at a level of $4V_{p-p}$. As you sweep from low to high, look for dips or peaks that suggest a parallel or series resonance connected to the line. Also, high-frequency roll-off in excess of that normally due to parasitic inductance and capacitance can betray a tap.

Next, disassemble each phone. Many bugs will be obvious; those made by duplicating the phone on a modified circuit board will not. Trace the audio path, look for daughterboards, unmatched wiring, fresh solder connections, a mic other than the one in the handset—generally things that don't belong. Keep in mind while searching that bugs disguised as large polyester capacitors are available through European vendors.

With a sniffer or spectrum analyzer nearby, power up the phone from a variable DC supply. An RF bug in the phone will register.

The fact that these measures check clean means nothing if the adversary is the govern-

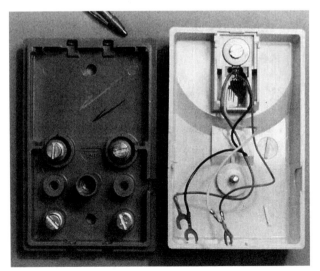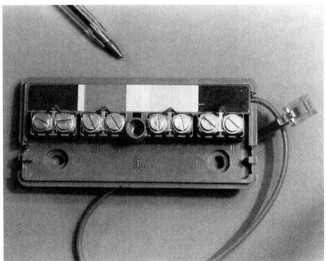

Why the counterbugger must disassemble and inspect the phone jacks. Each one contains enough room to hide a bug.

ment or a private party who has mustered a five-figure bugging fee. In those cases the tap exists far from the house, perhaps inside the local exchange. The strongest counter-tap technique deserves repeating: don't tell the phone what you don't want known.

THRESHOLD-BASED TELEPHONE COUNTERMEASURES

Some threshold-based autostart taps can be defeated by manipulating the variables those taps use to sense that the phone is off the hook. Voltage-sensing switches see 48V when the phone is on the hook. They trip when line voltage drops to 5V in the off-hook condition. The actual trip-point lies somewhere between 5V and 48V but is rarely higher than 30V. If the caller could raise line voltage without having the central station sense an on-hook condition, he could cause those taps to shut down.

To demonstrate the technique, wire a 10K 1-watt pot in series with the phone line and place leads of a digital voltmeter across the line. Set pot resistance to minimum. In the on-hook state, the meter reads close to 48V. When the phone is taken off the hook, line voltage drops sharply, to the vicinity of 5V. Dial "1" to kill the dial tone; slowly increase resistance. The user will find that line voltage rises but the line remains active. He will reach a point, usually in excess of 30V, where the central station senses an on-hook condition and drops the connection.

By dialing the number as usual, then adding resistance once the call is underway, the user can cause a voltage-sensing tap to drop out. Run the resistance a few volts below the point the central station cuts off to avoid having the call terminated in progress.

One sees intuitively that loop current also falls as loop resistance rises. If it falls low enough, a current-sensing tap will drop out. Repeat the procedure described above, but this time wire a milliammeter in series with the pot and the line. Note loop current, and note the current at which the central station returns to the on-hook condition. A resistance setting that

allows slightly more current to flow can defeat some current-sensing taps.

These threshold-based steps make the wildly optimistic assumption that the altered voltage/current has in fact defeated the threshold-based tap, and that no other type of tap exists on the line.

TIME DOMAIN REFLECTOMETRY

A short pulse injected into one end of a cable travels to the other end, then reflects to the injection point. This reflection is readily detectable, and the character of the reflection tells much about the state of the line. Also, the time taken for the round trip is easy to measure and allows calculation of the length of the line. These steps define a procedure known as time domain reflectometry. The technique applies chiefly to coaxial cable but suits the phone line in some cases.

Dedicated TDR instruments can be had but cost a bundle. The procedure takes only a squarewave generator and an oscilloscope.

Assuming the pulse travels at the speed of light (983,573,087 feet per second), the relationship between time (from onset of the pulse to onset of the reflection) and length of the cable is:

length = (reflection time × speed of light) / 2

or: $l = (t \times v) / 2$

Divide by 2, because the pulse travels the length of the line twice. Stating length in feet and time in nanoseconds:

$l = (t \times .984) / 2$

In fact, the pulse travels at some fraction of the speed of light, called the velocity factor (VF), expressed in decimal terms. A VF of 0.9 means nine-tenths the speed of light. Cable manufacturers specify VF along with other cable traits. If the VF is known for a particular line, the time the reflection takes to arrive allows calculation of line length. Conversely, VF is

TIME DOMAIN REFLECTOMETRY

Extremely simple TDR bench circuit. CMOS 555 timer running at ~300 KHz generates ~1.5µs pulses; uses fast 2N2369 transistor to drive line. Scope probe should be set to ×10 (which, paradoxically, means "divided by 10") to minimize ringing. Observe waveform in three cases. First, with line impedance perfectly matched to generator impedance. Wire a 1K pot across open end of line, trim pot until pulse appears as square as possible. Amplitude drops by half, in keeping with Ohm's law. Next, short the

line. The waveform acquires a sharp dip when the reflected pulse arrives. Finally, with the line opened, arrival of reflected pulse creates a sharp peak. Obvious from the setup that an impedance irregularity placed between the input of the line and termination can cause an additional reflection that shows up in the 250-ns window when the main pulse is in transit. 40-MHz or faster scope preferred for TDR. The bugger who anticipates skilled counter-bugging should test his taps on TDR.

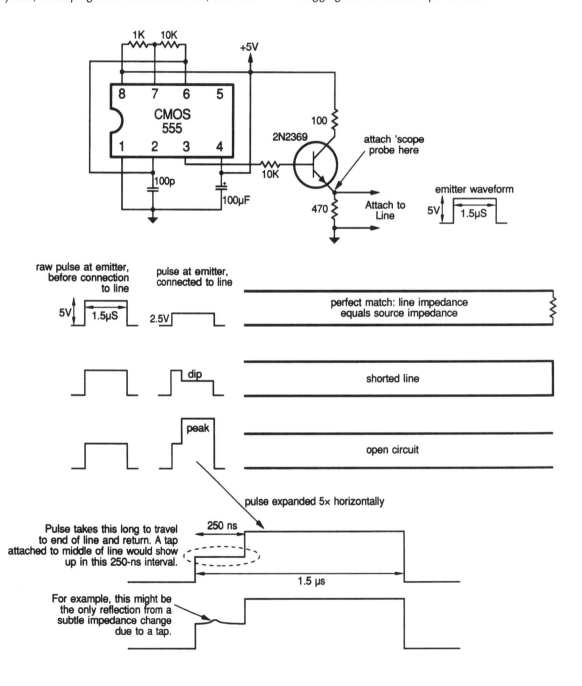

TIME DOMAIN REFLECTOMETRY

A) Unloaded output of pulse generator (emitter of 2N3969).

B) Line connected to pulse generator, 1K pot at termination of line trimmed to give best possible impedance match. Except for some ringing, pulse waveform intact, but reduced by ~50 percent, as predicted by Ohm's law.

C) Pot has been removed from end of line, leaving an open circuit.

D) Identical to C, but sweep has been expanded 5x. Pulse takes approximately 240 nanoseconds to make the trip from injection point to end of line and back. Because line impedance is much lower than pulse generator impedance, the reflection adds, making a plateau.

E) Line is shorted; reflection still takes 240 ns, but because line impedance is now much higher than generator impedance, reflection causes sharp dip. If a tap were connected to middle of line, its bump would show up in the 240-ns interval.

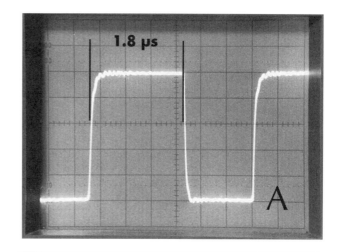

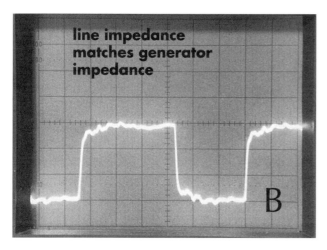

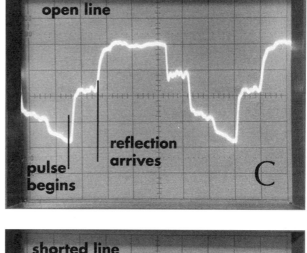

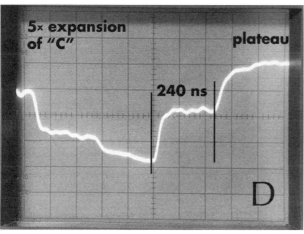

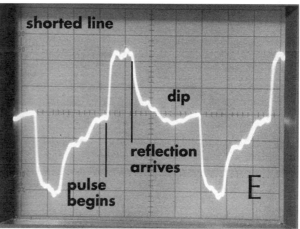

easily calculated from a known length of line. The revised equation states:

$$l = (t \times .984 \times VF) / 2$$

While TDR can detect taps that do not affect static variables, such as a tightly coupled inductor, the technique has limited counterbugging use. It should not be necessary if the entire line can be inspected.

Even when TDR applies, it rightly belongs with anticipatory countermeasures. The pulse profile tells a lot more when compared to a prior profile obtained on the line in a known, clean state. Accordingly, long lines awkward to inspect should be profiled (1) with the line open at termination, (2) with the line perfectly matched to the pulse generator, and (3) with the line shorted at termination. Keep photographs of these waveforms. Valid future comparison demands duplicating technique, preferably using the same pulse generator with the same scope, run by the same operator.

The experimenter can demonstrate TDR on a 20-MHz scope, but serious work calls for a 40-MHz or faster model.

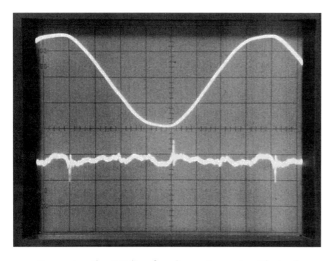

Screening the AC line for ultrasonic carrier. Photo shows input (top) and output (bottom) of passive network built from a couple of 0.01 µF capacitors in series. Top scale 100V/div (voltage measured relative to ground, not to the neutral AC terminal); bottom scale 1V/div. Filtering exposes high-frequency transients on AC line.

CARRIER CURRENT COUNTERBUGGING

Commercial carrier current detectors work well as far as they go. Most consist of an isolation network feeding a highpass filter, feeding a 567 tone detector tunable over the range of interest. Older designs use a manually tuned bandpass filter feeding a meter. The counterbugger can get a better picture of the line by viewing it on an oscilloscope. This method shows signals on the order of a millivolt, which may not trip a detector, as well as spectra outside detector range.

The AC line presents the problem of detecting millivolt signals in the presence of interference thousands of times greater. Practical carriers live above 10 KHz, a point that makes a good cutoff for a highpass filter to attenuate the 120V power signal.

A thorough job must examine all wiring, including phone, power, thermostat, doorbell, exterior low-voltage lighting, cable TV, and intercom (many homes built between 1964 and 1974 were wired for intercoms during construction; few intercoms were ever used).

Carrier current products based on the X10 protocol emit 120-KHz bursts readily distinguished from carriers bearing audio. The counterbugger should keep in mind that the bugger might have hidden a carrier current bug in an X10 carrier current control block.

If a carrier shows up the counterbugger must pinpoint the source. First, find the AC outlet where the carrier has greatest amplitude. AM carriers and wideband FM carriers respond visibly to sound, making a walk-test helpful in locating the bug.

If the source of the carrier is not obvious, have a helper unplug each AC-powered device in the house while the agent watches the scope. Keep in mind that the bug could be hidden in an AC outlet, in the attic, or under the house; and that the mic could be separated from the modulator.

Presence of a carrier implies a receiver somewhere on the same side of the power transformer, or that the carrier current transmitter is part of a repeater.

CARRIER CURRENT COUNTERBUGGING

- the most effective measure is to examine suspect wiring on an oscilloscope
- studying power lines demands fastidious isolation technique and is STRICTLY FOR EXPERIENCED, QUALIFIED PROFESSIONAL TECHNICIANS

A) Passive highpass network is adequate for most screening; substitution of capacitive reactance at different frequencies illustrates what's happening. At the 60-Hz line frequency, 0.01µF capacitor appears as a 265K resistance. By divider action with the 6.8K resistors, only a fraction of a percent of 60-Hz energy gets through; $170V_{p-p}$ comes through filter as ~100 millivolts$_{p-p}$. At a typical 400-KHz carrier frequency, 0.01µF capacitor appears as 40-ohm resistor; 99 percent of 400-KHz energy gets through this network. Note that the scope's

ground strap should NOT connect to any part of the isolation network, because the scope is already grounded through its 3-conductor power cable.

B) Passive isolation network feeds active highpass filter that cuts off below ~10 KHz, virtually eliminates 60 Hz from signal; second op amp boosts carrier by an amount that depends on amp's open-loop gain and the frequency of the carrier; 5532 works fine in this application. Can reveal carriers <1 millivolt. Note that this circuit demands an AC isolation transformer between scope and AC power supply; the op amps must run on batteries. The text presents this information to illustrate certain concepts involved in attenuating the AC line voltage to allow the counterbugger to screen for ultrasonic carrier signals. Reading this material does NOT qualify anyone to conduct the procedure, and it does NOT guarantee safety.

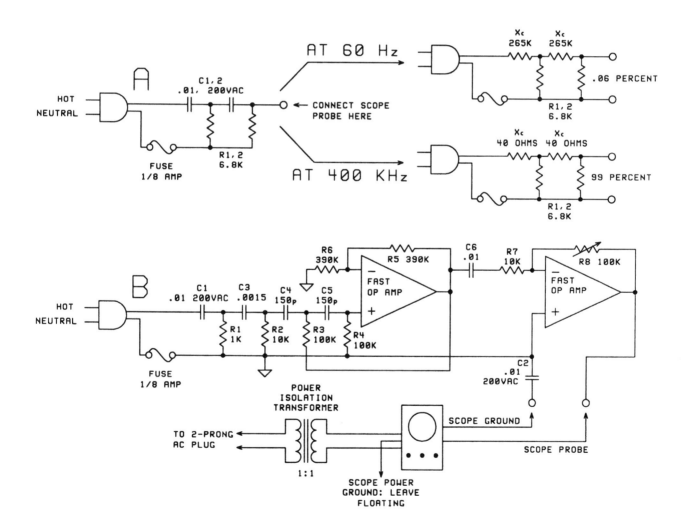

Note: Screening the AC power line exposes the operator to potentially lethal shock. For that reason the text warns anyone other than experienced, qualified professional technicians not to attempt it. Details offered elsewhere in this chapter are meant to inform the reader generally regarding means to attenuate the AC line voltage to facilitate detection of a low-level carrier. Reading these details will not qualify anyone to conduct the procedure. Again, if you are not already an experienced, qualified professional, do not attempt to examine the AC power line.

RF COUNTERBUGGING

If RF bugs abound, RF counterbugging is the most highly refined facet of the art. The nature of RF makes it omnidirectional, in a form whose detection is a mature science.

Counter-RF tools consist of the following:

- RF sniffers
- frequency counters
- spectrum analyzers
- radio direction finders

RF SNIFFERS

A sniffer senses RF energy and reads relative intensity on a meter or bargraph. "Stealth" models, worn concealed on the person, signal the user by a tone whose earbud pitch changes with signal strength.

Most sniffers consist of the following:

- an antenna
- a rectifier
- an integrator
- a meter or bargraph
- optionally, an audio driver

The antenna is a simple telescoping whip; special applications use tuned antennas. The rectifier is almost always a small-signal diode, such as 1N914; but germanium types (1N34A, 1N60, etc.) work better; hot-carrier diodes (1SS99) better still. The diode converts AC RF to a string of DC pulses. An integrator stores these pulses in a capacitor, converting them to a voltage suited to drive a meter.

Sniffers display RF intensity on a bargraph or a meter. The bargraph has no moving parts and no latency but offers less resolution than a meter. A 50-μa meter can display raw integrator output without further processing. A bargraph requires a driver following the integrator.

Sniffers come as amplified/unamplified, tuned/untuned, and meter/audio. Unamplified sniffers consist of a diode/integrator wired directly to a microammeter. Amplified sniffers boost RF before it gets to the diode, or they boost the output of the integrator. The RF amplifier can consist of a microwave transistor or an MMIC (miniature microwave integrated circuit). Gain blocks can give a sniffer as much sensitivity as desired, even to the point that local radio transmissions peg the meter. At that point gain defeats the sniffer's purpose.

Untuned sniffers do not limit bandwidth coming in, except perhaps AM radio, to counter strong local signals. Bandwidth is a function of the diode. Tuned sniffers use LC networks to narrow the band of interest to screen out interfering RF.

Meter-only sniffers are a lot less useful than those that include an audio feed to allow concurrent screening of meter peaks. Strictly speaking, the diode/integrator is an AM detector, but it is also a circuit that can detect FM at reduced volume.

Sweeping with a sniffer involves manually playing the antenna over the entire inner surface of the area being swept, while watching the meter and/or monitoring the audio. The initial sweep will find countless hot spots, few bugs. Hot spots coincide with metal objects acting as antennas, such as folding-door tracks, electrical wiring, metal runners at sheetrock corners, thermostat control wiring, etc. Many consumer electronic products generate enough RF to nudge the meter.

The novice can hone his skills by using a sniffer to sweep for low-power bugs that a

RF SNIFFERS

A) Simplest sniffer, totally passive. RF couples from antenna through C1 to anode of D1, which rectifies signals that exceed D1's forward voltage drop. RF DC is lowpass filtered by R2–C2, reads directly on microammeter. The fact that the antenna load is pure resistance (R1) means circuit has no discriminative ability and will read any electromagnetic radiation up to frequency limit of diode.

B) R1 has been replaced by inductor L1. In this case, C1 and L1 form a series resonant network. Frequencies below resonance will be shunted to ground and will not read on meter. Frequencies above resonance will be shunted through D1 and will read on the meter. Note a second network, L2–C2, that, optionally, gives one means to tune the sniffer. Replacing the meter with a crystal earphone makes this circuit a crude AM receiver. "A" and "B" are low-sensitivity devices useful mainly in detection of high RF levels, not much use in counterbugging.

C) A practical debugging design. Here diode output is amplified by op amp; choose C2 to limit response to audio frequencies. Meter is driven directly, allowed by meter zero control R1. Optionally, feeding op amp output to audio amp will let the sweeper hear the meter drive voltage. Strictly speaking, an AM detector still demodulates FM enough to identify a bug.

D) Example of a sniffer whose detection stage is preceded by a wideband RF amplifier, in this case a member of the MAR series of monolithic microwave integrated circuits (MMICs). Four-lead device is biased off R1–L1–C3. C1 and C2 are microwave-capable surface-mount chip capacitors. Remainder of circuit similar to unamplified types, but note meter drive could just as easily feed a bargraph display.

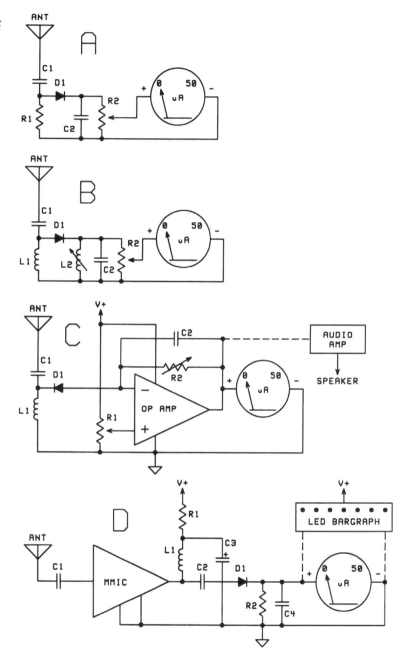

helper has hidden. With a little practice the user will learn to gauge the power of a bug from the sniffer's reaction. Very low power means that the listening post is nearby, or that the transmitter acts as the first stage of a repeater.

A key but seldom-asked question concerns what range needs to be sniffed. The bugger can build bugs covering 1 MHz to 2.4 GHz using off-the-shelf parts; a simple sniffer will spot those emissions. The bugger can also gut a couple of radar detectors to build a 24-GHz system whose carrier lies far beyond the average sniffer's range and is directional to boot. Sniffers and spectrum analyzers tend to peter out above 3 GHz. Hardware that can scan the radar bands costs so much that only clandestine services and the military can afford them.

FREQUENCY COUNTERS

If the sniffer turns up a bug, the next logical step is to tune a scanner to the bug frequency to hear what the bugger has been hearing. A frequency counter is a device that measures frequency of RF emitters.

This detection/frequency-count sequence happens so often in counterbugging that several firms market combination sniffer-counters, but the price of that combo is also the point at which moving up to a spectrum analyzer starts to make sense.

RF SPECTRUM ANALYSIS

A spectrum analyzer senses RF energy and displays signal strength vs. frequency on an oscilloscope. If the SA shows a presumptive bug peak, the operator can flip a switch and convert the SA to a radio receiver, tune it to the peak, and listen to the signal. This confirms most bugs. SAs possess submicrovolt sensitivity, enabling scan of a house or a small business from a single point.

Late models port to computer sound cards, and here the coffee starts to darken, for the sound card opens the door to storage and analysis of vast blocks of data, in turn enabling detection of bugs that might otherwise escape.

It becomes child's play to subtract one reading from another to expose a faint signal. This capability is particularly useful to detect off-hook phone transmitters. Store the spectrum display; store another reading with the phone off the hook; subtract the first from the second, and the peak stands out.

Commercial SAs suitable for counterbugging start at twenty grand. Microwave models top fifty grand.

Building a spectrum analyzer is a simple affair. The result will not give world-class performance and lacks the usual convenience features but could enable a skilled operator to catch perhaps 90 percent of RF bugs. For less than $200, oscilloscope owners can build a tool covering 10–500 MHz. The open literature offers several designs, all based on voltage-controlled cable tuners plentiful on the surplus market.

While spectrum analyzers excel at detecting RF, they have three weak spots. First, it is possible for a bug to generate a signal lost in the RF noise floor. Reception requires a sophisticated receiver, pretty much limiting the mode to situations with a modest fortune on the line.

Second, the SA has a resolution limit. This tells the narrowest signals the analyzer can resolve. A bug might show up as a bump on the shoulder of the legitimate peak or might not appear at all if the analyzer has poor resolution. Buggers use their knowledge of resolution limits to hide signals.

Finally, the SA cannot pinpoint an RF source. The usual step following identification of a probable is to sweep the premises with a sniffer.

Although SAs are potent counterbugging tools, they're just as handy for working up RF bugs. At a glance, they show the builder center frequency, harmonics, and type of modulation. They make transmitter alignment a snap, and they give the builder a preview of what a counterbugger will see in the event of a sweep.

RADIO DIRECTION FINDING

If spectrum analysis uncovers a bug that the sniffer can't find (implying that it's not inside the dwelling), a radio direction finder (RDF) can be

SPECTRUM ANALYSIS

While a spectrum analyzer can be a complicated instrument (and certainly an expensive one), the operating principle is extremely simple. A voltage-controlled tuner sweeps over a range of frequencies at a rate controlled by a ramp generator. The output of the tuner is a constant intermediate frequency, which feeds a radio receiver tuned to that frequency. Receiver output goes to vertical deflection control on oscilloscope. Horizontal scope feed is the same ramp (level-shifted, if necessary) that controls tuner, so scope sweep and tuner are always in sync. Scheme is so simple that oscilloscope owners can build a 500-MHz SA for less than two bills. Bottom diagrams depict typical SA display; left in very wide sweep, several tens of megahertz; right has been expanded to show part of commercial FM spectrum. One station seems to have picked up a little hitch-hiker . . .

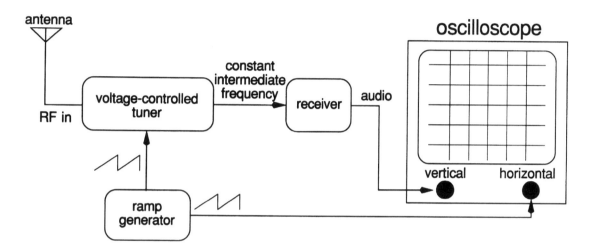

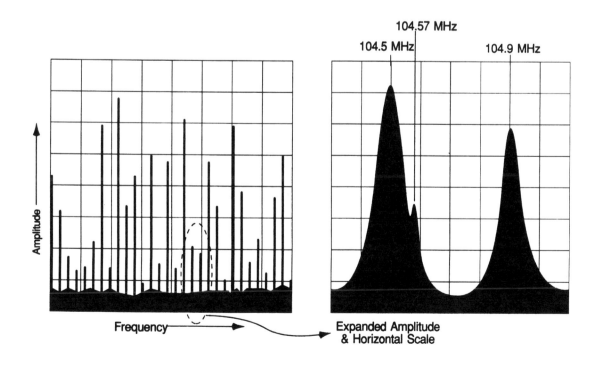

useful. RDF is based on several principles: the null of a loop antenna, interferometry, and the Doppler principle. The RDF must first know the frequency of the bug.

METAL DETECTORS

Metal detectors are useful for finding metal where none should be—tracing a buried hardwire line, for instance—but otherwise have limited counterbugging use.

NONLINEAR JUNCTION DETECTORS

A nonlinear junction detector (NJD) emits RF and detects harmonic energy generated by semiconductor junctions (anything containing transistors or diodes) reacting to this energy. The former Soviet Union doped brick with diodes, then sold the brick to America to build the U.S. Embassy in Moscow, because American NJDs could not tell diodes from bugs in the brick.

NJDs can detect inactive bugs as well as active ones. The drawbacks include a glut of nonlinear junctions in the average house (the hinge of a door, for instance). NJDs present no serious obstacle because every bugger knows they exist. Wrapping the bug in tinfoil foils the NJD.

DEBUGGING HARDWIRE

Properly concealed hardwire can be extremely difficult to find. Some hardwire lines hide in plain sight, by consisting of doorbell cable, phone line, or power cable. The sweeper should apply a high index of suspicion during the physical search. Never assume a wire belongs because it looks like it belongs. Confirm that each wire is what it appears to be.

DEBUGGING ULTRASONIC

Other than finding the bug on physical search, the only way to detect the signal is to listen for it with an ultrasonic transducer. If the counterbugger is lucky, the bug is running at 40

KHz and will be easily detectable by a 40-KHz transducer. If he's not lucky, the ultrasonic frequency could lie anywhere in the range 25 to 400 KHz. A complement of transducers to hear over that range is rarely found in the average counterbugger's bag.

Physical search should concentrate on likely transducer sites: near vents at the base of the house, under the eaves, etc. Ultrasonic bugs tend to be outdoor, line-of-sight devices. Discovery of the transmitter should locate the receiver by following the direction of the beam.

DEBUGGING INFRARED

Optical bug radiation shows up very well on a camcorder video display. Thus, viewing the target through such a camera, preferably in total darkness, with lamps extinguished to avoid masking, can be an effective countermeasure—unless the bugger has hidden the IR emitter in or near a lamp. His receiver uses an optical bandpass filter combined with a carrier system to kill the 60-Hz interference.

DEBUGGING FIBEROPTIC

Like hardwire, fiberoptic systems leak nothing if properly installed, and they don't show on metal detectors. Physical search is the best bet.

DEBUGGING DIRECTIONAL MICS

Inspect the perimeter, asking yourself where you'd hide a directional mic. If searching several square miles proves impractical, counsel the client not to speak secrets in the open.

INTERMITTENT BUGS

If an intermittent bug happens to be sleeping during the sweep, the counterbugger cannot depend on the usual active leakage. If the client's habit patterns suggest that exchange of intelligence happens only at odd hours, run the money-sweeps (SA and telephone) at that time.

DEBUGGING REPEATERS

Finding the first stage of a repeater is no different than finding a unitary bug. But any bugger who has taken the trouble to install a repeater has probably rigged some sort of tamper switch at the first node. And a repeater tells the target that he is not dealing with an amateur; somebody wants info badly enough to front the price of a new car to get it.

ANTICIPATORY COUNTERMEASURES

If the target cannot eliminate the risk of being bugged, he can make the job harder on the bugger. Something as simple as vacuuming the carpet before going out sets a trap. Only the best professionals leave no tracks. Padlocks, while easily defeated, put just one more barrier between the bugger and the target. Arm vulnerable nodes, such as the entrance to a crawl space, the external phone junction box, or the phone itself, with tamper seals; inspect them weekly.

BEHAVIOR MODIFICATION

While specific procedures will find specific bugs, the most effective tactics involve behavior. They distill to keeping secrets out of compromised media (meaning all media) and cultivating a lifestyle rich in disinformation.

Personal data once obtainable only by stealth now resides in the open. Only by willfully skewing a lifestyle can one shape that data to convey a false flavor. "Disinfoliving" does not take effect overnight; expect a minimum wait of several years. But after enough years of disinfoliving, personal data becomes disinfodata. Snoopers might find it difficult to reconcile a subscription to *The Daily Worker* with one to *Soldier of Fortune*, or a subscription to *Commentary* with one to *Hustler*. It might also be difficult to explain how a member of the John Birch Society managed to participate in a Greenpeace rally; and so forth.

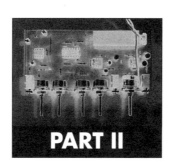

PART II

In the Field

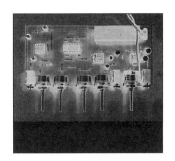

Another Note from Shifty

Collector current? Please. Exegeses leave me lunging for the rum. Believe it, buggers don't bore their clients with EQ curves and offset trim. We speak in terms of paper bearing the mug of a beloved president who dug kites; plaster the bloody watchtower with that paper.

The retentive digest you read in Part I gives a place to start and lets us speak the same language, the language of bugging. Raw circuits tell nothing of how buggers put science to work in the field, a perverse world where the bugger is one of few species who keep a sense of autonomy.

If these tales delve deeper than bug buffs are used to seeing, understand that they tell nothing of the Big Secrets, the heavy stuff that would make me a pariah and maybe get me whacked. And I can't guarantee that I'm not drizzling a bit of syrup to draw the ants away from my own little carrion heap. What I can show is how a bugger thinks, how he projects science beyond the lab, in hardware that the average tech-junkie could build and test.

To prevent demurs bound to plague claims of having run gigs for alphabet-soup agencies, I have lumped all official factions other than local cops under the rubric of the Government Printing Office, or GPO.

So let's go.

CHAPTER 22

Can You Bug This Microphone?

July, 1970. I had just left a meeting with Malloy at Lindy's Drive-In at the west end of Sylmar Avenue. The fact that Malloy tried to hire me to bug his own client said several things.

One: no lawyer would attempt such a hiring unless he could count on immunity if he were found out. Ergo, Malloy had to be a government snitch.

Two: the only way a guy with a clean record became a government snitch was to commit a government felony, be caught, and be offered snitch-hood as a means to halt prosecution. I had never seen anybody cooperate with the Government Printing Office who did not live in the shadow of prosecutorial blackmail.

Three: from now on everything Malloy's clients told "their" lawyer was going straight onto quarter-inch tape running at 7/8 ips on the Uher 4000-series open-reel deck that had been a GPO mainstay for the past decade.

Strangest of all, the pitch sounded so phony on its face that I would have been a fool not to smell a rat.

Not a complete shock. Eight years in the trade had taught that each new snitch was forced to entrap others, usually small fry like

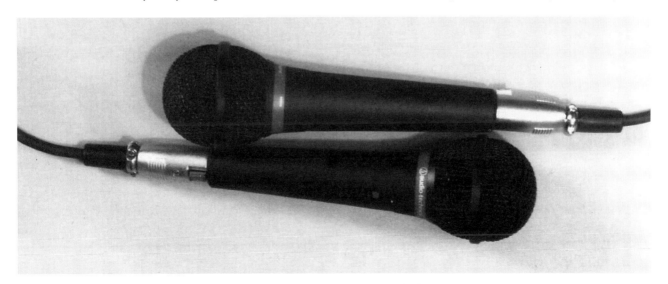

One of these mics is 100,000 times as sensitive as the other. Can you tell which?

bookies and unprotected pimps, or free-lance wiretappers like yours truly. Snitches begat snitches. The question now was not what the gig entailed, but what lay beyond the gig in terms of personal peril. I had agreed to a second meet to weigh those particulars and judge the color of Malloy's kale.

We met next day at Ships at the corner of Ventura and Doheny. Malloy insisted we take a window booth on the Doheny Street side. As we sat down I made a point of accidentally catching his coat on the edge of the table. The coat pulled tight, outlining the Nagra taped to his lower back.

A waitress brought us ice water and menus. While Malloy hit the head to activate the Nagra I ordered a bacon sandwich with coffee and cadged an abandoned *Times* off the counter. I pretended to read the sports section but was actually scanning the immediate vicinity for coverage that had to be there. By the time the grub arrived I had fixed on the one incongruous feature, a third-floor office in the building directly across the street from Ships. The bottom half of one window was mirrored. A 500-mm lens behind that two-way could read headlines on my *Times*. Anything longer could read serial numbers on currency. I did not need X-ray specs to see that Allen Funt wasn't behind the mirror yukking it up with a crew from *Candid Camera*.

Malloy returned as the jukebox issued the opening riff of a song I hadn't heard, called "Ohio." I ate while he declared his pitch in language diagnostic of entrapment. After the waitress hit us twice to freshen our coffee, Malloy assured her that we would be fine for the rest of the meal, then used the Style section of my *Times* to shield a stack of unbroken bank bundles he fanned out on the Formica. I counted 10 of them. To hook him I pretended to be tempted, but pumped him with questions I was careful to phrase in the hypothetical. Once I had milked all I could, I shook my head and laid this on him:

"As a member of the Bar, you should know that what you ask constitutes a felony. In fact, solicitation is a crime. However, because I do not have a tape of our conversation . . ."

As they say, duh.

Malloy's face fell, then brightened, as though receiving wisdom from the mothership. He scooped up the bills, said he'd call after I slept on the offer; he might have mumbled something about a bonus. Then he left me holding the check.

I had nixed the gig in blessed rites and would do so again when Malloy called. But I decided to wire him to get to the bottom of this cheeky scam. What was important enough to front twice the biggest fee I had ever earned? Ten grand was worth two Caddies and change in those days. The crux now was who had been behind that mirrored window, and why they wanted so badly to bag me.

* * *

Three weeks of surveillance (as appealing to tell as tar) confirmed GPO's ownership of Malloy. The boys never hit his office, nor he theirs. They talked everything but business on the phone. Another month passed before I learned that handlers met snitch every Thursday at 3 P.M. in the control room of a recording studio in the basement of the Ponsonby Building, two blocks from the Capitol Records tower. (GPO came to command the studio when a semi-famous record producer delivered himself by being pinched with just enough snow to qualify for dealer sentencing.)

Bug-proof "bubble rooms" did not exist back then, though one secretive government annex had built something akin to the cone of silence of *Get Smart* fame. Besides the fact that studios were supposed to be soundproof, the boys might have heard that those built since 1960 shielded their walls with grounded copper mesh that kept out powerful commercial radio signals, and which would keep a bug's RF in. Malloy's handlers had to relish these steps that seemingly kept them safe from guys like me.

Once I knew the location of the target, I schooled myself in its secrets. For commercial structures that meant perusing the blueprints kept at City Hall. Anybody could walk in and view the stuff. Prints showed crucial details like stairwells, windows, and doors. They plotted A/C ductwork and refrigerant lines and corresponding control feeds (one of the best carrier-current lines because hardly anybody swept them). Blueprints specified wall thicknesses and construction materials. Occasionally they told what make and model of lock was to be used on what door. To a pro this was like being given a passkey.

After I sketched key entry/escape routes I skimmed the electrician's schedule and caught a bonus. Besides power wiring, the diagram routed studio sound cables. Recording studios use balanced, low-impedance transmission lines as a universal link. The many discrete connections necessitated a plethora of lines. At a quarter-inch apiece, a bundle of cables could hardly be run under a door. So, studios built multiple lines into the walls during construction. These cables terminate in XLR jacks that line studio walls like electrical outlets.

The cable diagram told me that the audio complex had originally included an office and two broadcast booths for a radio station on the floor above the recording studio. Each broadcast booth tied through a numbered, balanced line that came out on a wall jack in a studio on the floor below but did not reach the control room. I noted these jack numbers, then split.

* * *

The intercept consisted of human speech originating in a "soundproof" room, which meant maximum attenuation on the order of 60 dB. The building prints confirmed copper mesh shielding in the walls. Access to the control room would be tricky, but access to the two studios relatively safe.

Rather than forcing a fixed gimmick to fit the scene, let the scene define the gimmick. (A bug is known as a gimmick, a maguffin, or just "it.") In this case, the variables defined a hardwire bug that would lurk in the studio adjacent to the control/meeting room. It would feed the former broadcast suite on the floor above, available for rent in two-hour blocks, through the existing hardwire connection that probably had not seen use in a decade.

I would make up the attenuation due to the control room by inserting an extra 60 dB of boost in the system. This added gain, excessive for a noisy environment, became practical in the preternatural quiet of a recording studio. And I would hide the gimmick in the least conspicuous item possible.

* * *

With specs defined, design became a matter of rote. Check out the sender schematic. Seven Panasonic WM-60AT electret mics run in parallel off common bias resistor R1, whose value was found empirically to optimize output from the string. R2 and C2 form the decoupling network often required for stability when electrets use the same power bus as a high-gain amplifier. C1 shunts RF.

Array output couples through C3 to the noninverting input of U1-a, half a 5532 dual op amp configured as a frequency-dependent amplifier. I chose the 5532 because it gave adequate gain and could drive 600 ohms. Its voltage noise was less than thermal noise of the electret bias resistor. (In fact, the 5532 had been a pipe dream in '70. I used a chip with similar capabilities that cost an amount equal to $200 in today's dollars. The 5532 is a close modern equivalent.)

All Part I's dread lore about noise and frequency contours—here it is, fleshed out in a bona fide bug. Gain equals one plus the ratio of impedance R4-C5 to the impedance of R3-C4. Since each network's impedance varies with frequency, so does gain.

U1-a output couples through C6 to primary winding of T1. T1's secondary winding ties to the XLR connector pins shown in the diagram.

T1 secondary also carries phantom power for the system, taken off the center tap.

U1-b is configured as a voltage follower whose input is biased at 1/2V+ by divider R6-R7. Its output serves as the artificial ground for U1-a.

C7, C8, and C9 bypass the supply.

* * *

The receiver's input stage uses the same transformer as the remote. The center tap of this winding ties to 9V battery No. 1, to phantom-

GIMMICK #1

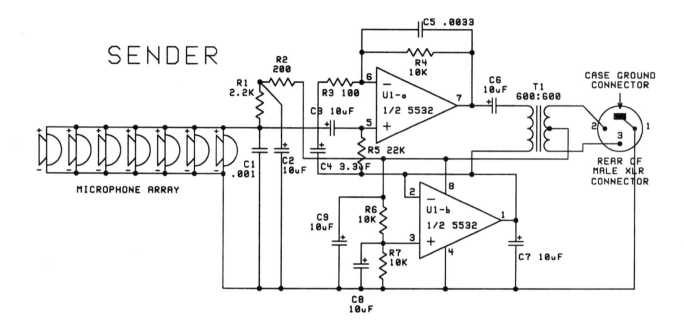

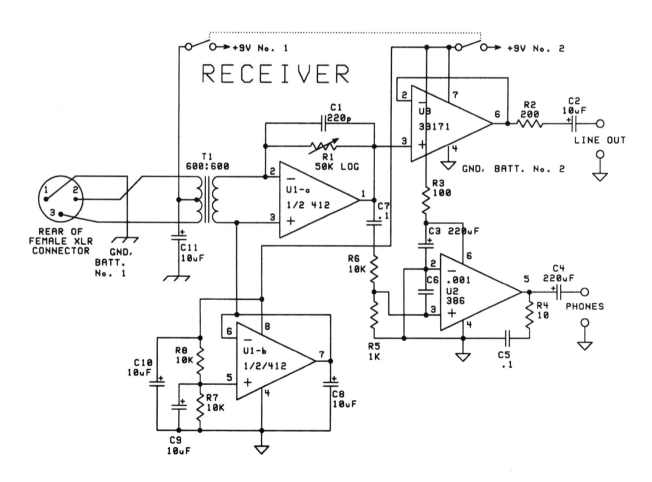

(SENDER) GIMMICK #1

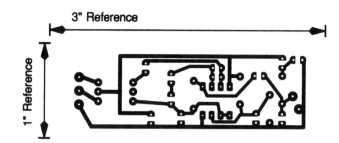

3" Reference

1" Reference

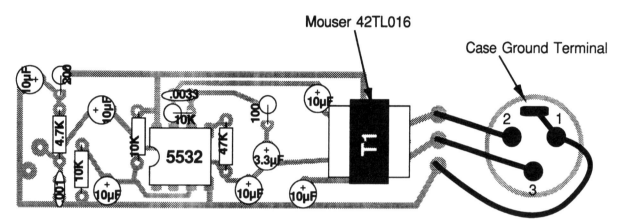

Mouser 42TL016

Case Ground Terminal

rear (solder) side of
male XLR connector

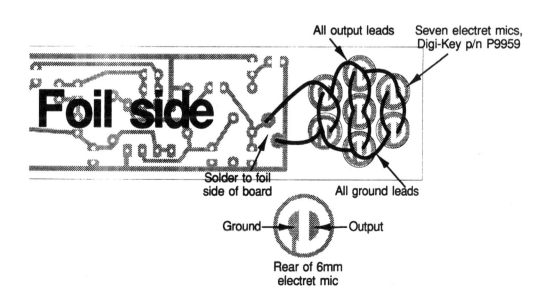

All output leads

Seven electret mics,
Digi-Key p/n P9959

Solder to foil
side of board

All ground leads

Ground — Output

Rear of 6mm
electret mic

power the sender. C11 decouples the sender end of this path.

T1 secondary couples directly to the inverting input of U1-a, whose gain is variable by pot R1 up to 38 dB. Note that T1 secondary acts as the input impedance for U1-a. C1 rolls off high-frequency response.

U1-a output couples directly to voltage follower U3. U1-a output is biased at 1/2V+. Since U3 output = input, direct connection to U1-a biases U3 at an appropriate operating point. Signal couples through R2-C2 to line output. Use of R2 is a common engineering practice to load the op-amp output, because some output stages exhibit instability when connected directly to a capacitive load. C2 isolates the output from the DC offset present at U3 output.

U1-a output couples also through C7-R6-R5 to noninverting input of audio power driver U2. R6-R5 acts as a voltage divider reducing U2's maximum gain to ~6 dB. Audio couples through C4 to headphone/speaker output. R4-C5 serves as a snubber. C11 shunts RF at U2 input.

Each electret element measured 20 dB more sensitive than the stock dynamic element. Running seven electrets in parallel does not yield linear signal addition; more like four times the output of a single (12 dB). The preamp applies about 32 dB of gain in the midrange. The receiver adds ~38 dB; a few dB more for the headphone output. Compared to the original mic, this system is 102 dB—123,000 times—more sensitive, despite gain stages running far below their limit. This gain proved more than adequate to the intercept. The experimenter may wish to note that the system performs significantly better using full-size electrets, such as Panasonic WM-034BYs or Radio Shack 270-090s.

* * *

I could summarize planting the gimmick with some vapory statement like, "Using techniques well known in the trade—stealth, deceit, diversion, lock-manipulation—my agents effected entry to the studio and connected the sender."

That leaves too vague a picture. The trade's blackest secret is that no bugger works alone.

We always hire help, because one guy can't be in three places at once, and because surrogates are often the only antidote to entrapment. What began in the '50s as a rare resort in matters of national security had by 1968 invested policy. You could lay odds on every third government job as a trap. GPO did not seek to kill freelance wiretapping. Too much intelligence flowed through that channel. They sought to proscribe the practice unless somebody they owned ran the gig.

So premier buggers stopped pulling exposure. We would design and usually make the maguffin, sometimes lay out the op. But when the deal went down we managed to be playing a nassau in view of 50 witnesses at Pebble Beach.

The talent pool willing to pull heavy exposure included some of the most volatile characters found outside a maximum security wing. They came from mixed backgrounds. In no particular order, you might find elite forces' NCOs drummed out for filching the odd claymore. Ex-cops exiled when they came to see life through Dirty Harry wraparounds. Third-rate buggers who got a little too cozy with Austin Nichols. And if you ever wondered how corrupt cops got once they left prison, hey, my lips are sealed. These and more comprised a pool whose existence no one will confirm. Pressing the point is like soliciting a tibial fracture.

These minions of dissimilar commencement share the fact of being bereft of conscience. Whacking a squealer is the moral equivalent to squashing a bug. No code, no moral quandary. Half of them seem to have been born without scruples. The rest lost them to erosion by fate or dilution in sauce. The surest among them affect Luca Brasi's remorseless fealty to The Godfather. Such operatives have to be handled like fulminate.

Aides' menacing mien stems from the fact that proper credentials cannot be gained voluntarily. An agent will have taken enough felony busts to sneer at one more. He (occasionally she) must be able to get along in the joint and keep his wits alive and his mouth shut until the bondsman arrives. That savvy comes naturally after a nickel in a maximum pen for violent offenders.

(RECIEVER)

GIMMICK #1

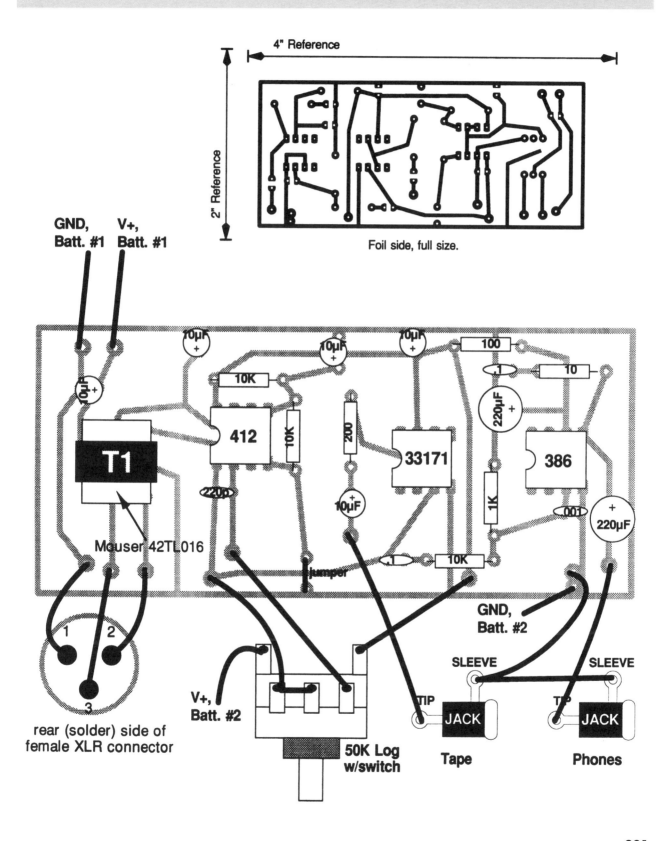

4" Reference

2" Reference

Foil side, full size.

GND, Batt. #1

V+, Batt. #1

10µF +

10K

10µF +

10µF +

100

10K

.1

10

10µF +

220µF +

412

10K

200

33171

386

T1

1K

.001

220D

220µF +

10µF +

Mouser 42TL016

.1

Jumper

10K

GND, Batt. #2

1

2

SLEEVE

SLEEVE

3

TIP

JACK

TIP

JACK

V+, Batt. #2

rear (solder) side of female XLR connector

50K Log w/switch

Tape

Phones

You cannot fully trust agents, nor they you, but crossing them has always proven incompatible with the act of breathing. GPO wanted no part of them because it could not control them—and because they bore such sordid histories that putting them on the stand would have been equal to calling Ted Bundy to testify in small claims court.

For their part, aides would have no truck with the Enforcement Community but saw guys like me as okay, even a solid meal ticket. About the only thing they respected was our autonomy.

When I speak of my agents, this is the pool.

* * *

Using techniques well known in the trade, my agents effected entry to the studio and connected the sender, hidden inside a gutted dynamic mic. For five Thursdays thereafter one of them taped/monitored from the old radio booth on the floor above.

I secreted the receiver in an open-reel tape deck my agent carried as part of a cover package that included wallet clutter, contracts and scripts for mythical promos he was supposed to tape. Somehow the voice talent never showed. The photos illustrate the practice of hiding a gimmick in a consumer electronic product; tap into the power bus, add input jacks. This piece is not the actual one used, which has long since gone to open-reel heaven.

My agent managed to record 40 minutes of Malloy and his handlers, maybe 20 minutes of handlers talking among themselves.

The tapes told me this: had I taken Malloy's money and executed the gig on his behalf, I would have been pinched, charged, denied bail, and cooled in the calaboose for a month. GPO would have offered to forget the charges if I pulled a gig involving the embassy of a Red Bloc power. The gig entailed heavy exposure inside the embassy. They wanted me because I was one of four wiretappers (about whom they knew) who could handle the technical end, but the only one with no prior official ties. That rendered me worthless for political hay if I were captured. And, as a deniable entity, no help would have been forthcoming, the classic profile of a doomed spy. Had I managed the gig undetected I could have kept the cash, so long as I declared it as income. The 70-percent top marginal rate at the time convinced me to pass.

* * *

This caper's gimmick proved formidable enough to join a hoard I kept for special clients. Four pieces eventually sold for $5K each. One found a home in the covert-ops cabinet of an American embassy somewhere in the southern hemisphere. The boys from state (yeah, sure) never explained why they wanted the thing. The other three, from what I heard, were adapted to oversize parabolic mics that could hear anything that went down in a spread the size of Laurel Canyon. The last one left the lab just after *Hollywood Chainsaw Hookers* premiered.

There was one more, the cryo version, but I can't talk about that. I can point out that electronic noise derives from atomic motion within materials that ceases only at absolute zero, but slows down plenty in a bath of liquid nitrogen.

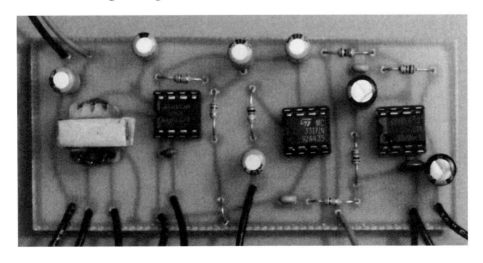

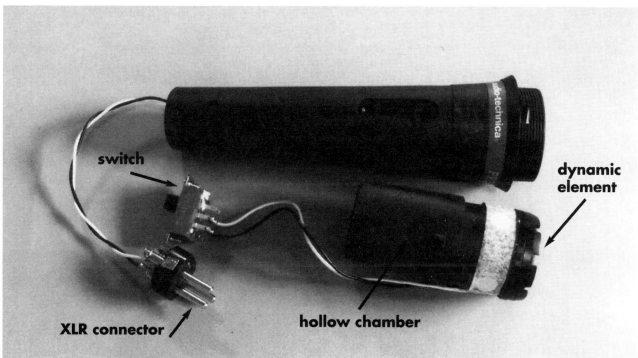

Disassembly of stock dynamic mic. Unscrewing ball cover reveals dynamic element, held in hollow rubber chamber that pulls out easily. Internal wiring is simple. Gimmick fits in place of stock parts.

Top: First gimmick
sender board.
Bottom: Mic end of
board has been
trimmed for easy fit
behind metal mesh
screen.

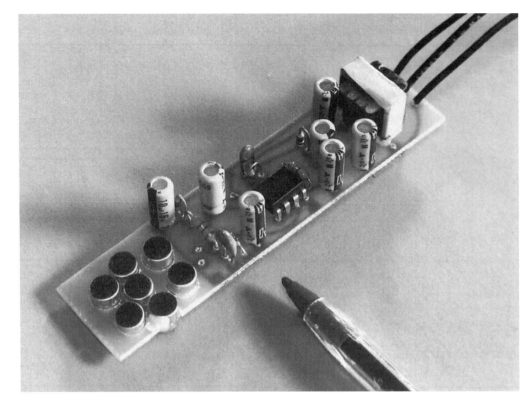

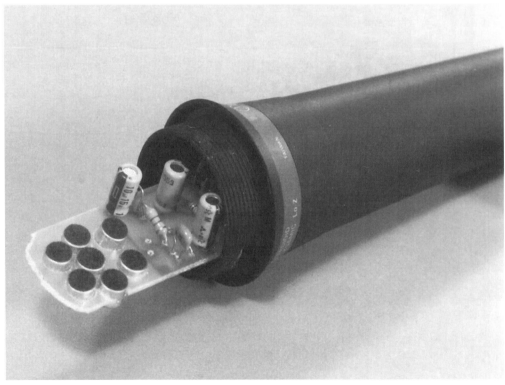

Top: Exterior view of XLR connectors illegally installed in consumer tape deck.
Bottom: Interior view of setup; stereo microphone preamp leeches power from the deck's bus.
Same technique used to hide gimmick in an open-reel deck in 1970.

CHAPTER 23

Muzak® in the Air

The first actual bug I ever built, the one that punched my ticket for the Dark Side, came about by an intercession of fate. In 1959 I landed a job at the Talladega (Ohio) *Sprite* on the strength of a résumé as long as a list of Marius Constant's greatest hits. But I had a GED, which in those days meant that I could actually read. (I also had an amateur radio license, but that hadn't seemed pertinent enough to list on the job application.)

Over three years I rose from gofer to copy assistant and finally to reporter, covering local news and sports. Eventually I began ghosting for the regular sportswriter when he was hungover, which meant anywhere from one column in ten to every other column. When cirrhosis called him to that great press box in the sky, I ascended the throne.

The EIC at the time, a chronic alcoholic named William ("Billy") Wunderlin, took exception to the way my columns treated the furry animal that symbolized his alma mater. What began as cheap office intrigue ballooned into a major personal vendetta: get the goods on Wunderlin.

A stratagem developed almost autonomously. The office was riddled with speakers oozing background music. Several writers and editors, Wunderlin included, had bribed Maintenance to disconnect the music feeds to their offices.

Knowing transducer basics from amateur radio, I wondered why I couldn't hit the maintenance room and tie some sort of amplifier to the speaker lead from Wunderlin's office and listen at my leisure.

Check out the schematic. The speaker feed ties directly to the 8-ohm winding of T1. One end of the 1K winding ties to the base of Q1; the other end of that winding ties to a bias potential taken off the collector through R1; C1 makes that end of the winding an AC ground. So the 1K winding of T1 both feeds audio to and biases the base of Q1. Q1 is configured as a common-emitter amplifier whose emitter resistor R2 is bypassed by C2. This causes it to amplify treble a lot more than bass—the "bug EQ" curve. Q1's collector load consists of the 600-ohm winding of T2. T2's 20K winding ties directly to the inverting input of U1. Direct coupling is possible because both LM386 inputs are biased to ground through internal 50K resistors. R3 acts as a volume control, and C4 acts as an RF shunt. C8 and S2 are optional, to kick U1 into high-gain mode. (The circuit board provides pads for S2 and C8, but does not show S2 or C8 installed. I haven't met a gig that needed the extra boost.) Audio couples through C6 to a speaker or a pair of phones. R5-C7 forms the standard snubber. C3, C5, and R4 bypass the supply.

GIMMICK #2

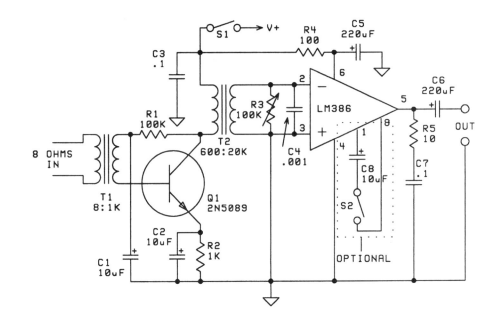

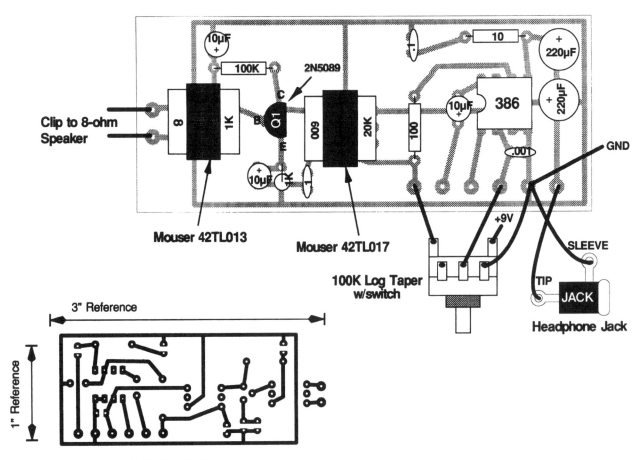

Foil side, 100%

Gainwise, the system stacked up like this:

T1   21 dB
Q1   40 dB (contoured)
T2   15 dB
U1   26 dB (46 dB in high-gain mode)

Total: 102 dB (122 dB in high-gain mode)

Such tremendous gain is tricky to stabilize without transformer isolation.

Use a metal box, of course, to shield the transformers and keep out RF. Twist input/output leads, and separate them physically.

This gimmick has enough punch to hear most anything within 100′ of the speaker. It's overkill for gigs where the speaker/mic is situated closer than 50′ to the target. Simple design typifies the gear buggers build for themselves and well-heeled clients.

This circuit has much to teach. Take the transformers. Common practice calls for loading each winding with a resistor equal to a few times the nominal impedance. Loading dampens inductors' tendency to ring, which manifests as nonlinear frequency response. Leaving the transformers unloaded gives the bugger a boost because a signal will induce more voltage in an undamped transformer than in one properly loaded.

Now and then a budding bugger asks about noise in a transformer. I tell him to consider two phenomena. First is how thermal noise and gain change from one winding to another.

Assuming no significant loss, gain of an 8:1K transformer = $(1{,}000 \div 8)^{0.5}$ = 11.2.

But thermal noise of 1K ohms (4.05 nv) and of 8 ohms (0.36 nv) also has the ratio 11.2:1.

Thermal noise vs. impedance and transformer gain vs. impedance ratio are square-root functions. Therefore, no change in S/N ratio occurs in a low-loss transformer.

$I_n \times R_s$ noise can change significantly, though. Consider tying a transformer winding to the input of an LT1028, which has a high I_n (1 pa / rtHz). One picoamp times 8 ohms is 0.01 nanovolts—practically impossible to measure, let alone hear.

But 1 pa times the 1,000-ohm impedance of T1's secondary winding is 1 nanovolt, a hair more than the chip's E_n. Not excessive, but you'd want to avoid higher impedances.

You would not want to hook a 1028 to T2's 20K winding: 1 pa x 20,000 ohms is 20 nanovolts of $I_n \times R_s$ noise and would make the super-quiet 1,028 many times noisier than it needs to be. Thermal noise alone comes to 18 nv.

The $I_n \times R_s$ calculation becomes particularly important when I_n exceeds 0.4 pa (discrete transistors running collector current >1 ma also exhibit high I_n), and with transformer winding impedance >1K ohms.

Incidentally, this gimmick proved great for screening transistors for "popcorn noise." Besides disparate betas, transistors of the same part number differ greatly in the amount of noise they generate. Noisy samples sound like Jiffy Pop®. A high-gain amplifier like this one exposes transistors that generate excessive noise. If you breadboard this thing and hear telltale pops and crackles, swap out the 5089. Test 10 samples. At least one should be pop-free.

Popcorn noise is an idiosyncrasy of the individual part, not something predictable from a curve of E_n vs. I_c.

* * *

And that's how my first gig went down in 1962. I got the goods on Wunderlin—a small matter of an unpaid gambling debt. We heard no more about the furry mascot; I left the paper with a sparkling recommendation.

Nothing might have come of this caper had I not mentioned it to my brother-in-law after a couple of Blue Ribbons at a backyard barbecue. He told a cop he knew. A week later the cop offered to pay me to build him a "bug."

The cop was evidently pleased with his purchase. Hardware requests grew more frequent and challenging, but more lucrative. My side business ballooned into a cottage industry. Other departments commissioned merch; GPO placed their first order in the summer of '67. I sank gradually into a world of black bags and wallet clutter, safehouses and alibis—a world where only chumps buy the Rule of Law.

When the time came to start planting gimmicks, fate had built me the best cover a bugger could have. Sportswriting confers an excuse to travel, crash in sleazy hotels, sop up booze like staves in casks of Jack, rent wheels and cruise the bowery at odd hours, and incur unexplained and unexplainable expenses. No one looks twice at a Visa chit made out to Midnite Massage or Dell's Stripperama. No one notices a sportswriter passed out at Studio 54 with his bookie and a pair of hookers. Sportswriting may be the only occupation for which serial DWI busts pass without comment. A sportswriter could, in short, do everything a confidential agent did without having to build a fresh cover each time.

CHAPTER 24

The Living Desert

Palm Springs, 1978. The hoods convened at the desert palace belonging to a retired television personality who called it Rancho Mirabella, but which the Enforcement Community had taken to calling Rancho Rigor Mortis, for the number of bodies believed buried in shallow graves in a vast plot that stretched from nearby Death Valley across the border into neighboring Clark County, Nevada.

Everybody who had tried to wire the house had either shied at the gate or failed to make the gig, the latter being smart operators who took the trouble to vet the targets. Too much about them said Heavy Connections.

I made a policy of never wiring connected guys, which these targets were not; more like business associates of connected guys. Still, the bugger who took this gig entered an eerie realm of risk. Detection was likely to end in premature retirement, a constant threat with targets who do not involve the legal system in their affairs. For these and various technical reasons I eschewed a direct attack against the house.

From what the boys told me, key conversations took place on the open back patio and mostly after dark. The hoods deemed the patio secure because it faced nearly a mile of wasteland, unbroken but for tumbleweeds out to where the San Gabriel Mountains met the desert floor.

I hiked up into the hills with my rangefinder and a pair of Bausch & Lombs. Distance from the hoods' patio to the nearest rocky cover measured nine-tenths of a mile, well within range of directional mics I had been using since a certain gig in Guatemala six years earlier.

I began the gimmick by gutting a cheap 5″ PA horn. I ripped out the dynamic driver and replaced it with an electret potted in rope caulk. The horn barely managed 26 dB of directional, contoured boost over the bare mic. This modified horn served as the basic sensor.

The horn mounted at the focus of a 10′ dish. Calculated dish gain exceeded 55 dB. Maybe 15 dB was lost to various inefficiencies; call dish gain an even 40 dB.

These physical (and thus noiseless) stratagems produced a directional mic whose bandwidth was limited by horn effect to tones of interest and was 2,000 times as sensitive as the electret in free air.

The photos show preparation of the horn, a type still found on the surplus market for less than a fin. I did not attempt to photograph the horn mated to the dish. I once photographed a big sonic dish whose exact dimensions evade memory. It was equipped with a then-unique sensor array that could hear into the ionosphere. The photo lab managed to lose that roll of film, and seemed unnaturally eager to get

Top left and right: Cheap 5" horn used for small alarm/public address system, front and rear views. Bottom: Removal of four screws and unit breaks down to individual components. (Large master-screw typically found behind a label that must be pried off.)

Modification continues with removal of magnetic driver and replacement with electret potted in rope caulk.

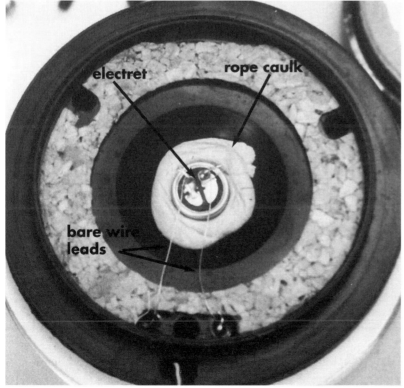

my name and address. Thereafter I took to having an agent print my pix.

Fringe directional mics demand high gain and extremely low noise. My preferred noise-reduction technique at the time was to limit amplifier bandwidth. That rationale flows from the fact that electronic noise varies as the root of bandwidth: narrow the bandwidth, lower the noise. Added to the observation that two formants yield fully intelligible speech, the preamp defined itself as a two-band tunable gain stage.

The problem with applying EQ after pre-amplification is that noise has already been boosted. A parametric equalizer would add even more noise from its multiple, cascaded op amps.

The simplest, quietest solution resembled block diagram A. This shows the use of LC networks to tune the gain stage. RF circuits use variable networks for tuning because variable inductors and capacitors are small and cheap at radio frequencies. Variable inductors tend to be impractical at audio frequencies due to the enormous inductances required (e.g., a 500-Hz tank would take a 0.1µF cap with 1,000 millihenries of inductance). Still, block diagram A would work if large, tunable inductors could be had.

From there the thinking leapt to the world of simulated inductance via op amps. Diagram B shows a generic configuration in which two op amps simulate an inductor tied to ground. This circuit can simulate inductance in the hundreds of henries. Furthermore, this inductance becomes variable if any of the four resistors is made a pot. In practice, the resistance values have to stay within a certain range to prevent

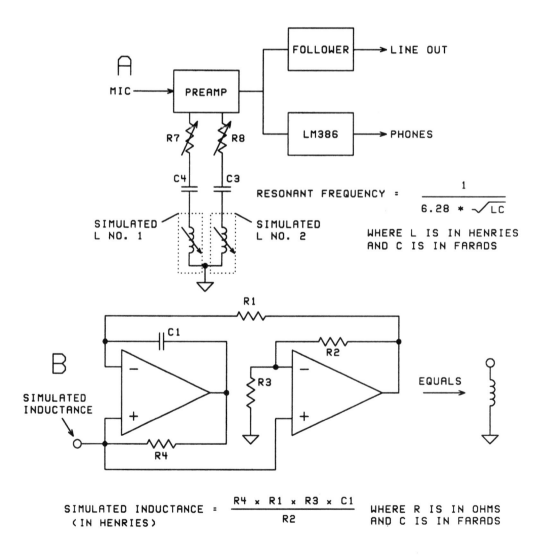

RESONANT FREQUENCY = $\dfrac{1}{6.28 * \sqrt{LC}}$

WHERE L IS IN HENRIES AND C IS IN FARADS

SIMULATED INDUCTANCE = $\dfrac{R4 \times R1 \times R3 \times C1}{R2}$ (IN HENRIES)

WHERE R IS IN OHMS AND C IS IN FARADS

A) Block diagram of desired preamp for long-range directional mic. Preamp tunable to two narrow frequencies by LC (inductor/capacitor) resonant circuits.

B) Shows how circuit is realized using op amps to simulate huge variable inductance.

oscillation. In the final circuit, R1 has been replaced by a 250K pot in series with 10K.

The basic preamp is a noninverting stage loafing along at about 33 dB of midrange gain. But look at the feedback loop. It's broken at the juncture of R2-R3 by an equivalent series tank to ground. At resonance, the impedance of a series tank drops (theoretically) to zero. Resonant frequencies leave the feedback loop by this path and don't make it to the inverting input. U1 is fooled into seeing an infinitely high feedback impedance for selected frequencies. Gain will approach that of an open-loop condition. Because this destabilizes some op amps, variable series resistors have been inserted to moderate the extent of the effect.

* * *

Referring to the full schematic, M1 gets its DC bias through R2, decoupled from the power bus by R1-C1. M1 output couples through C5 to input of U1, configured as a noninverting amplifier by R3-6 and C2. The feedback loop breaks out to two separate equivalent RLC series networks, one formed by R7-C4-U2-a/-b, the other by R8-C3-U2-c/-d. R24 and R19 control resonant frequency of their respective networks, while R7 and R8 control the degree of boost for each band. The component values shown tune the approximate range 700–3,500 Hz.

U1 output couples directly to the input of U3-a, an op amp configured as a DC voltage follower. Because U1's output is biased at 1/2V+, U3-a's output is too. Audio couples through R9 and C7 to tape output. R10 loads U3-a when the tape output is not used, to eliminate a potential feedback source.

U1 output also couples through C6 to divider R15-R14, serving as a volume control. R14's wiper is tied to the inverting input of U4, an LM386 power driver. C11 forms an RF shunt; C10–R12 form the standard snubber. Audio

couples through C9 to headphone output. R13 shunts audio to ground when no headphone plug is inserted to eliminate a potential feedback source. U3-b is configured as a voltage follower whose input is biased at 1/2V+ by divider R26–R27. U3-b output provides a stable bias reference for U1. C8, C14–16 and R11 decouple the supply.

Supply voltage dictated op amp selection. Nicad "9V" systems run closer to 7.4V. The Motorola MC3317X series is specified down to ±1.5V; the OP-27 down to ±3V.

As for electronic noise, the 10K source impedance generates 12.8 nv of thermal noise. The 10K impedance times the OP-27's I_n of 0.4 pa gives 4 nv. The chip's E_n is only 3 nv. These noise terms are insignificant next to R_s thermal noise. The OP-27 is as quiet as it's practical to get at this impedance. The calculation overstates audible noise because boost bandwidth is sharply limited.

In use, start with boost pots R7 and R8 full CCW. Tune one band, then the other, if additional boost is needed. (Tuning both bands on the same frequency results in no additional boost.) Some ringing, even oscillation, may be noted with maximum boost, particularly above 2 KHz.

* * *

The client gave me a tape of the hoods' voices that I used to pre-tune the amp. After painting the dish desert camo, I packed a thermos of Irish coffee and hit up to the gig. (I left my Camels. The flame of a Zippo can betray the agent from a mile away.)

Details of transporting and wrangling a dish border on trade secrets. I can say that the dish broke down into four sections that fit easily in an Econoline. With total dish weight less than 60 pounds, the bugger and one helper had little difficulty assembling the gimmick under an Ansel Adams moonrise.

GIMMICK #3

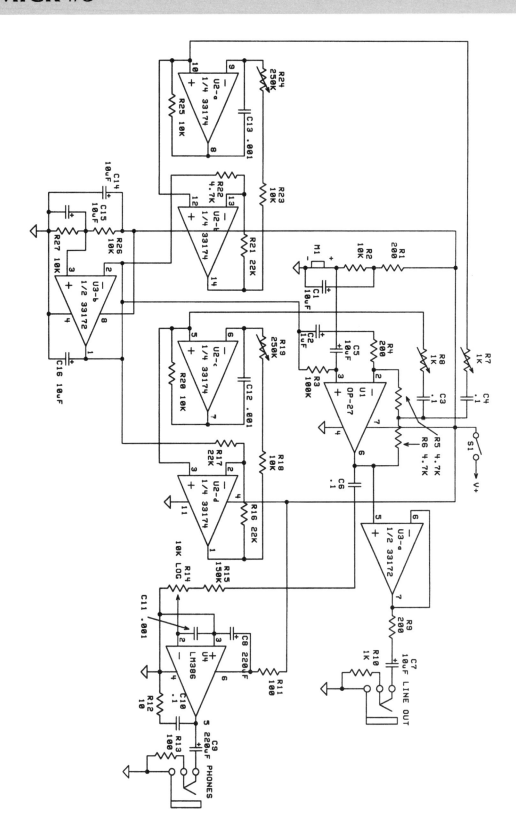

GIMMICK #3

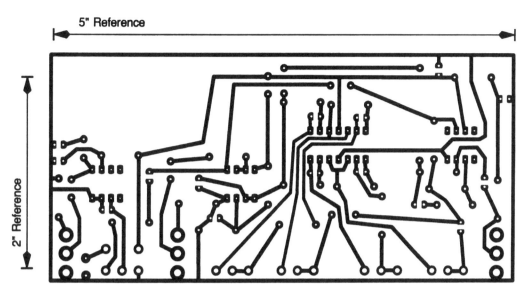

Foil side, full size.

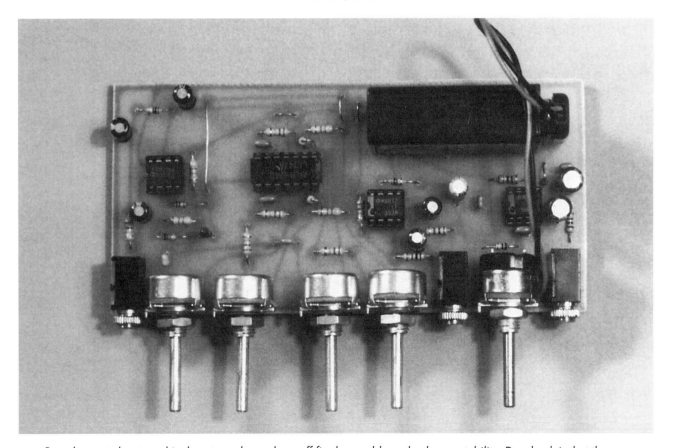

Board-mounted pots and jacks cut maybe an hour off final assembly and enhance stability. Drawback is that the case has to be drilled for pot shafts and jacks, which eats up the time saved. Board leaves room to attach a 9V bracket for (sideways) mounting of battery.

THIRD GIMMICK LAYOUT

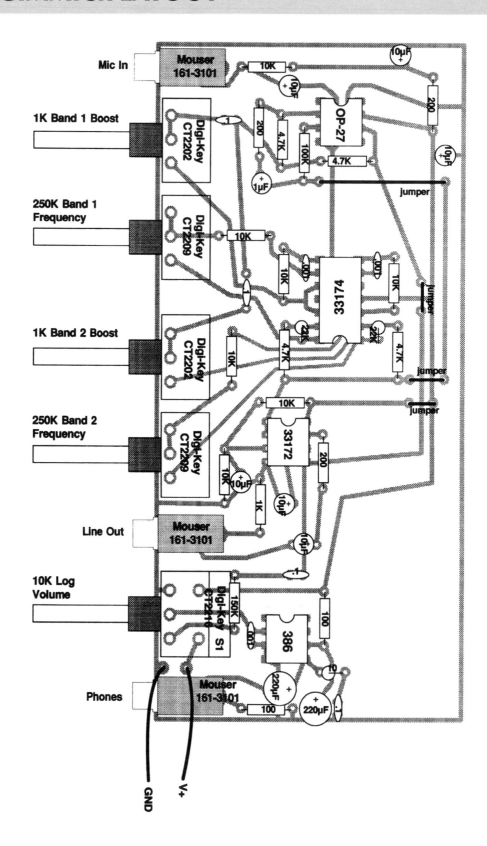

CHAPTER 25

Divorce

Malaōtec, the ancient Incan god of sports-writing, is known to have kept three wives: one to bear children, one to host soirees, and one for those times he felt trapped by the first two. Malaōtec managed with three wives what modern husbands are bound by law to manage with one. When one wife proves too few, fiscal spoils compare to fresh kill on the veldt, drawing scavengers from over the horizon.

Divorce constitutes a bugger's bonanza bigger than the War on Drugs, a rare blend of impunity and pelf, for the wrath of discovery shrouds the spouse, not the bugger. Dirt dictates the settlement in states that have eschewed no-fault divorce. Serious dirt demands a serious bugger.

Those who view divorce as fruit of soured vows should wake up and smell the kale. Every lawyer who sues on behalf of one spouse makes work for two lawyers to defend the other spouse—to say nothing of judges, bailiffs, process servers, and clerks. We're dealing with

GIMMICK #4

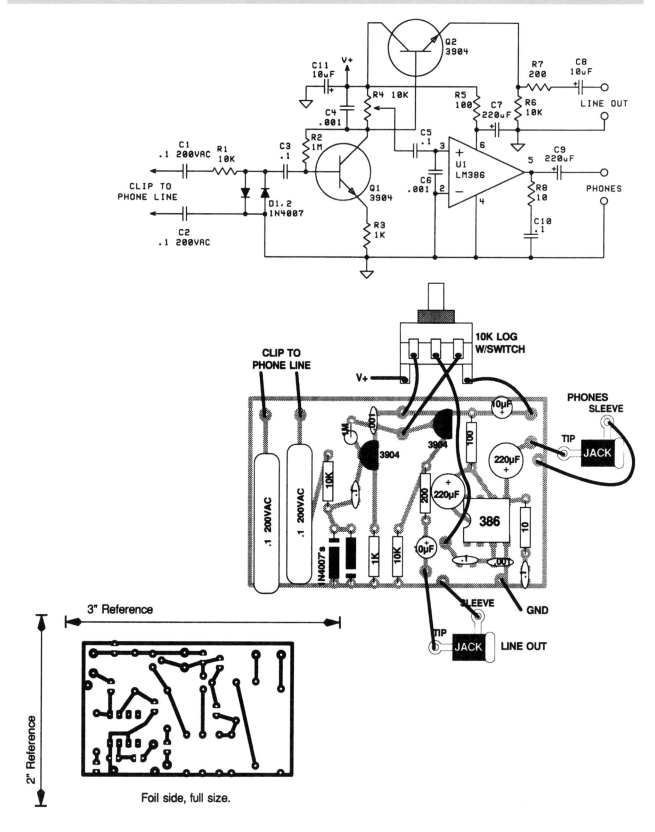

3" Reference

2" Reference

Foil side, full size.

another of America's great invisible industries. More urgent than the need to keep dope from being decriminalized is that of ensuring that divorce remains somebody's fault.

Whether it's true or not, adulterers presume private detectives to be watching. Many times they're right. They respond by becoming fugitive caricatures, not unlike Bogey in Dark Passage. They believe that silk scarves and wraparound shades render them invisible; that doubling back shakes any tail. The average divorce case involves tracking the perps to the splash pad. Photos of the parties' ingress and egress document opportunity; at least one shot of a syrupy kiss speaks to the point of intent.

We don't have to stick beepers on paramours' cars, because they tell us where they're going—over the phone.

* * *

This proverbial "one-evening project" is a single-ended quick-connect phone line monitor with a tape output buffer. At the 20-Hz ring frequency, C1 presents a reactance of about 80K, so current from the ring jolt will not be a problem; any overvoltage will die in clipper D1–D2. For safety (and perhaps an excessive precaution), system ground ties to the line through C2.

Audio couples through C3–R1 to input of Q1, configured as a common-emitter amp whose nominal gain is 10. C4 rolls off response above 15 KHz. Q1 output couples to U1 by divider action of pot R4, which also serves as Q1's collector resistor. Audio power driver U1 is configured in the usual manner.

Q1 output also ties directly to the base of Q2, configured as an emitter follower, a transistor circuit that has very high input impedance to avoid loading Q1, and low enough output impedance to drive a tape recorder input.

The agent should equip this piece with a pair of small, insulated alligator clips on one plug, a modular phone plug on another.

CHAPTER 26

Can You Bug Pebble Beach?

I checked into the Berkeley Hilton as Richard B. MacPhisto of Lemmington, New Jersey, and ordered up a case of Pabst on ice. Lombroso said he'd meet me the following day at ten. I'd sweat out the interim with brew and a dog-eared copy of *Forests of Flesh*.

While the brew was chilling I reflected on the way buggers deflect heat by mixing good works with bad. We used to get away with damn near anything by lumping it under the rubric of fighting Communism. Bugging and burglary slipped past the DEW Line so long as the targets were Communists or suspected Communists. For a while I took to setting up marks by subscribing in their names to the *Daily Worker* or the *Washington Post*, because GPO seemed to loathe one as much as the other.

That duck would not fly in a land where half the faculty still carried Party membership cards they had taken during the Hiss case, and where likenesses of Lenin nestled next to busts of Mao.

* * *

Next morning I picked up a Pinto at the Hertz counter and stowed my clubs in the boot. I took the Harry Dexter White Expressway down to the Rosenburg Cloverleaf, drove two miles beyond to the Jessup off ramp that opened onto Alger Hiss Boulevard. I parked

behind Lattimore Towers and walked two blocks to meet Lombroso in the coffee shop. I ordered skim milk and a Kim Philbyburger, and slipped the waitress a fin to bring me an Irving Peress from the bar (1 oz. vodka, 2 oz. Lavoris®, juice of half a lime; stir with cracked ice, strain into goblet, garnish with carious tooth; any bartender will spill this recipe, but nobody will say who mixed it).

I ate while Lombroso described the problem: bug two foursomes on a golf course. He, Lombroso, would be in one of them, but, unlike typical golf snobs, the others would not talk turkey on the links. They suspected him of not being a solid pinko, so they'd wait until they could ditch him back at the clubhouse patio.

Because the problem involved a group of persons constantly moving in an area with a radius of about 100′, I decided to use a mic that made talk sound 10 times closer than it was.

* * *

Check out the schematic. R1–C1 and R10–C11 form decoupling networks that kill the crosstalk between electrets running off different bias resistors on a common power bus.

Both preamps are identical; this describes the right channel. U1-a is configured as a noninverting amp whose gain equals one plus

GIMMICK #5

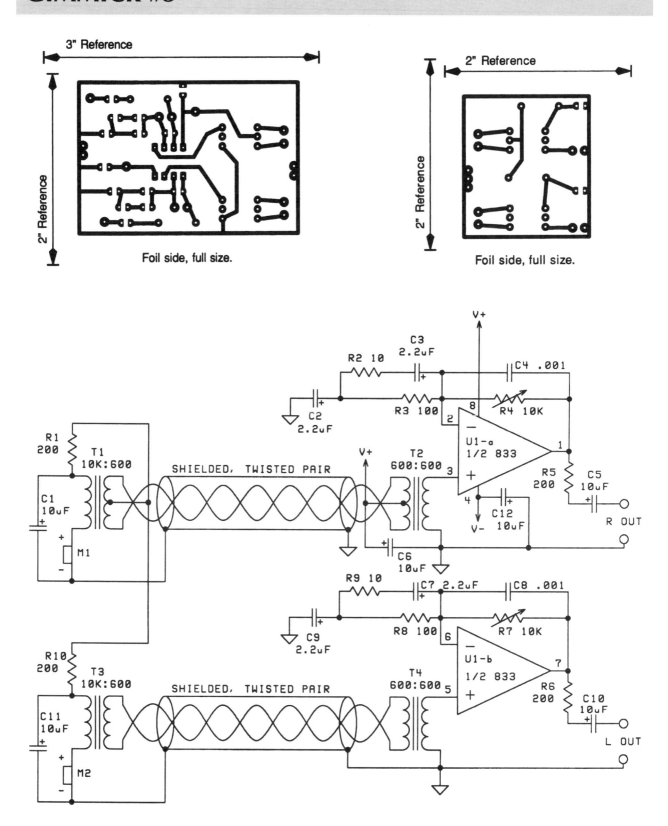

3" Reference

2" Reference

Foil side, full size.

2" Reference

2" Reference

Foil side, full size.

GIMMICK #5

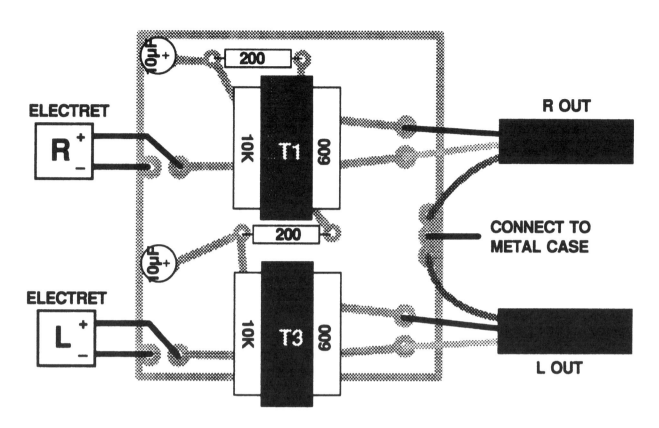

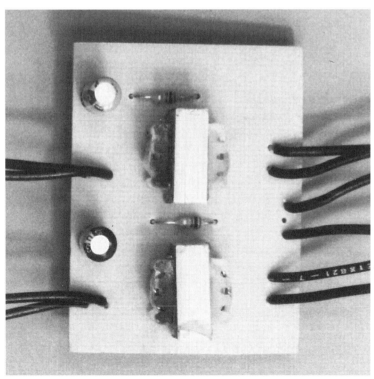

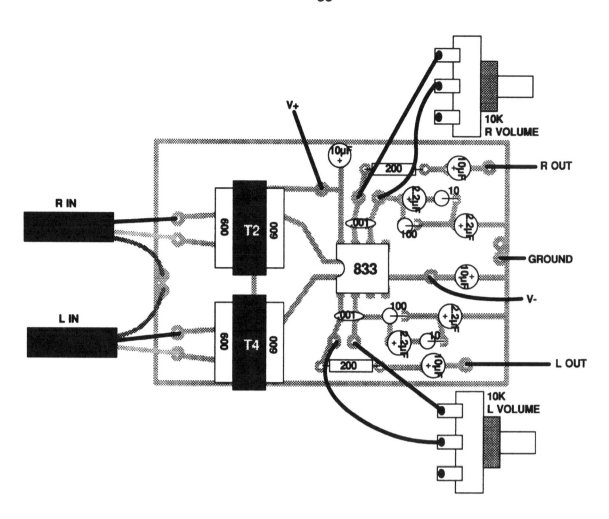

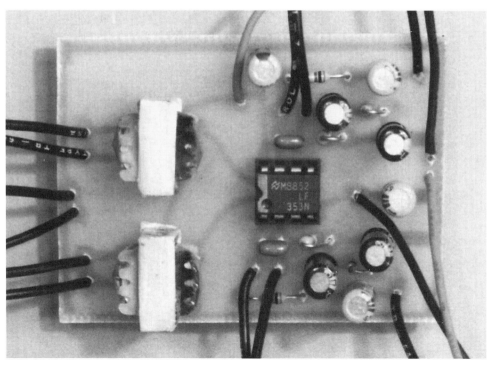

the ratio of the impedance of network R4–C4 to the impedance of network R2-R3-C2-C3. T2's secondary winding couples directly to the noninverting input and also serves to bias U1-a's input in an ON state. Audio couples through R5–C5 to line output terminal. R4 and R7 control gain of right and left channels, respectively.

V+ ties to T2 center tap to supply phantom power to both mics in the remote.

So far, we have a two-channel phantom-powered mic/preamp system; low noise, reasonably high gain. The magic lies in how the mics mount. For testing purposes, use a box about 4″ × 6″ × 8″; mount the mics in holes centered on the 4″ × 8″ sides. Use an aluminum box for indoor gigs. Full-size electrets friction-fit in 3/8″ ID rubber grommets.

* * *

Lombroso got me into the club as his guest; the gimmick lay hidden with my clubs. Instead of changing into golf shoes, I donned workman's overalls with "Lou" sewn on the pocket. I set up a stepladder beside a lamp in the middle of the clubhouse patio, as if I were changing bulbs. I don't think any member even looked in my direction. Affecting the badge of a lower class rendered me invisible to the upper classes. While I installed the gimmick in plain sight, the thought occurred that, had Marx and Engels figured golf into their equation, Communism might today prevail.

* * *

Three days later I played the tape for Lombroso and his two principals on a mid-sixties Norelcor that could play (but not record) stereo. We heard the first five minutes through speakers, in mono. This left everybody unimpressed, as per plan. I suggested we listen on headphones, and I'd crank up the volume. I produced three pair of Sennheiserr open-air phones, hooked them up and rolled tape, again in mono. Then:

"Oops—I switched to stereo. Sorry."

If truth is the bugger's biggest bane, surely showmanship is his best friend. I tried not to smirk while they tried to keep that how'd-you-do-that look off their faces. Binaural sounded like they were there, only better. Despite the targets' standing maybe 30 yards away, we could hear change clink in their pockets, ice burp in their drinks. We could tell that one guy scratching his chin needed a shave. And we heard every word, even the whispers, which any bugger will tell you are often more intelligible than normal speech.

I never told them they were hearing binaural, as if that fact might have clicked. In those days only buggers and the editorial board of the *Journal of the Audio Engineering Society* had heard of the concept.

* * *

Okay, it wasn't Pebble Beach. But it was a country club whose world-renowned golf course drew pinkos from all of southern California. When I went back wearing my "Lou" overalls to recover the gimmick, I found myself momentarily alone in the clubhouse head. I pulled out a felt-tipped pen, meaning to write **PINKOS ARE FINKS** on the wall above a urinal but paused, seeing this outlook as passe. I thought for a moment, then wrote **DEMOCRATS INVENTED DISCO**, knowing this was one dig they couldn't refute—and that no one would ever live down.

CHAPTER 27

Hardware à la Carte

For nearly 22 years prior to a self-imposed exile I did a lively trade in hardware to go. I never actively cultivated this market, but if a client described the need in sufficient detail and fortified his pitch with the right shade of kale, I generally came through. In fact I kept a stable of stock designs that I adapted to match requests. Many times I turned down orders I could have taken. Every bugger draws a line between what he will deliver unto strange hands and what he uses to do the impossible.

Hustling bugs involves more than building hardware. The sale is a ritual in which the customer expects the seller to shepherd him through a Black Art, despite that art being less complicated than compound interest. The wise seller dons his hat as shaman (or pimp, depending on your point of view). After 15 years in sportswriting I felt easy with both.

Because my customer base harbored a deep-seated need to be conned, every 13 months I obliged them with the Classified Con. I revealed the existence of, but refused to sell, certain pieces, on the grounds that they were Classified. When I finally "declassified" them 13 months later (often in a haze of contrived penury), stooges fronting for the GPO lined up like I was parting out a '55 Chevy.

* * *

A little knowledge is more than a dangerous thing. To a bugger it can spring the door to Pandora's safehouse. Back around election eve of '72 I made the mistake of introducing a veteran vice cop I'll call Sarge to the wonders of optical bugging. I sold him a simple IM infrared bug and companion receiver that would feed back from maybe 20′ without optics. Sarge was smitten, bought the gimmick on the spot for $2,800 in today's dollars and had great success in nocturnal ops using his 6X Weaver ahead of the receiver.

Predictably, Sarge got hung up in cases involving incandescent light, which swamped the receiver with hum. He asked me to build him something that would keep the fantastic audio but lose the hum.

A carrier-based system would have solved the problem. I couldn't sell him one because those systems had not then been declassified (for real). Had I tried, a gray suit would have materialized at the time of delivery to buy the piece. The amount would have been robust enough to guarantee that I would never again deal with someone this far down on the depth chart.

Well, drat the luck. Sarge was too flush a customer to lose. His request forced me to come up with a noncarrier-based optical receiver that could reject 60 Hz.

I knew from testing countless prototypes that highpass or notch filtering accomplished little after preamplification. A proper solution would notch 60 Hz at the phototransistor output, ahead of the preamp. A series network placed at the high-impedance (100K) output of the phototransistor would shunt 60 Hz to ground.

The chief obstacle to realizing this design was finding a 21,340-millihenry inductor to resonate at 60 Hz with the 0.33µF capacitor I had in mind. Such an inductor would dwarf a canned ham and weigh enough to anchor a dinghy. It would suffer low Q, high series resistance and would generally not perform up to snuff.

But a couple of op amps could simulate that inductance. More, the nature of the simulator made it tunable with a single pot. Putting the notch dead on 60 Hz would be a snap.

Check out the schematic. Phototransistor Q1 is biased off R4, decoupled from the supply by R3-C2. Q1 can be any general-purpose infrared phototransistor, such as Radio Shack 276-145 or Digi-Key QSD123QT.

Q1 output is taken off R6, a pot which also serves as the collector load. Note the way Q2's gain has been contoured by the ratio of collector impedance to emitter impedance. At 60 Hz, the amp actually attenuates the signal slightly. Above 72 Hz, gain rises @ 6 dB/octave because the emitter impedance drops due to falling capacitive reactance of C4. C5 helps

counter what could become a destabilizing treble emphasis.

Q1 output also sees an equivalent series tank made up of C13 and a simulated inductance of ~21 henries, provided by U2 and surrounding components. Trimpot R13 tunes the inductance. S2 is optional but lets the user switch the tank in and out of the circuit for an A/B comparison.

The audio driver is a 386 in standard config-uration. I used the noninverting input because Q1 is an inverting amplifier. Inverting the signal again would put the output in phase with Q1 input, making feedback oscillation likely.

D1 is an IR LED, such as Radio Shack 276-143 or Digi-Key QED233QT, placed directly behind Q1. R2 adjusts the brightness of D1, whose radiation turns Q1 partly ON. This greatly improves receiver sensitivity when the unit is used in total darkness. Q1 must have a plastic case, or dithering won't work.

To tune for best notch depth, power up the system, switch on an incandescent lamp, place the unit such that Q1 picks up plenty of hum but does not block. Trim R13 for greatest attenuation of hum. (Do not use a fluorescent lamp for this phase. Fluorescent emissions contain frequencies besides 60 Hz which the tank will not notch.)

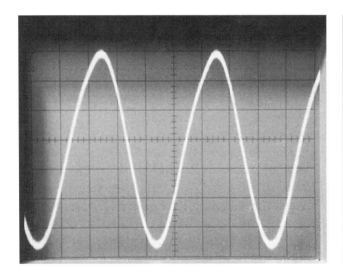 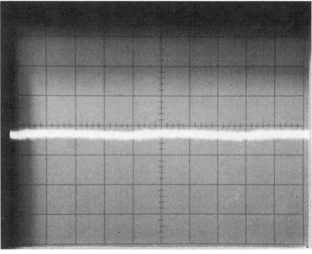

Left: U1 output, volume cranked all the way up, notch circuit switched out; 60 Hz tops 3V$_{p-p}$.
Right: Notch switched in. Hum remains audible, if invisible on scope, but does not interfere with intelligibility of signal from IM bug. Device is in a room with a 100W ceiling lamp; phototransistor is shielded from light just enough to keep it from blocking. Vertical scale of both photos 500 mv/div.

GIMMICK #6

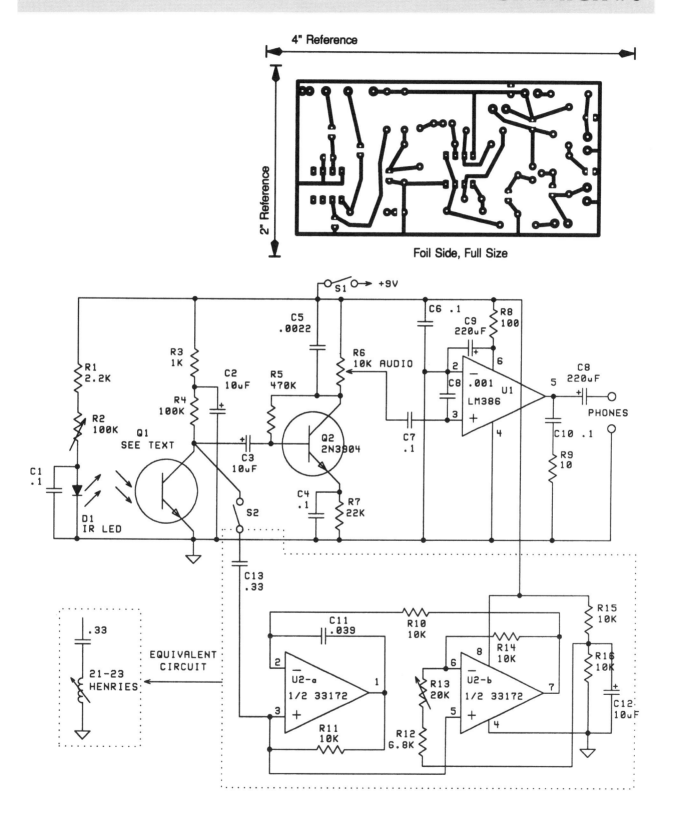

4" Reference

2" Reference

Foil Side, Full Size

231

GIMMICK #6

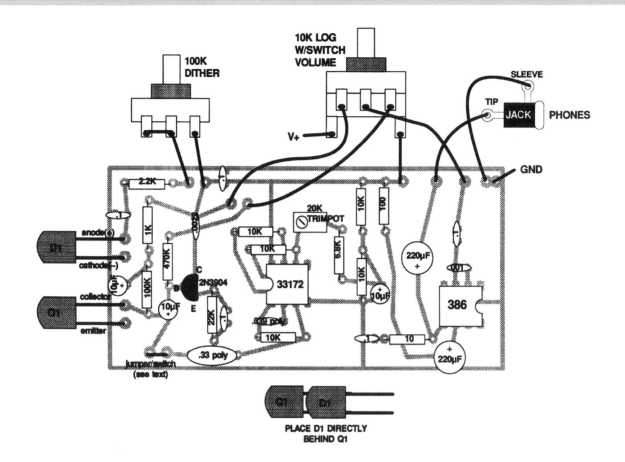

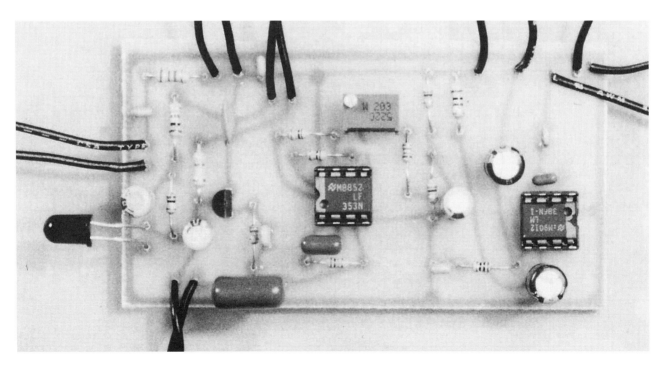

* * *

I called the companion transmitter the T-88 but nicknamed it "the Optoblaster," a name typical of those I whispered to customers at 13-month intervals. It's a super-simple constant-current intensity modulator based on a 386. The fact that the chip biases its output at 1/2V+ automatically provides constant current. Resting current is determined by supply voltage and the value of Rx. Any combination of resistance and LEDs is possible, so long as it observes the voltage/current limits of the chip and the LEDs. The sample built for this book made Rx a conservative 100 ohms. The Optoblaster was the only bug I ever sold that customers complained was too sensitive. Omit C8 to reduce audio gain by 20 dB.

The receiver will pick up intelligible audio from ~40′, without optics, and with the Optoblaster sitting directly beneath a 60W table lamp. With optics . . . let's just say Sarge's raves earned me a hundred grand in new business through the end of '77.

* * *

The point of a contact mic system than can hear really well below 20 Hz escapes most civilians, and is perhaps best left implicit in the unmentionable notion of safecracking.

Ontology aside, check out the VTC-9X, much the same high-gain subsonic amp I once built for, er, special clients. The mic is an electret whose aperture has been sealed to make it a contact mic, detailed in Part I's discussion of the topic. M1 is biased and decoupled in the usual fashion but couples directly to the input of U1-a, a noninverting amp whose 40 dB gain is only 3 dB down at 3 Hz. The value of C3 determines the preamp's high-frequency corner; 0.01μF (1,600 Hz) makes a good starting value; increase the value of C3 to decrease high-frequency response.

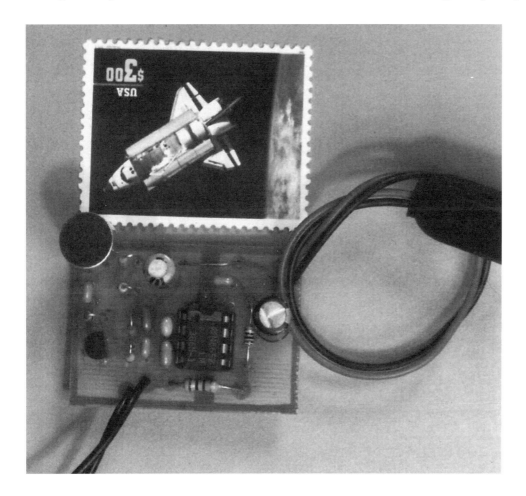

GIMMICK #7

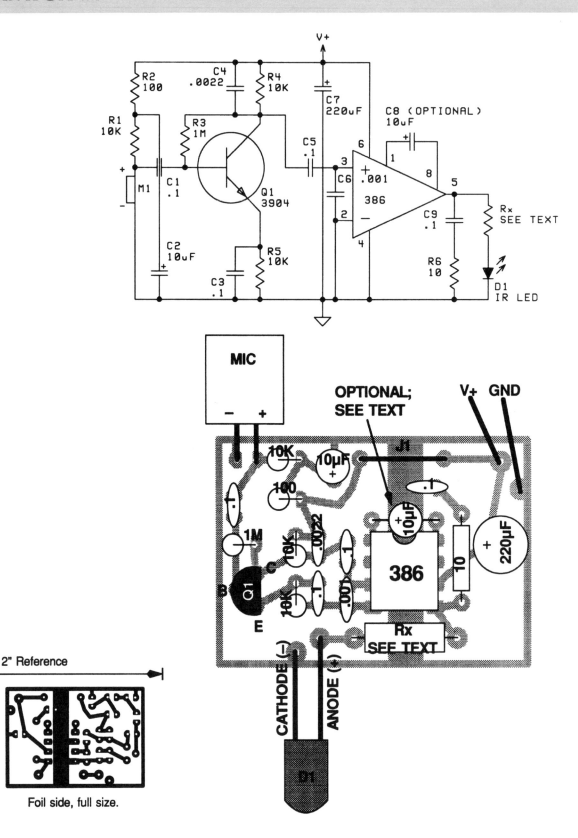

2" Reference

1" Reference

Foil side, full size.

DC coupling preservers 100 percent of M1's subsonic output but creates a huge DC offset at U1-a output. R4 exists to null this offset (trim R4 to give 1/2V+ at U1-a output).

U1-b is configured in the usual fashion to provide a stable bias reference for U1-a.

U1-a output couples through R6 and C4 to U2, an MC34119 audio power driver configured for 20 dB of gain and further attenuating treble by action of C6. Twist U2's output leads tightly. High system gain requires short leads and a neat layout.

U1 and U2 run off separate 9V batteries. The system exhibits subsonic oscillation, at least at more than moderate volume levels, if powered off a single battery.

System response extends so close to DC that the subsonic AC generated when volume is adjusted will mute the output for a second or two. This is expected from the nature of the circuit.

Device requires high-quality, sealed, low-impedance headphones to realize full performance. "Hearing" subsonic tones takes practice. They register as a pressure not unlike the sensation of tensing the ears in anticipation of a loud noise. These tones are readily perceived after modest practice. Viewing the (DC-coupled) output of U1-a on an oscilloscope while listening gives feedback that speeds learning. When beginners ask for a good safe on which to practice, I usually recommend the Diebold 1200-E.

* * *

If you plan to sell hardware to go, remember these rules:

1. Never keep finished gear on hand. What does not exist cannot be filched or photographed. Building the piece from scratch, often under time pressure, smacks of magic that magnifies value. Building from scratch meant a couple extra bills in days when eggs cost $0.29 a dozen.

2. Always understate performance. If years of testing show that a body wire will give one mile under good conditions and a quarter-mile under the worst conditions, never claim more than 200 yards. Pieces that beat their claims are rarities. They grow to legend by word of mouth. Pieces that don't meet spec have a way of putrefying in gossip, along with the builder's rep.

3. Name every piece. Use a code, such as PDL-979, or something lurid, such as "Subsonic Detectigon." Buyers expect a name. Given a choice, they buy named gimmicks six to one over superior but nameless ones.

4. Have the client test the gimmick in your presence to confirm that it performs to spec and, more importantly, to his satisfaction. Offer no static if the buyer wants to back out. One disgruntled customer will cost plenty in lost sales.

5. Make certain the client understands current drain and likely battery life using a fresh battery of a specific type. He should also grasp the difference between carbon-zinc and lithium as the difference between three hours and 30 hours of operation.

6. "idiot-proof" pieces that could be damaged by momentarily reversed battery polarity by soldering a rectifier diode in series with the appropriate power lead.

7. Know the buyer. You may legally sell surveillance gear only to bona fide law enforcement personnel. GPO's pet means of "recruiting" free-lance builders was to send a ringer masquerading as a cop to buy hardware. Failure to vet the badge was usually good for an indictment.

GIMMICK #8

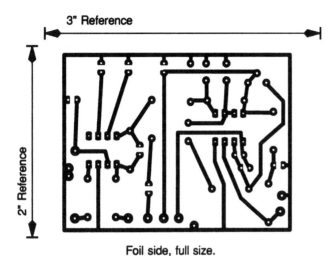

3" Reference

2" Reference

Foil side, full size.

NOTE: TWO BATTERIES,
COMMON GROUND

GIMMICK #8

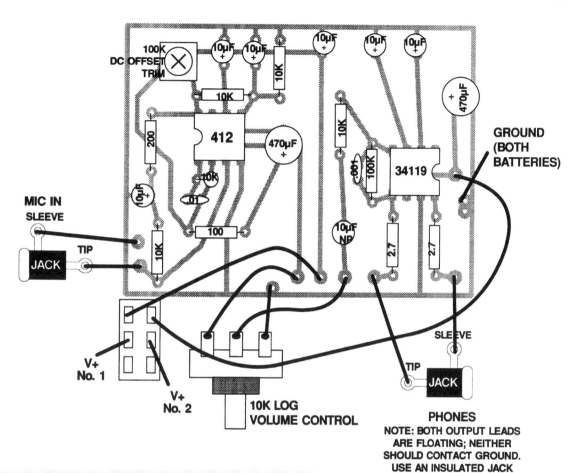

MIC IN
SLEEVE
TIP
JACK

100K
DC OFFSET TRIM

412

470μF +

V+ No. 1
V+ No. 2

10K LOG
VOLUME CONTROL

GROUND
(BOTH BATTERIES)

34119

SLEEVE
TIP
JACK

PHONES
NOTE: BOTH OUTPUT LEADS
ARE FLOATING; NEITHER
SHOULD CONTACT GROUND.
USE AN INSULATED JACK
WITH A METAL ENCLOSURE.

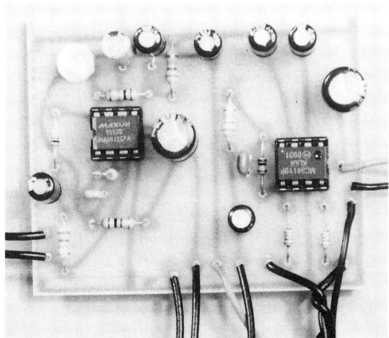

CHAPTER 28

Shifty (Counter)bugman

Welcome to what should have been the shortest take in the book. Counterbugging is the bastard issue of hope and denial; the blighted spawn of science and fraud. It's the doxy of greed, paramour of grift, and often poses a contradiction in nomenclature. Debugging is a thing taught with doubt, fraught with toil, laden with angst, and packed with profit. Yet the scope of the bugger's arsenal, his fiendish guile, make debugging a venture in futility against all but feckless attacks. I offer this assessment in lieu of what I cannot say, despite fictive auspices, but which the reader might infer from the text as a whole.

Every top bugger does or has done counter-bugging. Besides generating legit income, counterbugging gives an excuse to keep tabs on the competition, though I doubt I found competitors' best efforts any more often than they found mine.

Because he's paying his counterbugger an otherworldly sum, the client pretty well expects bugs to be found. He does not anticipate the snow-job that follows:

"Look what the synchroharmodyne turned up." I cradled the bug like the Star of India diamond. "Looks like a subcarrier transmitter. Must've cost somebody a bundle."

The client paled. "You mean they're listening now?"

I shook my head. "It's safe," I said. "I deactivated it."

I always said no when the client asked for the bug. The Laws of My Profession bound me to forward contraband to The Authorities.

. . . knowing that I had found a decoy, probably one of several. The real gimmick might take disassembly of the house to find, and a military satellite uplink to deactivate. And I wasn't going to flash my uplink for a civilian.

In fact, I had never given a bug to The Authorities. I made a point of studying every bug I found before I destroyed it, so I could mimic that style for decoys. GPO fell for them nine times in ten. If they recognized the style they'd confront the mystery bugger: "Isn't this your work, NAME?" NAME denied, knowing the game. The boys confronted me just as often when NAME mimicked one of my decoys.

Finding bugs is okay. Flaunt them. The client has paid for the privilege of fondling them. Fingering a fellow bugger is not okay, even if you know who ran the gig. The operator you debug today could next week be debugging you. To call counterbugging a font of moral dilemmas is the understatement of a career.

Professionals are obliged to think beyond the single gig, to ramifications affecting The Industry. Every bugger wants a viable debugging game with a stout rep. Clients need confidence in their debugger. Nothing builds confidence like finding bugs. Counterbuggers who can't make a living eventually drift back to bugging, at least if they don't debug just to cover bugging.

This partly explains liberal use of decoys. A decoy is a real bug, but one fated to surface in a sweep. Decoys help the bugger thwart discovery of the primary bug while making life easier for the counterbugger. Bugging and counterbugging are games in which everybody wins except the mark.

. . . and ones whose risk profile intensifies with prowess. At some point the diligent counterbugger starts turning up hardware planted by GPO or one of their contract agents. GPO will have known from physical surveillance that always accompanies a serious bug that debugging was underway. They will warn the debugger, who will heed the warning once he learns that cluing his client to the bug will cost him a deuce in Leavenworth. Seven different agencies make up GPO. Only three of them have names. They take a harsh view of counterbuggers raining on their parade. This is one reason the drug bund shuns free-lance technicians.

* * *

"What happens to bugs once the gig is done?"

I'm always tempted to say that they go to Bug Heaven, that great salvage lab in the sky, but that answer insults the intelligence of too many people. Usually I look grim and say that we send an agent to retrieve the bug, or that the bug is timed to self-destruct after ten days, or that its EPROM will fade at a predetermined point. I tune my lie to the asker's needs.

The truth is something else, a set of facts civilians are ill-disposed to see. In most cases, abandon the bug. Think about it. Capture is how they convict. If they didn't nab you going in, going back is the only way they can get you at all. We're talking about a gimmick that costs twenty bucks, tops, against a second mortgage in legal fees.

For cases that mandate recovery, like the hardwire gig in '70, the bugger always sends

an agent, if he can get one to take the exposure, and arms the agent with a pair of ViseGrips® to destroy the gimmick on the spot. If the boys don't see you crush it, they'll have a hard time proving that you didn't merely pick up the pieces.

The corollary explains why buggers never keep finished hardware around unless they mean to have it photographed or filched. Buggers may be the most common targets of GPO black-bag jobs. Accordingly, we offer up decoys the way mom 'n' dad leave cookies and Coke® for Sp. Agt. Claus. Now and then bugging gear is seized in a random traffic stop that took weeks to arrange. . . .

* * *

"What should I do if I find a bug?"

Weigh the wisdom of calling the heat. Government interest in catching some petty bugger rooting through a civilian's closet ranges from slim to nil. The bugger is probably on the team. To keep him as a resource they have to derail the complaint. That can mean derailing the complainant. Consider too that a complaint prompts GPO to pump the bugger for info about your little imbroglio, maybe get copies of choice intercepts, in case you turn out to be a telco exec or petty pol, or somebody else who looks good on a leash.

A bugger who is discovered faces no worry so long as he rats out his client and gives up his intercepts. Realize that if you're important enough for somebody to pay a professional to bug, GPO wants to know all they can about you and the party who hired the bugger. They already know about 90 percent of buggers.

If GPO does not already control the bugger, your complaint underwrites prosecutorial blackmail. Maybe you decide later not to press charges (the dread "refusal to cooperate"). GPO needs a way to make you say yes. At that point you may find yourself the target of a Columbo buffoon/bully number.

Forget the bizarre notion of justice, as in pressing charges and bargaining for a guilty plea resulting in a harsh fine or three months in Dannemora. That rarely happens because busted buggers cooperate. If you force the matter, the prosecutor will claim that the perp has reformed and is doing Important Work for the Government.

* * *

Counterbugging brings up one of my all-time best-sellers, a wideband RF sniffer, but one with a twist, an audio feed to let the user hear what the meter reads. Most surveillance guides talk about these things; few reveal how they work. Design flows from the fact that the meter-drive voltage is audio. To add sound to a sniffer, feed a tap off the meter to an audio amp.

Check out the schematic. Antenna feed couples through C1 to the junction of L1 and D1. This arrangement shunts signals above L1-C1 resonance to D1, and shunts signal below resonance to ground. You can screen out domestic AM radio signals by making L1 small enough. The prototype used 10µH, whose 1.6-MHz resonance with C1 gives a reasonable compromise between low-frequency sensitivity and rejection of interference.

RF is rectified by D1, which can be a 1N914, but a 1N34A gives the sniffer much greater sensitivity. A hot-carrier diode, such as 1SS99 or NTE112, works even better. The reason for this resides in each type's forward voltage drop. Silicon diodes take about 0.6V to conduct, germanium diodes about 0.35V, and hot-carrier diodes about 0.2V.

Note that D1 is oriented to pass negative peaks. These will be inverted by U1, whose gain is variable by pot R6. R3 and the surrounding voltage dividers R1-2-4-5 serve as a meter-zero control. C2 limits U1's high-frequency response to the audio band.

U1 output drives a 50µa meter directly. U1 output also couples through R7-8-C6 to input of U2, a 386 rigged in the usual fashion. C11 is optional and will kick U2 into high-gain mode.

House the sniffer in a metal case for best sensitivity and rejection of local interference. Be sure to insulate the antenna from the case with a rubber grommet.

To use the sniffer, connect a pair of fresh 9V batteries, power up, set audio gain to minimum, set RF gain to desired level, zero the meter using R3. To test, bring the antenna near a low-power RF transmitter, such as an old cordless phone (a walkie-talkie will cork the meter and could zap the diode). If no transmitter is available, hold the antenna a few inches in front of a television screen, or about 10 feet from a microwave oven heating a cup of water. The device has more than enough sensitivity for sweeping and works great for peaking RF bugs.

The front end is a classic AM detector. Despite this, it will demodulate wideband and narrowband FM enough to confirm a meter peak as an audio transmitter. The richness of the RF environment evident in the audio feed dramatizes why increasing sniffer sensitivity quickly passes the point of diminishing return.

GIMMICK #9

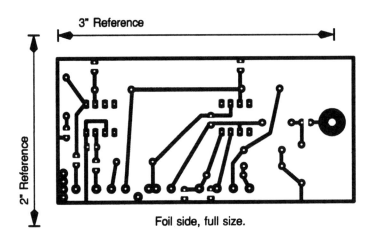

3" Reference

2" Reference

Foil side, full size.

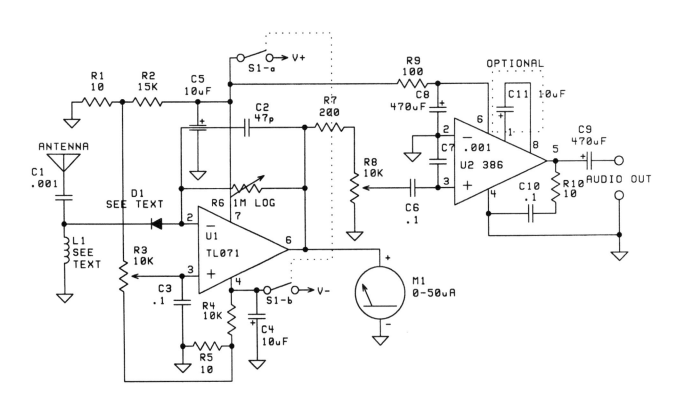

GIMMICK #9

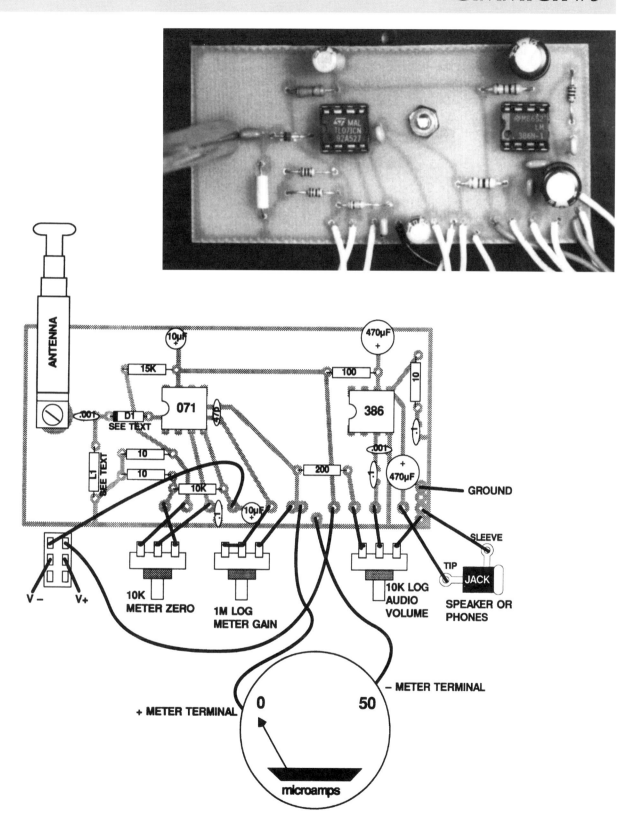

CHAPTER 29

Travelin' Man

I spent the first half of 1977 on the road, letting my rep cool off after something chronicled in still-classified RCMP files as the Maple Leaf Caper. The smart bugger always nixed gigs offered in the aftermath of a coup. Official clients rolled out their undoable files to see if they could fob them off. These gigs meant progressively heavier exposure without commensurately higher pay. Too heavy a rep also drew scrutiny that hampered movement, but which buggers used pretty effectively to run interference for each other. Gigs with five-figure fees could afford to bring in Chicago Mike and Long Island Tony and even Phoenix Phil, at least before his car blew up in '79, just to whip the locals into a swivet sufficient to cloud the real objective.

The bugger who found himself temporarily "hot" could cool off in many ways. He might take a day job, always in an industry allied to bugging—a stint as a telco lineman, or an exterminator, or a satellite TV installer or . . .

Or he might hit the sauce, affect an air of dissolution, maybe arrange a pinch for DWI. The boys would read the arrest report, shake their heads sadly. "Shifty's back on bug juice. We better give the El Cajon caper to NAME." The truth, of course, is that top-line buggers are never out of control, even when we appear most vulnerable.

Instead of staging one of these grand dramas I hit the road: Shifty Bugman, traveling salesman, driving from town to town with suitcases full of goodies for cops n' private eyes. This particular tour set out in Provincetown and wound up in Palm Springs. At every stop in between I made a beeline for the chief of narcotics. Eight times in ten I left with a check, because I always pulled something out of my bag that blew away whatever the customer was using. For a long time my best dazzler was a subcarrier RF transmitter and companion receiver. I'd give the head narc the frequency to dial into his scanner, which would lock on my bug's signal but not emit a peep. Then I'd activate my receiver, modified to decode the subcarrier. I made a point of cranking the volume so high that it would scream like the banshee while his scanner continued mute. Many times he'd be on the phone pressuring the brass to sign the purchase order while the receiver was still squealing. (Cost? Two grand in preinflation dollars, thank you.)

Traveling served a darker end. I called on cops because they were always eager to show me gimmicks that somebody else had sold them. Besides confirming that they did not know about, and thus could not counter, my serious stuff, sales calls were one way other

GIMMICK #10   LINE LOCATOR (RECEIVER)

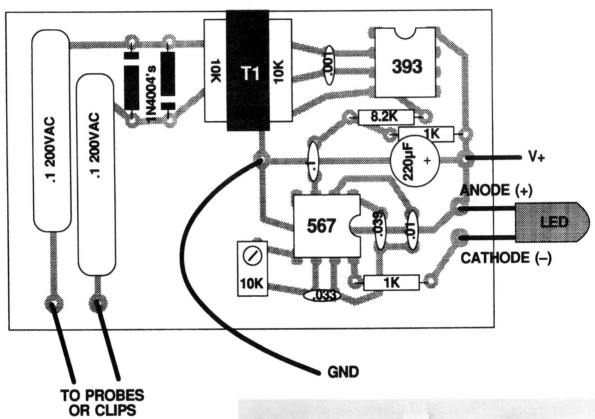

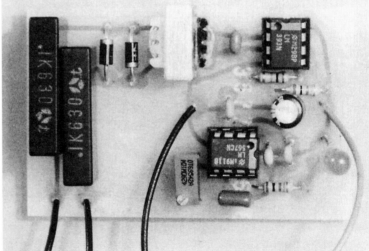

TO PROBES
OR CLIPS

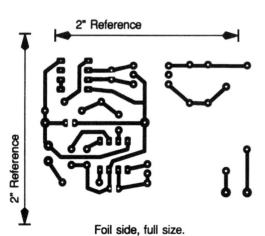

2" Reference

2" Reference

Foil side, full size.

LINE LOCATOR (TRANSMITTER)   GIMMICK #10

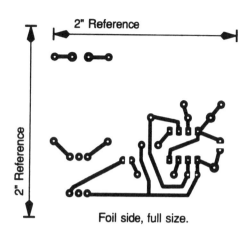

2" Reference

2" Reference

Foil side, full size.

TO CLIPS

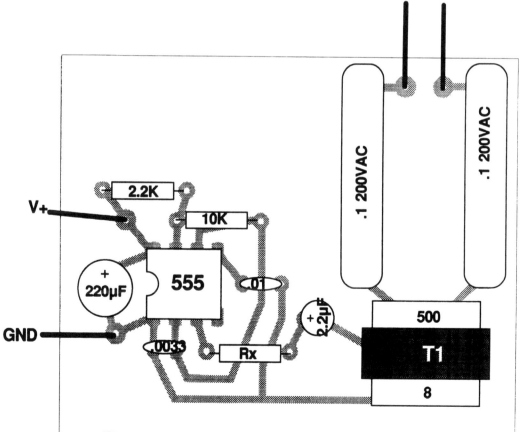

.1 200VAC

.1 200VAC

V+

2.2K

10K

+ 220µF

555

.01

GND

.0033

Rx

+ 2.2µF

500

T1

8

buggers and I controlled the state of science available to the hoi polloi.

* * *

A roadshow fave, always in demand among new PIs, this line locator system is the same one whose function was explained in Part I. For years it kept my ex-wives in mink, me in polyester and my bartender in a tax bracket higher than mine.

* * *

"Where do you keep the plans for all this stuff?"

In my head. I keep several crates of faux plans in various drops around the country, and a couple down Malaotec Way. My rented storage locker in San Berdoo has been burgled so many times the manager stopped wasting padlocks on it. Of late I have taken to posting apocrypha on the Internet, some encrypted, some in the clear.

CHAPTER 30

Bookie

I had refused to wire Maynard on ethical grounds. He was my bookie. If they took down Maynard I'd be left with no reliable place to bet.

Instead of hiring another bugger the task force actually changed its target to Lester Trillingham, also a bookie, a man I was never able to abide because he kept barely a nodding acquaintance with the main line in Vegas. If a bettor insisted, Lester would lay the Vegas spread, but double the vig. Lester also had a reputation for being hard to find on Monday after getting middled on Sunday.

My agent went up to Lester's office on the pretext of laying two pennies on Dallas against Green Bay and spotted the sniffer-disguised-as-a-pen-set on the desk. That ruled out RF, which only left me 50 options.

I walked off the distance between Lester's building and the apartment tower adjacent; call it 100′, tops. That sounded like ultrasonic range.

* * *

M1 gets its bias off R2, decoupled from the supply by R1–C2. Output couples through C15 to input of U1-a, an op amp configured as a noninverting amp with "bug EQ" built in. The treble pre-emphasis helps compensate for the difficulty of modulating the 40-KHz carrier as frequency rises. U1-b forms the standard bias reference for U1-a.

U1-a output couples through lowpass network R7-C9-C10-C11 to the FM port of U3, a bipolar 555 timer with a free-running frequency in the vicinity of 40 KHz, trimmed by R11. The carrier frequency is critical to clear transmission and will shift out of the sweet spot as the battery ages, so U3 runs off a supply locally regulated by U2.

U2 output couples through R12 and C14 to 8-ohm winding of T1, whose 1K winding drives the ultrasonic transducer. Depending on frequency, the output of T1 can exceed $60V_{p-p}$, enough to cause a nasty shock. The experimenter must exercise proper care when testing this circuit.

* * *

The receiver uses the same ultrasonic transducer as the transmitter; couples it directly to the input of U1-a. Pot R3 varies preamp gain from 0–40 dB. (At 40 KHz, the 074 runs out of gas at about 40 dB. If R3 is changed to 100K, a MAX414 will extend gain by ~20 dB.)

U1-a output couples directly to input of U1-b, which, with U1-c and associated components, forms a precision fullwave rectifier. DC coupling allows U1-b to get its DC bias from the output of U1-a. U1-c output couples directly to U2-a, an op amp configured as a quasi-18 dB/octave lowpass filter that cuts off ~7 KHz. Here also, U2-a gets its bias from the output of the prior stage. Recovered audio is taken off the output of U2-a.

U2-a output couples through C8 to U2-b, a highpass filter that sifts out low-frequency spuriae that plague ultrasonic transmission.

U2-b output couples through C11 to divider R20-R19, which serves as volume control to U3, a 386 configured in standard fashion.

To align the system, power up both pieces, set receiver preamp gain to minimum (0 dB).

Set volume about a quarter of the way open; monitor through sealed headphones. Aim the two transducers at each other about 3′ apart. Trim transmitter pot R11 to give best audio. Fine tuning for range and sound quality is best accomplished out of doors at the anticipated working range.

* * *

Natch, I got the goods on Lester, won my bet, and lived happily ever after.

(TRANSMITTER)

GIMMICK #11

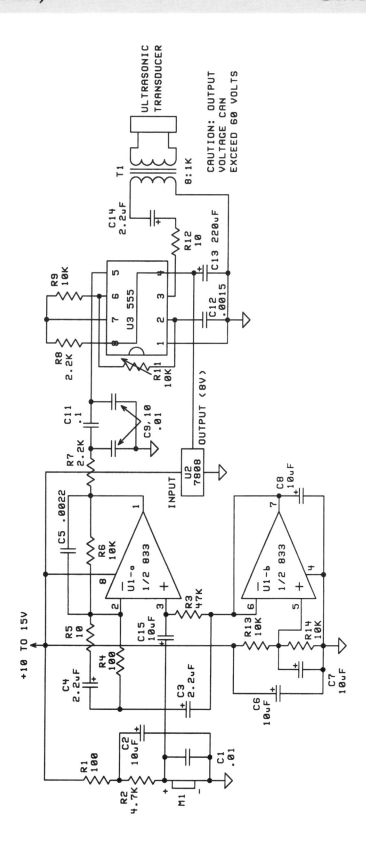

GIMMICK #11 (TRANSMITTER)

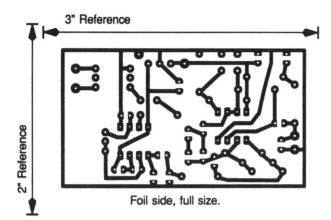

3" Reference

2" Reference

Foil side, full size.

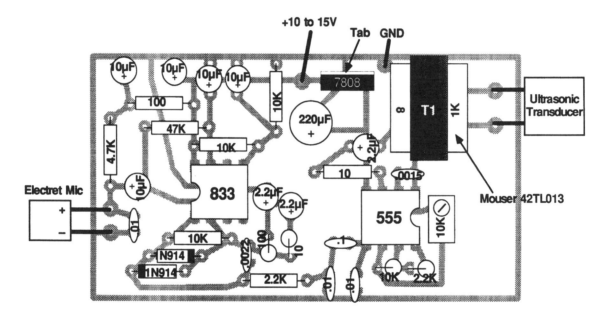

+10 to 15V   Tab   GND

10µF   10µF   10µF   10µF

100

47K

10K

4.7K

10K

220µF

7808

8   T1   1K

Ultrasonic Transducer

2.2µF

10

.0015

Electret Mic

+

−

10µF

.01

833

2.2µF   2.2µF

555

10K

Mouser 42TL013

10K

1N914

1N914

.0022

.01

.01

.01

2.2K

10K   2.2K

.1

.01

(RECEIVER)

GIMMICK #11

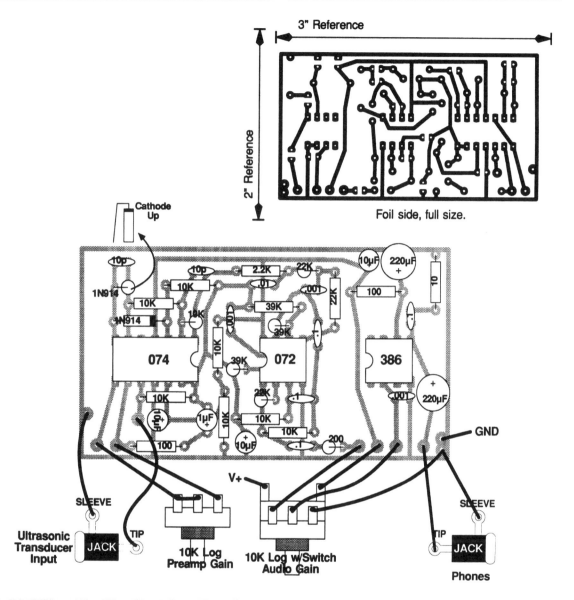

3" Reference

2" Reference

Foil side, full size.

Cathode
Up

10p

1N914

10K

1N914

10p   2.2K   22K

10K   .01

.001

39K

39K

22K

10K   39K   072

074

22K

10K   10K

10K   .1

10K   .1

10K

10µF   100

1µF

10µF

100

200

10µF   220µF
+

100

10

.1

386

220µF
+

.001

GND

V+

SLEEVE

Ultrasonic
Transducer
Input

JACK   TIP

10K Log
Preamp Gain

10K Log w/Switch
Audio Gain

SLEEVE

TIP   JACK

Phones

GIMMICK #11 (RECEIVER)

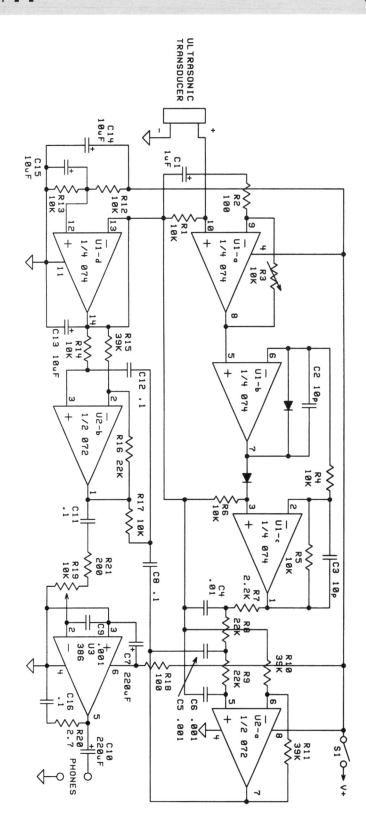

CHAPTER 31

Can You Bug This Mime?

Weirdest gig?

Wiring a mime.

Let me qualify that. Nobody wanted to wire the guy for being a mime; for miming, as it were. His bag spoke of raptures past the ken of sensible men, barring them perforce from a sportswriter's orb. Sportswriting ran with its own convoluted and generally indecipherable logic that made just enough sense to wed the norm.

But sportswriters and mimes?

As well teach the tundra to a leech.

Nor, obviously, did the client want to wire the guy in the act of miming. Good mimes were as talkative as pecky cyprus paneling in Perry Mason's office.

The mime lived in an apartment complex, a fact that called up one of bugging's oldest identities: APARTMENT COMPLEX = CARRIER CURRENT, because whole wings, sometimes the entire complex, ran off the same side of the power step-down transformer. With apartment occupancy averaging 68 percent near the end of '76, my agent had no trouble letting a pad month-to-month in the same wing with the mime.

Once we acquired the target I sent an agent in to take Polaroids of the pad. Apartment locks are master-keyed at so many levels that they can be opened, literally, with straightened paper clips. For cover my agent wore overalls and carried a spraying rig, prefiguring a particularly sordid caper still nine years away.

After perusing the Polaroids I decided to plant the bug in the mime's 8-track tape deck. I might have chosen another appliance but for the mortifying fact that I owned an identical Realistic® TR-882 8-track tape deck. I could work up the gimmick without having to buy a new TR-882 and thus leaving an extra trail.

* * *

The carrier current transmitter uses pretty much the same audio stage and FM core as the ultrasonic bug. The difference lies in the ~400-KHz frequency, and the fate of the FM signal. Coupling to the AC line is achieved through impedance transformation. A transformer steps down the high impedance present at Q1 collector; resonance prevents the AC line voltage from penetrating the modulator to any significant degree. The coupling cap shows 60 Hz a high impedance.

T1 was custom-wound by gutting one of the Mouser 42IFXXX transformers. The primary consists of 20 turns of 30-ga. magnet wire; the secondary, three turns of 30-ga. wire (wind the secondary first). This has much less inductance than the stock transformer and requires a much larger capacitor to resonate at 400 KHz. The lower L/C ratio lowers Q of the tank, making it easier to modulate.

T1 can be used in its original state but has such a high Q that a parallel resistor is required to get the tank to accept modulation. The custom design described has proved a good compromise between drive voltage and Q.

* * *

The receiver couples to the line using the same transformer gimmick, only in this case a Mouser 42IF103 is used in its stock configuration. The resonant winding ties to the inputs of comparator U1 to form a zero-crossing detector; C2 brings resonance down from 455 KHz to the 350–400-KHz range. The coupling network includes clipping diodes to protect the comparator input stage from being blown by a strong carrier; and R1 to lower the Q of the tank to allow good modulation transfer.

Comparator output ties directly to the input of the 4046 CMOS phase locked loop. The 4046 exhibits the greatest tracking range of all common PLLs, besides running on low voltage and costing pocket change. It lacks an LED to indicate lock, and its VCO is extremely sensitive to supply voltage. Even the on-chip zener won't hold solidly enough, so the comparator and the 4046 run off a supply locally regulated by a 5V 3TR.

PLL output passes through a buffer and a lowpass filter to strip the carrier, then to a standard 386 driving a speaker. The receiver makes no provision for driving headphones, a little safety measure I insisted upon in gear I built for others to use.

* * *

Tune the system on the bench before connecting it through a line. Power up the transmitter, but not the receiver. Connect scope probe across the output of T1 (transmitter). Peak the carrier. Now connect transmitter output to receiver input through a 100K resistor. This keeps the receiver's transformer output below the clipping threshold of D1 and D2, and should give ~50 $mv_{p\text{-}p}$ measured across the comparator inputs. Tune T1 (receiver) for peak signal. Now power up the receiver and tune R4 (receiver) for best audio.

Note that you do not have to connect the system to the AC power line to experiment with it. Connect it through an ordinary twisted pair, shunted by a few ohms of resistance. Only experienced, qualified professionals have any business connecting a carrier current system to the AC power line. A mishap can be fatal. **Again, if you are not an experienced, qualified professional technician, do not connect this system to the AC power line.**

(TRANSMITTER)

GIMMICK #12

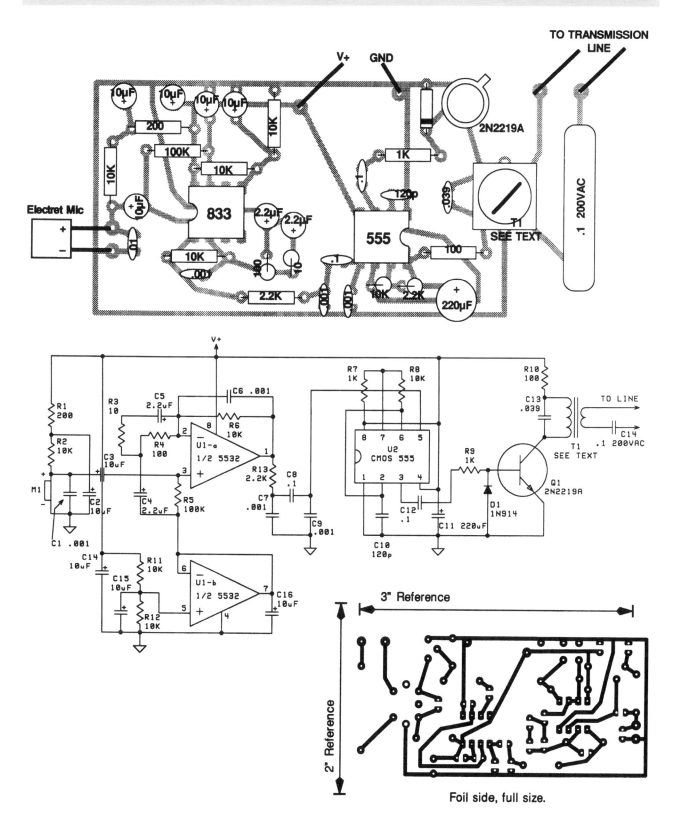

Foil side, full size.

GIMMICK #12 (RECEIVER)

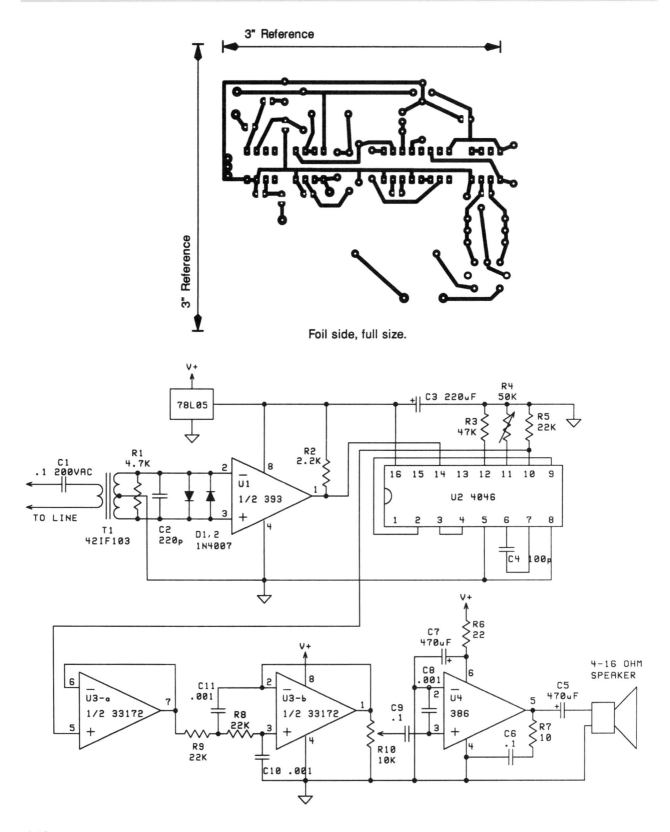

Foil side, full size.

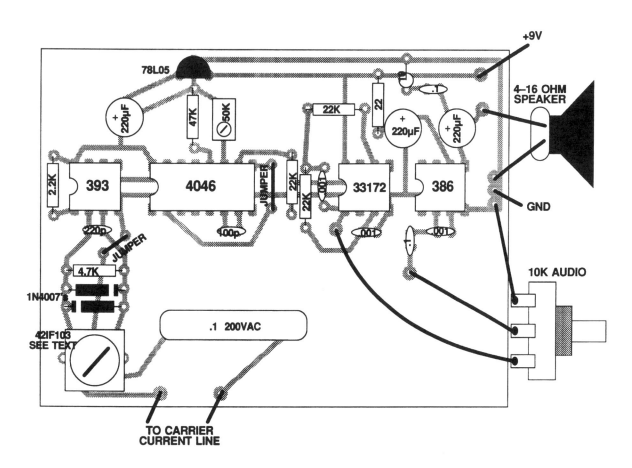

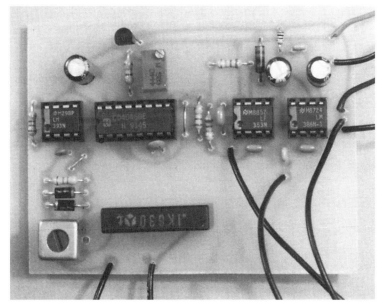

***

My agent rented an apartment month-to-month on the mime's wing. I had to front the security deposit and first month's rent, along with light and water deposits; build a phony identity for the agent; buy two work cars and meet other expenses nobody anticipates when they hire a bugger.

My agent managed the installation under the same pest-control pretext, only this time we posted lookouts and hired a gorgeous female shill to run interference if the mime returned unexpectedly ("Oh, sir, my tire's gone flat. Could you help me?"). Because the hardware my agent carried would get him busted, he wouldn't take the gig unless I provided adequate protection.

Screening the tapes took nerves of steel. The mime got off on Donna Summer, Abba, K.C. and the Sunshine Band. After the first hour I was close to nausea, gulping seasick pills with my head in the bowl.

As the gig wore on we learned that the mime never spoke, even off duty. He did not place or take phone calls, never had pizza delivered, never did anything, it seemed, but mime.

At 12:02 P.M. each day, the mime drove to some public thoroughfare and executed his standard repertoire: he pretended to pull a rope; pretended to be trapped in a shrinking box; pretended to pet an invisible dog; pretended to be a supermarionette. He mimicked facial expressions of passersby, patted babies in strollers, under the watchful approval of their mothers. Et cetera, ad nauseam. I could never watch the mime for very long before my hand reached absently for the .45, as though the subconscious knew exactly how to deal with a problem.

One night the ritual changed. The mime started playing 8-track tapes of Miles Davis, Brubeck, vintage Sinatra; a week later he switched to Buck Owens and George Jones; a few more days and we were back in Disco Hell.

These shifts gave the first clue to what was happening. The mime always left the apartment in mime getup. His musical taste exhibited wild, periodic swings, because somebody else returned under the whiteface. The mime's pad was a safehouse. Occupants entered and left in mime getup, the only legal way to appear masked in public, and an ideal cover, because mimes and lepers were the only creatures whom people walked a block to avoid.

As to who maintained that safehouse, and why . . .

***

After this gig I banked my cut and dumped my TR-882 at the Goodwill.

CHAPTER 32

Play by the Rules

Sure, professional bugging has rules:

1. Never screw the client. A satisfied client is the best and only advertising. The sharper your rep, the higher your fee and the better cut of client you tend to draw. A hardy rep confers the option to choose among sweet gigs instead of having to take the dregs.
2. A rep can get too hot. Appreciate the difference between not screwing a client and doing the impossible every week.
3. What's not on the tape isn't your fault. The fact that the client paid for the tape does not entitle him to specific content.
4. Share the wealth. Some gigs are impossible without greasing a few palms. Bribes are one reason for the high cost of professional bugging.
5. Run a gig for three reasons:

    A) to earn money
    B) to earn a favor
    C) to pay back a favor

    "Favor" implies an area unsafe to plumb. Money tells half the story. The other half of bugging is wired into an underground economy in favors owed and favors paid.

6. Cabbage that isn't cash isn't money. Every agent you hire expects payment in cash. Checks are OK for hardware-only sales to official parties, at least if the buyer wants to clue the world. Any client who insists on paying by check to have you plant a bug is setting you up.
7. The corollary to rule #6: Declare every cent of cash income. The oldest setup is to pay cash, then arrange an audit. The fact that it still works means some haven't gotten the message.
8. The corollary to rule #7: Never put yourself in a position of having to run a gig to get/stay out of jail.
9. Never tell anybody how you did it. If pressed, spin a yarn that leads to a decoy. How you did it is a trade secret. Nor should you spill your MO in a Basement Bugger's Bible.
10. Major private bugging is okay, even routine, so long as GPO knows about it. Major gigs from which they're frozen out provoke rancor that keeps high-line buggers in the passing lane.
11. Never run a gig for personal reasons. Many talented buggers falter at the summit of restraint. You can get away with serious bugging only so long as you enjoy official protection, or the

presumption of that protection. Personal gigs are renegade ops that never enjoy protection.

12. Refuse any feat except bugging. The deal sours this way: NAME hires you for a straight wire gig, pays just enough over the going rate to arouse suspicion. NAME's instructions end with, "By the way, drop this behind the couch." NAME proffers a plastic bag holding an ounce of hemp.

   Don't take it. NAME doesn't want an intercept. He wants a patsy to plant contraband. That means the risk is too great for NAME to take. The correct response is to return the front money and walk away. Taking the gig has two outcomes. One is an instant bust. The other is for succeeding jobs to demand progressively darker plants, ending in the framing of an innocent party for murder. At that point NAME owns you.

13. Trust two types of people: (A) your family, so long as they remain drug-free civilians with clean records; and (B) men to whom you owe your life and who owe their lives to you. These latter bonds form almost exclusively in war. Only close kinship and trust forged in the arena of death can survive the pressures. The rest of the world defaults to a pool of real and latent snitches with whom you may fraternize, and certainly use, but never trust.

A word to those who see themselves hiring a pro. Every bugger a layman is allowed to hear about, and especially ones who seem to come with impeccable credentials (like having their names mumbled by a two-time loser in a biker bar, or wafted on gin-breath from the sleaziest lawyer in town) lead directly to the Government Printing Office. If you want to appear on GPO's version of *Cut-Up Camera*, solicit for bugging.

CHAPTER 33

Build It

The end has come without our having said in so many words that professionals build all their own tools. I thought everybody knew. My reticence roots in caution. Like most members of a culture built on lies, I have learned to treat truth like a rabid hound. Despite this aversion, I could hardly claim to have scoped out a gig, then called Bugs 'R' Us to have #58 airmailed to a drop in Watts.

Buggers build all their own tools, from scratch, to suit specific gigs. That excludes bench gear, though we have been known to tweak the odd spectrum analyzer. Civilians seem perplexed by this revelation. Pros see no other way. Look back over prior segments and consider what on the shelf now, nevermind then, could meet spec. With little perusal one finds that catalog pieces lack the requisite gain, or the right EQ, or exist hidden in the wrong prop, or draw too much current—they suffer a host of failings, in fact.

Had I commissioned a gimmick from another free-lancer (which I did, occasionally, to make GPO believe my expertise had limits), the odds approach nine in ten that word would have leaked. Free-lancers know when they're asked to build something Too Hot. The free-lancer could have trebled his take by selling me out.

Had anyone tried to move one of my serious gimmicks, even on the Enforcement Market, he would have been bought out or warned off. The trade is rife with gossip of this occurrence:

"Newark Lou tried to sell a synchro-harmodyne to some hayseed cop in Dubuque."
"What happened?"
"NAME stepped in. They bought him out."

Commercial hardware's gravest flaw lives in the fact that no "bug" vendor operates without GPO consent. The rarity of bug-related indictments belies a sinister truth. Anyone who has bought surveillance gear and done something naughty with it is owned by GPO, whether he knows so or not.

On the bonus side, parts form the cheapest facet of most gigs. Homemade gimmicks cost less than the sales tax on manufactured ones. Homebuilt allows 100 percent quality control and burn-in testing. Buggers sometimes plant bugs in temperature extremes, such as furnaces, freezers, and unmentionable nooks. We have to test those gimmicks at the anticipated operating temperature. Factory gear seldom gets the requisite screening.

Custom bugs leave no trail if built correctly. Pros don't buy parts. We secure them, meaning we get them through invisible channels which I am not about to tell.

Incidentally, the parts list of every tool I have shown now resides in a threat-recognition database. Believe it, ordering a 5532 and a couple of Mouser 42TL016's (combined with the public record of having bought this rag) will draw notice in dark quarters.

Mass-produced tools live five to ten generations behind the state of the art, which civilians never see. Those who claim to expose The State of the Art are ill informed or scamming. Cutting-edge hardware lives chiefly in privateers' labs. I hate to downplay my own tome, but I haven't shown it here.

Not that commercial hardware serves no purpose. It comes with a UL listing and a warranty. It suits a clientele of limited expertise and ample budget, a species the Drug War has succored in spades. Commercial pieces make dynamite decoys. They bear a slick, finished look alien to real bugs that wows the starch out of the client. They work great against backwater bumpkins and cheap hoods. But when we crack the big time, the world of free-lancers against whom no target is too secure, custom bugs prevail.

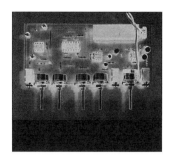

Epilogue

For the first five years in the life I fancied myself a confidential agent, not a bugger, but that semantic sheepshank never cleared my conscience. Another five passed before I managed to build a truth worthy of absolution. Buggers sneak, creep, even lurk. We absolve ourselves by kidding no one about it.

Despite the wealth of tutorials in print, and the simplicity of the concepts involved, few individuals bug at the professional level. The rest, in my view, have a right to mull a strange state of affairs. Bugging thrives in a world where laws apply only to chumps, but your neighborhood bugger isn't the one perpetuating this state and certainly did not inaugurate it. Extrapolators can take that as a starting point.

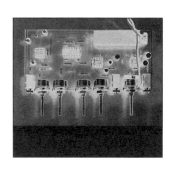

Appendices

APPENDIX I

How to Build Bugs

"DEAD BUG" CONSTRUCTION

Soldering parts together by their leads results in a product that has been likened to a dead insect. Ham radio operators use the technique to minimize parasitic inductance and capacitance. Wiretappers occasionally build one-transistor RF bugs this way to get something about as big as a pearl, including a mic and a hearing-aid battery. Assembly requires a stereoscopic magnifier and micro-tipped tools. The method suits only selected bugs.

Perfboard

"Perfboard" is short for perforated circuit board, a phenolic or glass/epoxy material 1/16" thick, riddled with holes on variable centers, including the 0.1" grid that fits DIPs. Perfboard construction involves plugging parts into holes and soldering their leads together on the underside of the board. Few perfboard projects show the underside of the board because the maze of wiring only confuses the viewer. Despite the messy look, careful technique has enabled complex devices to be built on perfboard. This is

Two types of raw perfboard. Left shows 0.165" center, suitable for large irregular parts. Right shows holes on standard 0.1" centers suitable for DIPs and small electronic parts. Material cuts easily with tin snips.

*Top left and right:
Two views of universal
printed circuit boards.
Builder must adapt circuit
to existing patterns.*

*Bottom photo shows
common breadboard
and companion universal
circuit boards. Bread-
board and circuit boards
are keyed to same
coordinate system.*

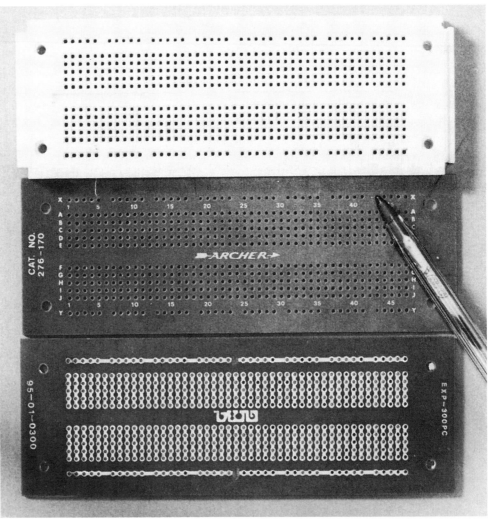

a key option for those who don't care to etch and drill a printed circuit board.

Perfboard comes in a subtype that places a copper ring around each hole on one side to facilitate soldering the part to the board. This lets the builder flip the stuffed board and wire point-to-point without having parts fall out.

Universal Printed Circuit Boards

A step up from perfboard includes predrilled boards with copper traces adaptable to many circuits. One common type has its holes numbered according to the same grid system as a companion breadboard. Many projects will not use the whole length of this board, which the builder can truncate.

Custom-Printed Circuit Boards

The bulk of bugging gear is built on custom-printed circuit boards. Bare boards have a layer of copper completely covering one or both sides. The builder transfers the circuit pattern to copper using some form of etch resist, then dissolves unprotected copper, leaving the circuit pattern. The remainder of construction involves drilling, stuffing, and soldering. Custom boards demand the most work but confer unlimited versatility.

Raw circuit board stock comes in 1/16″ and 1/32″ thicknesses. The currently prevalent FR-4 material is a composite of glass fiber and epoxy. The standard one-ounce copper thickness is adequate for most applications. Board stock comes in several standard sizes, 3″ to 18″ square, and convenient rectangles, such as 3″ × 4.5″ and 4″ × 6″. The 1/32″ stock is preferred because the builder can cut it with tin snips; because it costs slightly less than 1/16″ material; and because it does not dull drill bits as fast as 1/16″ material.

Etch resist is a generic term for material that protects copper from attack by etching solution. Manually applied etch resist comes in sheets of donut pads and traces coated with adhesive. Transfer is effected placing the pad over the desired spot and burnishing it with a medium-tip ballpoint pen. The pad or trace remains when the sheet is lifted away.

Traces also come in rolls of black tape 0.015″ to 0.187″ wide. Boards in this book have been laid out to accommodate #4 tape (0.031″). Common masking tape works great to fill large patches of board.

Etching dry tape results in a board useless due to undercutting. Etchant flows under the tape and eats through the copper. Undercutting

Examples of rub-on pads and traces and rolls of etch-resist tape.

can be prevented by presoaking the taped board in water for an hour prior to etching. The first soak takes 20 minutes in lukewarm water; the next two, 20 minutes each in water at least as hot as the etchant will get. Using thumb and fingertips, press the tape firmly onto the board between soaks. Presoaking usually results in a 100-percent functional board.

Undercutting tends to occur under sharp turns in the tape and where strips cross. To reduce the risk of undercutting, avoid sharp turns with tape and apply a spot of rub-on material where tape strips meet or cross.

Other Resist-Transfer Methods

One of the oldest methods of transferring a printed circuit pattern requires boards treated to respond to ultraviolet light. The pattern is laid out on a sheet of Mylar®, placed over a sensitized board held in a glass frame, then exposed to a source of ultraviolet light. The exposed board is placed in developer, which washes away the exposed parts and leaves a coating of etch resist where the opaque traces blocked the ultraviolet. The board is then etched in the usual manner. The process demands an initial equipment outlay of ~$100 and a fair degree of skill.

Two recently developed methods tap the growing availability of personal copiers and laser printers. One method prints the circuit pattern to a special plastic sheet, which is then placed on bare copper and ironed. Heat melts toner on the plastic; fused toner sticks to the copper and remains when the plastic is peeled away. A similar method uses paper coated on one side with water-soluble glue. The pattern is copied to the glued side of the paper, then ironed on as with plastic. The adhesive melts when the board is soaked in warm water, the paper floats away, leaving the etch resist pattern on the copper.

Both toner methods await definitive versions that work often enough to justify their cost.

Drilling

Drillbits #65–#67 suit holes for common electronic parts. Some parts, notably rectifier diodes, have leads too big for #65 holes and require a #62 or larger bit. Ordinary drill bits cost about a buck each in quantity 10. Carbide bits cut quicker and last longer, but their brittleness leads to frequent breakage in manual drilling.

Drilling requires a proper support, such as an old magazine or a half-inch of newspaper; and a suitable drill, preferably one equipped with variable speed.

Lock the bit in the chuck with about 3/32″ of the shaft exposed. Any more disposes to bending and breakage. Hold the drill such that the bit is perpendicular to the board. The weight of the drill is the only pressure needed to get a hole started. Sharp bits punch through crisply; moderate pressure may be needed as bits age.

Drilling makes a residue of fiberglass and copper slivers. The builder should clean them from the board reasonably often during drilling. Drilling also leaves burrs on both sides of the board. The builder should sand these smooth with a copper scrubbing pad before proceeding with construction. The entire process demands appropriate precautions to avoid getting splinters in the hands.

Etching

Etching describes the process of dissolving copper not protected by etch resist. Two commonly used etchants are ferric chloride and ammonium persulphate. Etching involves an exchange of ions; iron for copper in the case of ferric chloride, ammonium for copper in the case of ammonium persulphate. Because the reaction products are soluble, etchants dissolve copper.

Ferric chloride stains just about everything, especially fabrics and skin. It eats most base metals, including stainless steel. It comes as a powder (4 oz. for each 16 oz. of water) and in solution.

Ammonium persulphate comes as a white powder that forms a colorless aqueous solution. One pound of ammonium persulphate dissolved in one gallon of distilled water makes the standard solution. The builder can mix less, keeping the same ratio of ingredients. Though not as messy as ferric chloride, ammonium persulphate does not etch as fast.

HOW TO MAKE A CIRCUIT BOARD

Step 1

Gather materials, including PC board stock, rub-on pads and tape, masking tape, scissors.

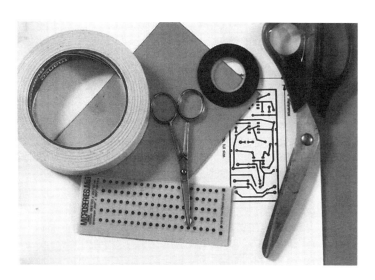

Step 2

After cutting the board to desired size, cut out the printed circuit pattern and tape it to the FOIL SIDE of the board with masking tape.

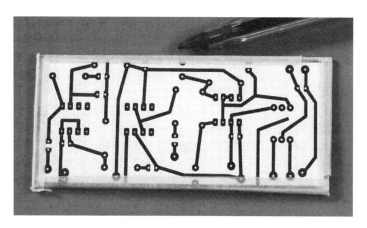

Step 3

Place the board on some suitable padded surface, such as a half-inch stack of old magazines. Drill holes in center of each pad, through paper and board beneath. Note that only about 3/32" of bit protrudes from chuck.

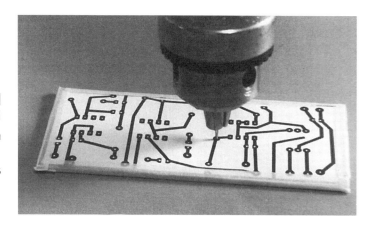

Step 4

Once holes are drilled, carefully peel off the paper circuit template. Save it. Note burrs on both sides of the board.

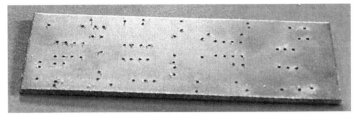

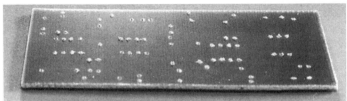

Step 5

Under running water, using a copper scrubbing pad and taking appropriate precautions to avoid splinters, smooth burrs off BOTH SIDES of the board. Result should be clean and smooth.

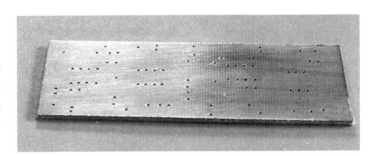

Step 6

Using the paper template as a visual guide, apply rub-on pads and tape to the foil side of the board.

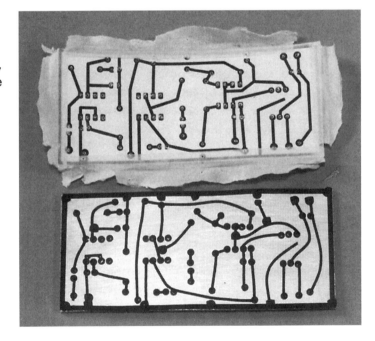

Step 7

Etch the board. Photo shows board ~80-percent etched in a solution of ammonium persulphate.

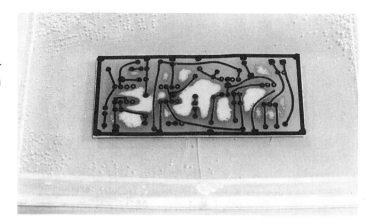

Step 8

Once etching is complete, rinse board under running water for several minutes. Peel off tape and scrub off rub-on pads using copper scrubbing pad under warm running water. Inspect traces for undercutting and incomplete etching. Repair as needed; square up rough board edges using a file.

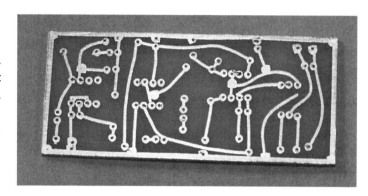

Step 9

Gather materials: soldering iron, solder, parts, damp sponge, wire clippers, etc.

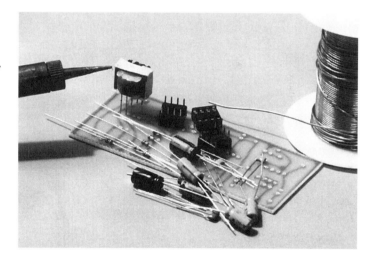

Step 10

Solder parts in holes, trim leads, double-check parts placement. Result is ready for wiring to external components and mounting in case.

Both etchants should be heated to the temperature of comfortably hot water (~120 degrees Fahrenheit) prior to etching. Otherwise, etching takes a very long time.

Etchants are poisons. The user *must* keep them *securely* out of reach of children and other irresponsible parties. Etchants can burn the skin and the eyes, dictating appropriate protective measures when handling them. The etching process leaves poisonous byproducts that, in some jurisdictions, may be defined as hazardous waste requiring disposal in a specified manner.

Etch boards in a glass or plastic tray. The type sold for manual photo processing is ideal. Use enough etchant to cover the board with ~1/16″ of solution. Constantly and gently rock the tray side to side. Reheat the etchant periodically. I remove the board and heat the etchant for a few seconds in a microwave oven; oven power setting and heating time depend on the oven and the volume of etchant. Avoid excessive heating; generally, do not exceed 120 degrees Fahrenheit, because wax-based etch resist can melt or lift off the board. Extremely hot etchant increases the risk of undercutting. Etching with ammonium persulphate takes 15–20 minutes; ferric chloride averages somewhat less. Etching demands appropriate precautions to protect the eyes and skin.

Dispose of used etchant in a safe manner and in accordance with local laws. Never store etchants in a metal container.

Rinse the freshly etched board in warm water for several minutes, then peel off tape. Scrub off rub-on patterns using a copper scouring pad (the flat, rather than the bulbous type). This process goes more quickly if board and pad are held under hot water for a few seconds prior to scrubbing. Some sources recommend organic thinners to dissolve etch resist, but these have not proved necessary in my hands. Also, the copper scouring pad should be used solely for circuit boards and not in any aspect of food preparation or dish washing.

The post-etch stage is a good one to file down rough board edges.

Inspect the board, under low-power magnification if necessary. Look for undercut traces and incomplete etching. Thin bridges can be broken with the blade of a small-tipped screwdriver. Undercut traces should be bridged with a wire fragment and solder.

Prototypes shown in this book were built by printing the circuit pattern on copy paper, then cutting out the pattern and taping it to the foil side of a piece of circuit board stock precut to size. The board was placed on an old magazine and holes were drilled through the pattern and the board behind it. Then the paper template was peeled *intact* from the board. Both sides of the board were smoothed under running water using a copper scouring pad. The circuit pattern was then transferred to the board with rub-on pads and tape, using the saved template as a visual guide. The board was then etched as described above.

Creating a Ground Plane

A ground plane is a layer of copper on the component side of the board, unbroken but for lead-holes. To create a board with a ground plane, start with 1/16″ double-sided board. Tape and drill as described above; mark the circuit-pattern side to be able to identify it later. Remove the template and sand down burrs on both sides of the board. Before applying pads and traces, cover the ground-plane side with overlapping strips of masking tape. The tape must cover the entire board on that side and be tightly burnished with, say, the back of an old tablespoon. Then apply pads and tape to the other side of the board. Etch in the usual manner. The builder will note some discoloration where etchant flows through the holes, but usually no significant loss of copper on the ground-plane side.

Once the board is etched and cleaned, create a space around each lead-hole on the ground-plane side, so component leads do not touch the ground plane. A quarter-inch drill bit works great for this. Press the tip into the hole, turn to rout the copper. A gentle touch with a low-speed drill speeds this process. These extra steps are one reason ground-plane boards are reserved for applications that demand them.

Ground plane #1   **Space**   **Ground plane #2**

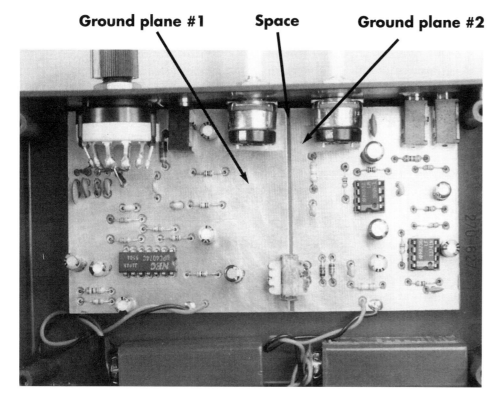

Example of a device built with a ground plane, two of them, in fact, one each for two separate ground systems. Note that board has been routed away from lead holes. Device function and specs are classified.

Bottom left: Typical drillbits—#66 for average leads, #62 for larger leads. Carbide bit meant for high-speed drilling machines; difficult to use manually.

Bottom right: Solder, desoldering wick. In this case, wick is for heavy-duty joints. Can be made suitable for normal desoldering jobs by cutting down the middle with tin snips. Two former soldering tips now used for desoldering. Small, undamaged tip used for conventional soldering.

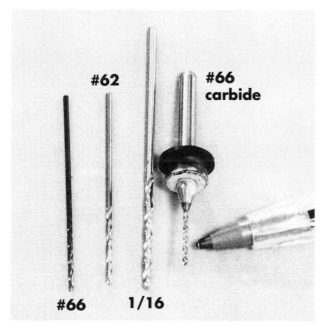

#62   **#66 carbide**

#66   **1/16**

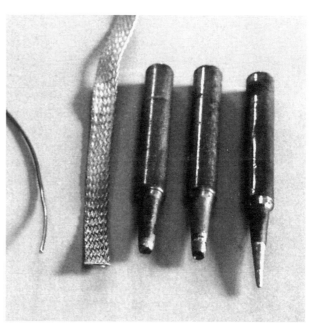

Soldering

Soldering is best learned through practice. Description alone cannot convey proper technique. Soldering requires a 25–35 watt soldering pencil with a 1/16″ chisel tip.

Solder used in electronic assembly is a 60/40 alloy of tin and lead. It comes in spools of wire; 0.031″ or 0.025″ thicknesses suit light electronic work. Solder contains a core of flux, which wets the copper and promotes bonding among the metals. The builder can choose between two types of flux in electronic solder: rosin, which is soluble in an organic solvent, such as absolute isopropyl alcohol; and water-soluble flux. Circuits that work at and above ultrasonic range should be cleaned of flux.

Soldering can damage or destroy parts by heat. Heatsinking transistors and diodes is widely recommended and rarely practiced because skilled soldering rarely results in heat damage. If semiconductors will be subject to undue heat, as might result in certain desoldering operations, heatsink the lead being heated.

The builder should solder in an adequately ventilated area and should avoid inhaling the rich white smoke that rises off freshly melted solder because it contains lead.

Soldering goes easier by installing components in like groups. Start with sockets, followed by flat-mounted resistors, then upright resistors, disc capacitors, finally electrolytic capacitors and special parts, such as transformers and trimpots. After each category is soldered, clip leads close to the board. Lightly grasp the lead being clipped to keep it from flying into your eye.

Heavy-duty soldering calls for a soldering gun. The tip heats only when the trigger is pulled. Avoid using soldering guns near parts, especially circuits with transformers, because the powerful AC field around the gun can induce injurious currents in the circuit.

Desoldering

Salvaging parts or swapping them out calls for desoldering. Light desoldering is conveniently managed with desoldering braid, a woven copper impregnated with flux to promote wicking. The end of the braid is placed on the joint to be removed, then the soldering tip is placed on the braid. Solder melts and wicks into the braid, freeing the lead.

Desoldering wick works best when pressed into the boule with moderate pressure. That pressure eventually abrades a hole in the plating on the tip. The exposed core of the tip dissolves in solder, and shortly the tip becomes useless for soldering. Such damaged tips can be treated roughly and make great desoldering tools.

To Socket or Not to Socket

Socket most audio integrated circuits. Sockets enable hassle-free salvage, facilitate replacement in the event of failure, and allow testing of different op amps in the same circuit.

Practicality of socketing falls as system frequency rises, such that RF components should solder directly to the board. Sockets increase lead length, which increases parasitic capacitance and inductance. The higher the frequency, the more problems result. Generally, avoid sockets in circuits working above 455 KHz.

Sockets impede the transfer of heat. Power drivers, especially the LM380, sink heat into the circuit board. Sockets interpose a thermal barrier that can defeat this process.

Common DIP sockets come with a notch on one end, known as a key. When soldering the socket to the board, place the key where the notched end of the chip will go. This aids proper orientation of the chip.

Socketing and desocketing take practice. Before socketing a virgin chip, gently bend its leads inward, toward each other, until they are centered in the socket holes. Push gently down with enough force to seat the chip. Inspect to see that no leads have bent under the chip.

Using the fingers to desocket a chip usually results in bent leads and a punctured finger. The correct method is to insert the blade of a small-tip screwdriver under one end of the chip; rotate the blade so that the end of the chip lifts slightly; do the same at the other end; repeat until the chip lifts freely from the socket. Prying in one step frees pins at one end but bends pins at the other. Leads bent too many times grow brittle and break. Properly treated chips will survive hundreds of socketing cycles.

Troubleshooting

Despite my years of experience building electronic devices, up to 10 percent of the author's boards fail to work when first powered up. On a rough percentage basis, these failures trace to:

soldering errors	65%
wiring errors	13%
component stuffing/socketing errors	13%
circuit board design errors	6%
board fabrication errors	2%
others (unspecified)	1%
defective component	very rare

Soldering errors include solder bridges, which are easily seen when they bridge open traces but are often invisible beneath flux between tightly-spaced pads. Scraping the flux between the pads often cures the problem. Cold solder joints denote apparently sound but electrically corrupt connections. The prevalence of soldering errors dictates that the builder inspect the board after soldering.

Wiring errors involve leads to pots, switches, and jacks. These, too, drop out in a methodical post-soldering inspection.

An incorrectly oriented polarized cap in the signal path can lead to low signal, no signal, distortion, or seemingly bizarre DC offsets. Improperly mounted bypass capacitors can heat up, smoke, vent gas, and even burst. Tantalum bypass caps quickly become dead shorts, if wired incorrectly and subjected to voltage, and have to be replaced.

Circuit board layout errors occur during design, or during the application of etch resist. After designing a board, it's a good idea to wait a day before building the prototype. Recheck the board layout when you're fresh. Take another break after applying etch resist, and inspect the board prior to etching.

Post-etch inspection should concentrate on the junction of traces and pads, where undercutting happens most. Inspect closely spaced traces using a magnifier for copper bridges too small to be seen with the naked eye.

Defective components are rare enough that the wise troubleshooter eliminates other causes before imputing malfunction to a bad part. Socketed chips are readily swapped out.

Initial power-up is sometimes called "the smoke test," because a major wiring error will zap a chip or melt insulation. To minimize this risk, screen the board prior to powering it up. Place the leads of an ohmmeter set for 20K across the power leads (in the case of a dual supply, between the positive lead and ground, then between the negative lead and ground). The ohmic reading will depend upon which meter lead ties to which battery lead, and will shift over several seconds due to capacitor charging; but in no case should a dead short or even an unusually low ohmic reading be obtained. The likely current draw of the circuit can be estimated by knowing current consumption of each op amp, transistor, or LED. By Ohm's law this corresponds to a certain minimum resistance. For example, a circuit using a TL072, an LM386, and an electret microphone should show a resting current drain no greater than:

$$(2 \text{ x } 1.4 \text{ ma}) + 8 \text{ ma} + 0.5 \text{ ma} = 11.3 \text{ ma}$$

Call it 15 ma at the outside. Given a 7.5V battery, minimum resistance should read no less than 7.5V / 0.015A = 500 ohms. A reading across the supply less than this demands investigation prior to powering up the circuit. If a board fails to work after initial power is applied, repeat the ohmmeter test before applying power again.

When a device that passes the ohmmeter test fails to perform, a few quick checks usually diagnose the failure. First, with power applied, verify voltage at all supply pins. An artificial ground should read very close to 1/2V+. Check all points with a known bias. For example, a noninverting amp whose input is biased at 1/2V+ should read very close to 1/2V+ at the output.

Troubleshooting the signal path requires a signal generator and an oscilloscope. Apply the signal to the input and trace it stagewise to the output. The function of the stage dictates the appearance on the scope—100 mv applied to the input of a 20-dB preamp should emerge from the preamp as 1V; a 60 KHz sinewave into a fullwave rectifier should emerge rectified; and so forth.

Cases

Bugs often stop at the bare-board stage because many gigs give no reason to encase. The prospect of NJD countermeasures, or the need to suppress harmonics of an RF bug, dictate a metal case that must entirely surround the device. Bug sniffers and custom radio receivers gain about 6 dB of sensitivity when housed in a metal box, which should tie to circuit ground; insulate the antenna from the case using a rubber grommet.

Cases other than these are matters of convenience—something to hold the battery and mount knobs and jacks. Plastic is cheap and easily worked. Several plastic cases come with 9V battery compartments. Metal is harder to work, usually more expensive, and uglier once worked. Steel, in particular, requires considerable skill and precautions to avoid injury. Though aluminum is optimum for neither electrostatic nor magnetic shielding, it will suffice in environments not particularly rich in interference. A plastic box whose interior is lined with aluminum or copper foil can replace some metal cases. Metal-doped plastic cases that claim 50–55 dB of shielding have recently hit the hobby market (Digi-Key).

The bugger should bear in mind that any case offers many square inches of fingerprint space and countless crannies for trace evidence.

APPENDIX II

Parts ID and Pinouts

INTEGRATED CIRCUITS & SURFACE MOUNT PARTS

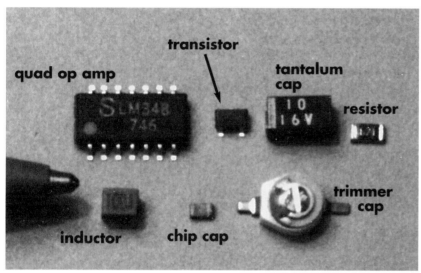

quad op amp

transistor

tantalum cap

resistor

trimmer cap

inductor

chip cap

Most ICs come in dual inline package carriers typical of the top photo. Designated as 8-pin DIP, 16-pin DIP, etc. Pin count begins lower left-hand corner and proceeds counterclockwise around the chip; left to right on the bottom row, right to left on the top row. The key end is identified by a pit, notch, white stripe, or some combination of these markings. Resorting to surface-mount parts is not often necessary, but the bugger should be aware of the option. The parts are soldered to the foil side of the board. Surface-mount parts are small enough that most jobs require magnification, mini-tools, and a steady hand. The fraction of parts available in surface-mount packages is growing. Usually cost a premium over full-size, or are available only in qty. 10 or more. Surface-mount soldering involves first tinning the board, tacking down one lead, then soldering the others. Desoldering surface-mount parts with ordinary desoldering aids is often difficult enough to mean sacrificing the part. Bottom photo illustrates a few surface-mount case styles.

notch

14

8

stripe

1

pit

POTENTIOMETERS

Potentiometers, or "pots," are variable resistors that come in two common tapers, linear and logarithmic (also called audio-taper); diagram illustrates the difference. Log-taper pots are preferred for volume controls because they give greatest control at lowest volume. Linear-taper pots are usually labeled "B(value)"; B100K = a 100K linear-taper pot. Log-taper pots are labeled "A (value)"; A250K = a 250K log-taper pot. Common pots that cost $1–$4 from major suppliers exhibit a wide tolerance, such that a pot rated 10K might measure 8.5K to 11.5K total resistance. Board-mounted, screw-adjustable pots serve as trimmers or "trimpots." Controlling more than a few milliamps of current requires taking power into account. Carbon film pots should not be pushed past 1/4W; wirewound pots are designed for high current.

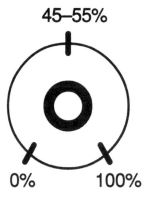

Linear-Taper Potentiometer

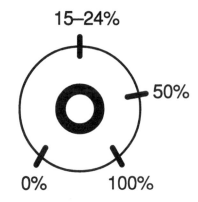

Audio- or Log-Taper Potentiometer

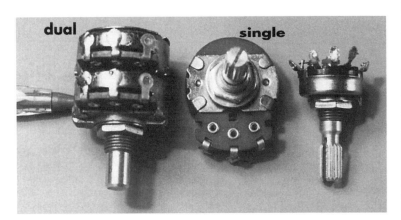

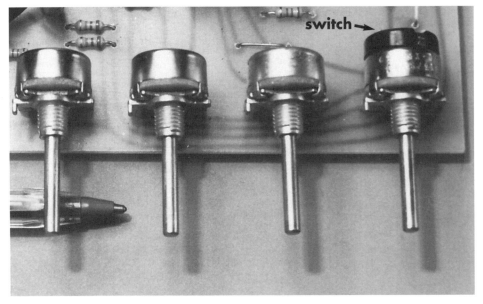

Board-mounted full-size pots are neat and convenient, but board must be layed out specifically to accept their leads.

CAPACITORS

- Capacitor markings vary greatly. Some are obvious, such as "0.01," the value in microfarads; others, such as "103M," have to be interpreted. The first two digits are a number to which the number of zeros specified by the third digit are appended. For example, a capacitor labeled "104" means 10 + 4 zeros = 100,000 picofarads = 0.1µF; "103" means 10 + 3 zeros = 10,000 pF; "221" means 22 + 1 zero = 220 pF. Values below 100 pF are taken as they are, e.g., 6, 18, 82pF, etc. If in doubt about a capacitor's value, measure it on a digital multimeter.

- The letter after the multiplier tells capacitor tolerance: Z = -20 percent / +80 percent; M = ±20 percent; K = ±10 percent; J = ±5 percent; F = ±1 percent. So, a capacitor labeled "332J" means 3,300pF (or 0.0033µF) at 5 percent tolerance.

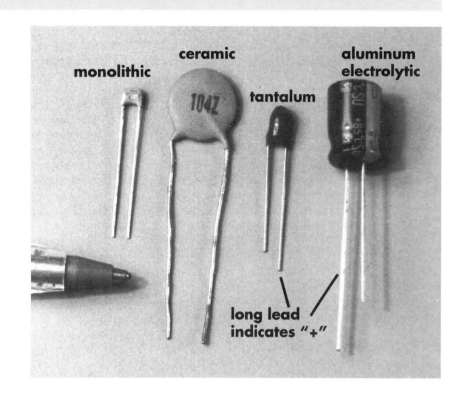

- Ceramic bypass types vary greatly with temperature, typically -20 percent to +80 percent, but offer low impedance to high frequencies, which suits them to bypass use. They are not suitable for the signal path.

- Caps suitable for the signal path include poly (polypropylene, polycarbonate, polystyrene, Mylar®, etc.); tolerance 20 percent or better. Caps used in active filters should be 5 percent or better. Caps used in the tank of an RF transmitter don't need tight tolerance but do need temperature stability to minimize drift. Silver-mica and types labeled "NPO" suit this use.

- Take particular care to install polarized capacitors correctly. In all cases, the cap's positive lead connects to the more positive DC potential. Incorrect wiring can lead to heating, smoking, or venting of gas that can be explosive. Generally, a cap so damaged should be discarded. Tantalum bypass capacitors do not vent, but quickly become a dead short if wired incorrectly across the power bus and have to be replaced.

- Be certain that the capacitor's rated working voltage exceeds the highest DC or AC voltage to which it will be subject. A bypass capacitor for a 9V circuit should be rated at least 10V; and so forth.

- Use bipolar (nonpolar) electrolytic caps when a DC offset is expected to reverse in normal circuit operation.

FIXED RESISTORS

The most common 5-percent carbon film resistors are identified by colored bands that tell value and tolerance. First three bands decode according to table below; fourth band indicates tolerance; gold = 5 percent; silver = 10 percent. Carbon composition resistors are preferred at VHF and above. Devices shown in this book use 1/8W and 1/4W 5 percent carbon film resistors interchangeably, except where specifically noted. Quarter-watt resistors cost less than a penny apiece in quantity 200. Fixed resistors can mount flat or stand on end. Resistor should not get more than barely warm in normal operation. (An exception to that rule occurs with metal-oxide power resistors, which can get hot enough to burn the skin in normal operation.) To calculate a power rating, multiply voltage times current flowing through the resistor. For example, take a 100-ohm resistor in series with an LED running on 18V. The forward drop across the LED is 1.7V, so current flowing through the resistor = (18V–1.7V) / 100 = 163 milliamps. Power dissipated in the resistor = VI = 16.3V x 0.166A = 2.66 watts; so the resistor should be rated at least 3W. Because metal-oxide power resistors are built to run at elevated temperature, they often mount 1/4"–1/2" off the board to facilitate airflow cooling.

Color	Abbrev.	Number	Multiplier	EXAMPLES
black	BLK	0	×1	BRN-BLK-BLK = 10 ohms
brown	BRN	1	×10	BRN-BLU-RED = 1.6K
red	RED	2	×100	RED-RED-RED = 2.2K
orange	ORG	3	×1K	BRN-BLK-ORG = 10K
yellow	YEL	4	×10K	YEL-VIO-YEL = 470K
green	GRN	5	×100K	BRN-BLK-GRN = 1M
blue	BLU	6	×1M	BLU-RED-YEL = 620K
violet	VIO	7	×10M	GRY-RED-RED = 8.2K
gray	GRY	8	×100M	BRN-BLK-BRN = 100 ohms
white	WHT	9	×1G	ORG-WHT-ORG = 39K

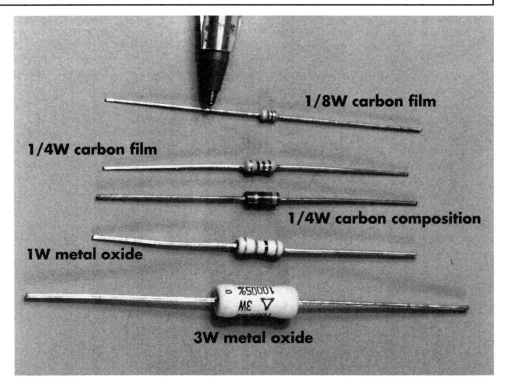

1/8W carbon film

1/4W carbon film

1/4W carbon composition

1W metal oxide

3W metal oxide

COMMON DIODES AND TRANSISTORS

Diodes are specified by semiconductor type (silicon, germanium, etc.). Small signal diodes are typified by 1N914 or 1N4148 silicon types; germanium types 1N34A, 1N270, 1N60, etc. Small signal diodes usually come in clear glass cases with a dark band to indicate the cathode ("–" terminal); germanium diodes are larger than silicon diodes. Rectifier diodes typified by 1N400X series: 1N4001 to 1N4007; they come in black cases with a white band to indicate cathode.

Most common bipolar small-signal transistors come in the TO-92 case and use the E-B-C pinout (emitter-base-collector, looking at flat side of case and reading left to right). Notable exceptions include MPSH10 and MPSH11, which go B-E-C. Same part numbers can be had in

different cases. Choose larger metal case to dissipate higher power. In TO-39 case a metal tab identifies the emitter; the collector is also tied to the case. Common FETs also come in TO-92 case but use D-S-G (drain-source-gate) pinout; one exception is the 2N3819, which uses D-G-S. FETs that come in metal TO-18 case often add a fourth lead which ties to case and is grounded to shield the die. Drain and source are interchangeable on most FETs. Power MOSFETs come in many case styles: TO-39, flat pack, TO-220. Identifying the leads of an unknown bipolar transistor is easy because it acts as two diodes wired in series and will read as such on ohmmeter. NPN transistor acts as two silicon diodes with two cathodes and a common anode; PNP transistors the reverse.

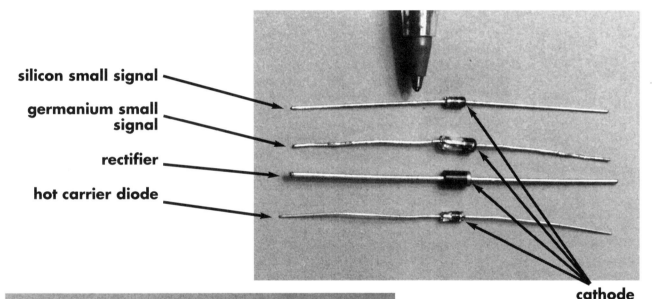

silicon small signal

germanium small signal

rectifier

hot carrier diode

cathode

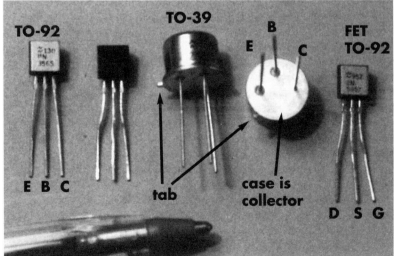

TO-92

TO-39

B

E

C

FET TO-92

E B C

tab

case is collector

D S G

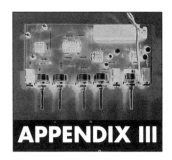

APPENDIX III

Basic Bug Math

If every bugger knows one epiphany, it has to be the realization that these tiresome formulas not only work, but they hold the keys to feats that will probably never make the open literature. Formulas let the designer predict and control circuit behavior. Performance at significant variance with predictions can tip the builder to a construction error or faulty part.

OHM'S LAW

$$E = IR$$

where E = electromotive force in volts
I = current in amperes
R = resistance (or impedance) in ohms

Example: An optical transmitter being built to bug the comptroller of Universal Widget Corp. will use a laser diode having a forward drop of 1.4V. The diode will run off a regulated 5V supply. What value of series resistance, Rx, is needed to limit current through the diode to 59 milliamps?

Solution: Refer to schematic "A." Because the diode drops 1.4V, the voltage across Rx will be (5V - 1.4V) = 3.6V. Given this voltage and the desired current flow of 59 ma, use Ohm's law to solve for resistance. Rearranging Ohms' law: R = E/I:

Rx = 3.6V / 0.059A = 61.02 ohms =
62 ohms closest standard value

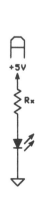

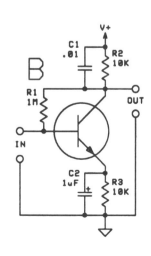

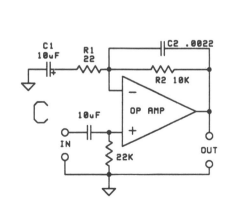

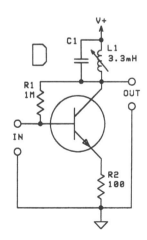

CAPACITIVE REACTANCE

*Capacitive reactance (Xc) at
frequency f = 1 / (6.28 x fC)
where f = frequency in Hz
C = capacitance in farads
(To convert µF to farads, divide by a million;
to convert picofarads to farads, divide by 10[12].)*

Example: You plan to impress a 500-KHz carrier on an active phone line. The coupling capacitor must show the line around 6,000 ohms of reactance at 3,000 Hz to avoid dampening the audio, but very low reactance at 500 KHz to ensure good coupling. Find the value of a capacitor that meets these criteria.

Solution: You can solve this by trial and error. First, calculate the reactance of a capacitor of convenient value, say, 0.1µF, at 3,000 Hz and at 500 KHz:

Xc = 1 / [6.28 x 3,000 x (0.1 / 1,000,000)]
= 531 ohms
Xc = 1 / [6.28 x 500,000 x (0.1 / 1,000,000)]
= 3.2 ohms

Nope. Xc is too low at 3,000 Hz. But you don't have to recalculate, because Xc follows a linear proportion. By reducing capacitance tenfold, reactance rises tenfold. So, a 0.01 cap has 5,310 ohms of reactance at 3 KHz, high enough to avoid loading the line; and 32 ohms at 500 KHz, low enough to couple the carrier.

SERIES RESISTANCE

*Series resistance = sum of resistances in series
(R1 + R2 + R3 + . . .)*

Example: A critical circuit needs exactly 663 ohms of resistance; such a resistor is not in your junk box and does not exist as a discrete value.

Solution: Wire two standard values, 620 ohms and 43 ohms, in series.

PARALLEL RESISTANCE

*Parallel resistance = (R1 x R2 x Rx) /
(R1 + R2 + Rx):
where Rx represents any number
of additional resistances*

Example: After designing an IR bug, you find that current-limiting requires a 250-ohm 1W resistor, which is not in your junk box. The client is chain smoking outside the lab, waiting on you to build the bug. What value of 1/4W resistors wired in parallel will give 250 ohms and 1W power capacity?

Solution: Using the formula: (1,000 x 1,000) / (1,000 + 1,000 + 1,000 + 1,000) = 250 ohms

But, since you're using resistors of equal value, simply divide the individual resistance by the number of resistors: 1 000 / 4 = 250 ohms. Eight resistors will give 125 ohms and 2W power capacity; etc.

SERIES CAPACITANCE

*Net capacitance of two capacitors in series =
(C1 x C2) / (C1 + C2)*

Example: You find that you need a 500pF cap but don't have that value. What two equal-value caps wired in series will give 500pF?

Solution: Using the formula: (0.001 x 0.001) / (0.001 + 0.001) = 0.0005µF = 500pF

PARALLEL CAPACITANCE

*The value of capacitors in parallel =
sum of individual capacitances*

Example: You've just built the carrier current transmitter described in Part II but cannot find a 120pF cap in your parts bin.

Solution: Wire 100pF in parallel with 20pF = 120pF.

IMPEDANCE OF A PARALLEL RC NETWORK

Impedance (Z) of a resistor in parallel with a capacitor = RXc / (R² + Xc2)⁰·⁵:
where R = resistance in ohms
Xc = capacitive reactance in ohms

Example: What is the theoretical gain of a common-emitter amplifier (schematic "B") at 50 Hz and at 3 KHz?

Solution: Theoretical gain of a class-A-biased common-emitter amp is roughly equal to the ratio of collector impedance to emitter impedance. If no capacitors were involved, we could divide R2 by R3 to get theoretical gain. But each resistor is in parallel with a capacitor, so the solution requires calculation of those two impedances at 50 Hz and 3 KHz.

First, find Xc of C1 and C2 at 50 Hz and 3 KHz:

For 0.01µF, Xc = 318K at 50 Hz;
Xc = 5.3K at 3 KHz

For 1µF, Xc = 3.2K at 50 Hz,
53 ohms at 3 KHz

Now calculate the two relative impedances at the two frequencies. For the collector impedance, 10K R2 is in parallel with 0.001 C1, so, at 50 Hz:

$(10,000 \times 318,000) / [(10,000)^2 + (318,000)^2]^{0.5}$ = 9,995 ohms (call it 10K)

Collector impedance at 3 KHz =
$(10,000 \times 5,300) / [(10,000)^2 + (5,300)^2]^{0.5}$
= 4,683 ohms

The emitter impedance at 50 Hz =
$(10,000 \times 3,200) / [(10,000)^2 + (3,200)^2]^{0.5}$
= 3,048 ohms

Emitter impedance at 3 KHz =
$(10,000 \times 53) / [(10,000)^2 + (53)^2]^{0.5}$ = 53 ohms

Gain at 50 Hz =
(10K / 3,048) = 3.3 = 20(log3.3) = 10.4 dB

Gain at 3 KHz =
(4,683 / 53) = 88.4 = 20(log88.4) = 39 dB

Measured gain will be less than predicted for two reasons. First, use of negative feedback lowers gain. Second, the lower the supply voltage, the more actual gain falls short of theoretical.

IMPEDANCE OF SERIES RC NETWORK

Impedance of a resistor in series with a capacitor = (R² + Xc²)⁰·⁵,
where R is resistance in ohms,
Xc is capacitive reactance in ohms.

Example: Find the gain of the op-amp preamp (schematic "C") at 50 Hz and at 3 KHz.

Solution: Gain of a noninverting amp = 1 + (feedback impedance / input impedance). In this case the feedback impedance is a parallel RC network, the input impedance a series RC network. To solve, calculate capacitive reactances at 50 Hz and 3 KHz; plug those values into the impedance formulas for each type of network and solve.

Xc of 10µF at 50 Hz = 318 ohms

Xc of 10µF at 15 KHz = 1.1 ohms

Xc of 0.0022µF at 50 Hz = 1.45 megohms

Xc of 0.0022µF at 15 KHz = 4,824 ohms

Impedance of the input resistor network at 50 Hz = $(R^2 + Xc^2)^{0.5}$ = $(22^2 + 318^2)^{0.5}$ = 319 ohms

Impedance of the input resistor network at 15 KHz = $(R^2 + Xc^2)^{0.5}$ = $(22^2 + 1.1^2)^{0.5}$ = 22 ohms

Impedance of the feedback network at 50 Hz = RXc / (R² + Xc²)⁰·⁵ = (10,000 x 1,450,000) / [(10,000² + 1,450,000²)]⁰·⁵ = 9,999.8 ohms = 10K

Impedance of the feedback network at 50 Hz = RXc / (R² + Xc²)⁰·⁵ = (10,000 x 4,824) / [(10,000² + 4,824²)]⁰·⁵ = 4,345 ohms

Gain at 50 Hz = 1 + (10,000 / 319) = 32.4 = 30 dB

Gain at 15 KHz = 1 + (10,000 / 22) = 455.6 = 53 dB

A little heavy in the bass, but perfectly OK if the transducer has a natural bass fade. If not, cut C1 to ~3.3µF and the amp should be ready to rock.

LC RESONANCE

Resonant frequency of series or parallel LC network = fR = 1 / [6.28 x (LC)⁰·⁵] where L is inductance in henries and C is capacitance in farads

Example: You decide to increase the selectivity of a 40-KHz ultrasonic receiver by making the preamp resonant at the carrier frequency. The preamp is a common-emitter amplifier whose collector resistor you'll replace with an LC network (schematic "D"). Using a 3.3 mH variable inductor, what value of capacitance will cause the tank to resonate at 40 KHz?

Solution: Rearranging the general formula and solving for capacitance at resonance:

$C = 1 / (39.4 \times f^2 \times L)$
$C = 1 / [39.4 \times (40,000)^2 \times (0.0033 \text{ henries})] = 0.0000000048$ farads = $0.0047µF$, closest standard value

The formula works equally well for calculating tank values for an RF oscillator:

Example: You plan to build an LC-tuned RF

bug to work at 160 MHz. The bug will use a canned RF coil whose nominal inductance is 0.0393µH. What value of capacitance will resonate with this coil at 160 MHz?

Solution:

$C = 1 / (39.4 \times f^2 \times L)$
$C = 1 / [39.4 \times (160,000,000)^2 \times (0.0000000393 \text{ henries})] = 2.5 \times 10^{-11}$ farads = 25 picofarads

Your starting capacitance on the breadboard should be maybe 10pF, because at least 10pF of stray capacitance accompanies the layout. In fact, stray capacitance may be so high that the coil resonates below 160 MHz with no added capacitance. You might have to go to a smaller inductance to get to 160 MHz. Fire up the SA and check it out.

DECIBELS

Decibels are a form of shorthand used to denote amplitude. Instead of saying "the circuit has a numeric voltage gain of 2,000," say "66 dB of gain." Decibels come in two types, amplitude dB and power dB. Amplitude (voltage) dB = 20 x log(value); power dB = 10 x log(value). All dB terms in this text are voltage dB. To express attenuation in dB, the numbers come out negative. Attenuation by a factor of 100 =

dB	NUMERIC	EXPONENTIAL
-60	0.001	$\times 10^{-3}$
-40	0.01	$\times 10^{-2}$
-20	0.1	$\times 10^{-1}$
0	1	$\times 10^{0}$
20	10	$\times 10^{1}$
40	100	$\times 10^{2}$
60	1,000	$\times 10^{3}$
80	10,000	$\times 10^{4}$
100	100,000	$\times 10^{5}$
120	1,000,000	$\times 10^{6}$

multiplication by 0.01; 20log 0.01 = -40 dB. So, a compressor set for its minimum threshold of -40 dB kicks in at 10 millivolts.

Two useful benchmarks:

1. Amplitude doubles or halves in 6-dB steps. If the voltage gain of a stage doubles, it has gained 6 dB; if a filter incurs a loss of 12 dB, it has reduced the voltage by a factor of 4, etc.

2. Amplitude changes 20 dB per decade. If gain of a stage falls by a factor of 10, it has lost 20 dB; if the output of an 80-dB preamp feeds a power driver whose voltage gain is 10, total system gain in dB becomes 100, etc.

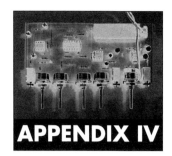

APPENDIX IV

How to Read
Schematic Diagrams

A schematic is a symbolic representation of how parts connect to make a circuit. Once symbols are known, reading schematics reduces to:

- recognizing standard subcircuits
- tracing the signal path
- tracing the power and ground buses

The text has shown dozens of standard subcircuits: op-amp-based devices, including the inverting amp, noninverting amp, subtractor, summing amp, voltage follower; several types of active filters; RF oscillators; common-emitter transistor amplifiers; the charge pump; specialized integrated circuits, such as an ultrasonic FM generator, phase locked loop demodulator; etc.

Good schematics utilize the *bus* concept. A bus (*buss* in some texts) is a common path to which several components connect. Single-supply circuits have two buses, the positive supply bus and the ground bus; dual-supply circuits add the negative supply bus. The positive bus is usually shown at the top of the diagram, the ground bus at the bottom. To enhance clarity, major subcircuits are arranged in a linear path, from left to right. Whatever the arrangement, the object of a schematic is to facilitate the viewer's understanding of circuit function.

Take the example below, the same schematic shown in the discussion of the poly-tube shotgun mic. The positive supply bus is on top; the ground bus on the bottom. The heavy line identifies the signal path. The mic feed enters Q1 base, emerges at the collector, enters pin 3 of a 386, comes out pin 5.

Circuit function is easily understood by recognizing the subcircuits. The first subcircuit is a common-emitter transistor amplifier. Nominal gain equals ratio of collector impedance to emitter impedance. In this case, and below 15 KHz, gain should be 100 = 40 dB; the low supply voltage dictates less gain. The ceramic mic can couple directly to the base because ceramics do not present a DC path.

Output comes off the collector. When the pot is turned fully counterclockwise, it contacts the positive supply bus, where no signal exists. When fully clockwise, it contacts the collector, where maximum signal exists.

The second subcircuit is an LM386 audio power driver. Q1 output feeds the noninverting input because the signal was inverted between input and output at the collector of the transistor. If it were inverted again, the output of the 386 would be in phase with the microphone input, a state conducive to oscillation.

The capacitor isolates the 386 input from the large DC potential at Q1 collector. If C3 were polarized the positive terminal would have to tie to the wiper of R3.

The third subcircuit is the bypass network. The 386 runs off the standard RC decoupling network mandatory in high-gain circuits; C2 serves as bypass for Q1.

More complicated schematics are just as easily analyzed by breaking them into subcircuits and tracing the signal path and power bus.

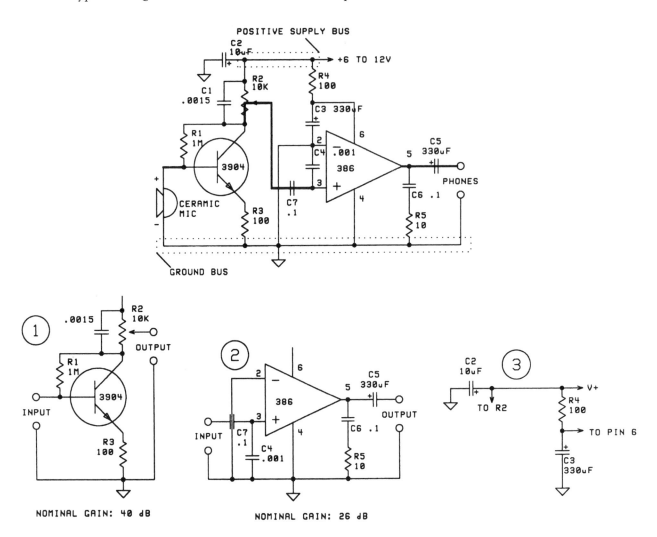

SCHEMATIC SYMBOL LEGEND

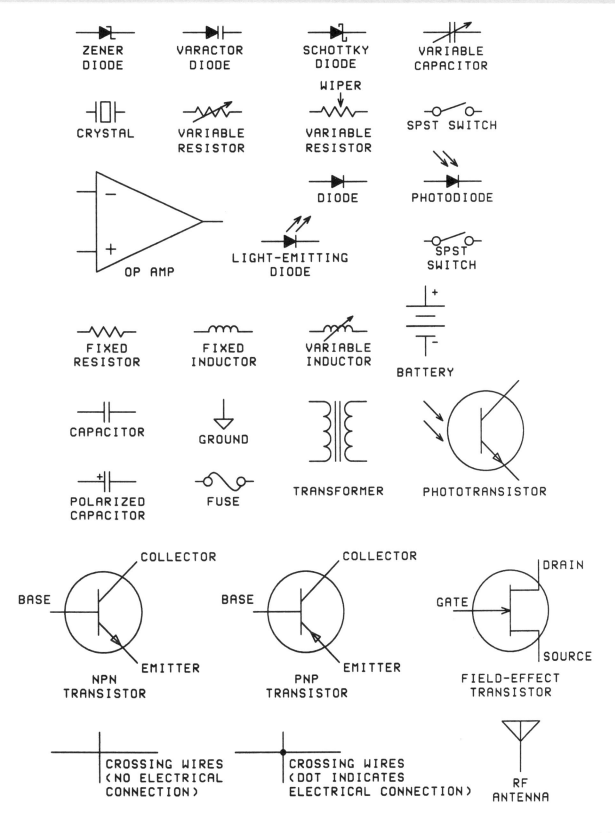

ZENER DIODE

VARACTOR DIODE

SCHOTTKY DIODE

VARIABLE CAPACITOR

CRYSTAL

VARIABLE RESISTOR

WIPER

VARIABLE RESISTOR

SPST SWITCH

OP AMP

DIODE

PHOTODIODE

LIGHT-EMITTING DIODE

SPST SWITCH

FIXED RESISTOR

FIXED INDUCTOR

VARIABLE INDUCTOR

BATTERY

CAPACITOR

GROUND

TRANSFORMER

PHOTOTRANSISTOR

POLARIZED CAPACITOR

FUSE

COLLECTOR

BASE

EMITTER

NPN TRANSISTOR

COLLECTOR

BASE

EMITTER

PNP TRANSISTOR

DRAIN

GATE

SOURCE

FIELD-EFFECT TRANSISTOR

CROSSING WIRES (NO ELECTRICAL CONNECTION)

CROSSING WIRES (DOT INDICATES ELECTRICAL CONNECTION)

RF ANTENNA

STUFFING DIAGRAM SYMBOL LEGEND

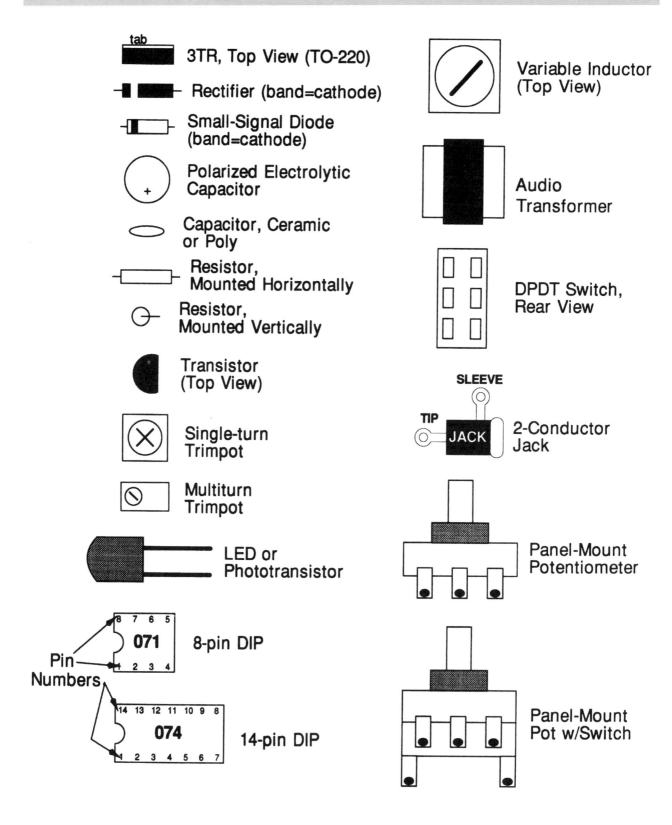

tab
3TR, Top View (TO-220)

Rectifier (band=cathode)

Small-Signal Diode
(band=cathode)

Polarized Electrolytic
Capacitor

Capacitor, Ceramic
or Poly

Resistor,
Mounted Horizontally

Resistor,
Mounted Vertically

Transistor
(Top View)

Single-turn
Trimpot

Multiturn
Trimpot

LED or
Phototransistor

Pin
Numbers

8-pin DIP

14-pin DIP

Variable Inductor
(Top View)

Audio
Transformer

DPDT Switch,
Rear View

SLEEVE

TIP

JACK

2-Conductor
Jack

Panel-Mount
Potentiometer

Panel-Mount
Pot w/Switch

APPENDIX V

How to Design Bugging Gear

Despite a leaden rep as blackest of the black arts, bug design follows a simple, logical routine:

- Define the purpose of the tool.
- Prepare a block diagram of the tool.
- If the block diagram looks workable, prepare a detailed block diagram that includes buffers and supply lines.
- If this also looks workable, substitute specific subcircuits for the blocks; at this point choose transistor vs. op amp; single supply vs. dual; battery vs. AC power; etc.; this stage ends in a complete schematic.
- Test the circuit on the breadboard; ascertain supply voltage, current drain, and bypass requirements.
- Revise and retest based on breadboard. results; finalize the schematic.
- Lay out a printed circuit board.
- Build a prototype.
- Lab-test the prototype.
- Field-test the prototype.
- Revise the design as needed.

Bug design is a matter of chaining sub-circuits. Consider a situation that might have occurred countless times in the real world:

Problem: Using discrete transistors, design an audio preamp having at least 50 dB of gain at 3 KHz, but no more than 15 dB of gain at 50 Hz. The stage should be suitable for 9V battery power; total current drain of the stage cannot exceed 2 ma at a supply voltage of 7.5V.

Solution: Fifty dB of gain isn't practical from one transistor at this low supply voltage, so the stage will chain two common-emitter amps. Coincidentally, this happens to deliver the specified frequency contour. Cascaded stages result in frequency-dependent gain that rises at 12 dB/octave.

Having chosen two transistor stages, select the transistors. Nothing in the spec dictates anything beyond the reach of 2N3904s. (Never choose a specialized and thus traceable part when generic parts will do.) Schematic "A" shows the result.

Problem: Make the stage you just designed part of something useful. Agent X, one of your regulars, has asked you to build a high-gain audio amp suitable for a ceramic contact mic. Headphones only, no tape output. X does not say—they never do—but you understand that he will use the amp to intercept speech.

Solution: Mate the preamp to an LM386. The most economical method is to replace Q2's collector resistor with a 5K audio-taper pot. Wire it such that the wiper is at V+ full CCW, at the collector full CW. Tie the wiper to the 386 input through a 0.1µF cap. You don't need a large cap here because preamplification has already occurred. Use the inverting input, because the output of Q2 is in phase with the input of Q1. If you used the 386's noninverting input, the headphone output would be in phase with the microphone input, making feedback oscillation likely. Schematic "B" shows the result.

Problem: Agent Y wants pretty much the same device, but he's working with an electret-based hose microphone. Adapt the existing device to an electret.

Solution: Don't start from scratch every time. Once you have a good basic block design, adapt it to other applications.

In this case, you have to add a bias network for the electret. Whenever you run an electret mic off the power bus of an amp flirting with 90 dB of gain, give the mic bias resistor its own decoupling network. Because the voltage present at the mic output is very much higher than the voltage present at the base of Q1, couple the mic through a capacitor. Use a large capacitor to keep low capacitive reactance, and thus low thermal noise and low $I_n \times R_s$ noise. The big cap has no significant effect on frequency response because the amp achieves contour by not amplifying bass. Schematic "C" shows the result.

Problem: Design a printed circuit board for this device.

Solution: *What* problem? Because the schematic applied the bus concept and a linear signal path, the circuit board designs itself. You can literally place part symbols over schematic symbols.

Laying out a board is easiest working right side up, as though looking down on the parts as they will sit on the board. Once you've got the layout, don't forget to *flip it horizontally to give the foil side of the board.*

This device exhibited conditional stability on the breadboard; it was stable running wide open, with a stout supply consisting of a fresh alkaline 9V or a 10-cell AA nicad pack. It was unstable

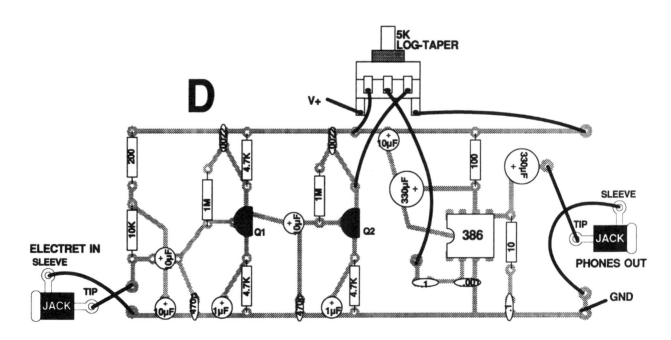

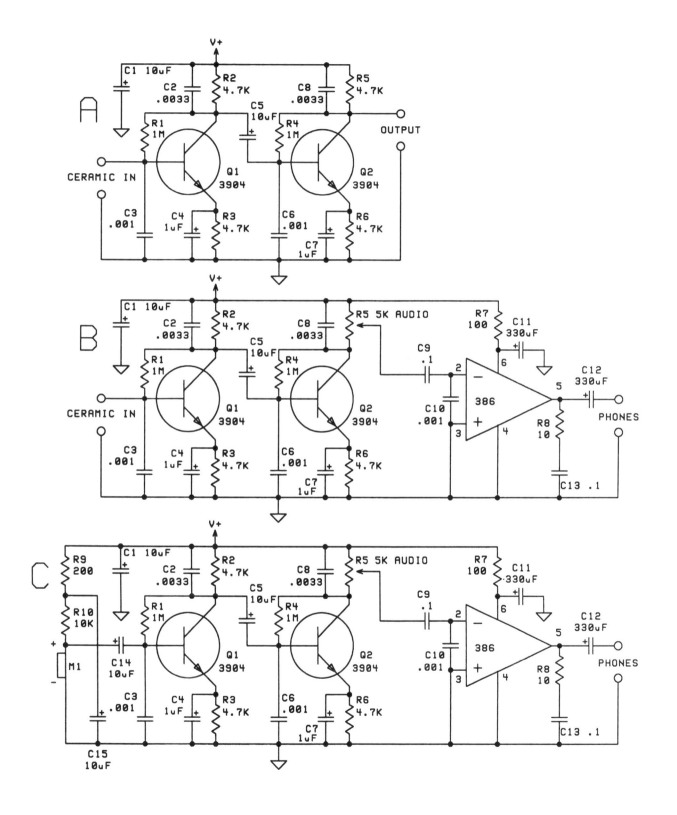

when running off a low-capacity 9V nicad. C7 might benefit from a switch, for the countless applications that don't need radical gain.

A prototype will introduce additional variables. Lead dress is key to stability. Input and output leads do not have to be shielded but should measure no more than 1″. Twist them tightly. Parasitic capacitance of 3′ of mic cable can destabilize some amps, so keep length of cable as short as practical.

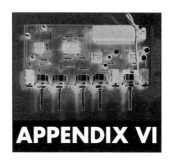

A Bugger's Glossary

absolute zero— -459.7 degrees Fahrenheit, the temperature at which no heat exists.

AC—Alternating current.

aliasing—The production of undesirable artifacts by modulating a carrier with a frequency higher than carrier / 2. Many ultrasonic carrier systems minimize aliasing by choosing a carrier frequency several times that of the highest frequency to be impressed on the carrier.

amp—Short for "ampere" (A), a unit of current; also short for "amplifier."

apocrypha—Literally, books of the Bible felt to be inauthentic; in loose usage, any literary work of doubtful authenticity.

beta—Loosely, the DC current gain of a bipolar transistor.

bias—For the verb "bias," substitute "apply a DC potential to." For example, ". . . whose input is biased at 1/2V+." "Bias" (noun) means the DC potential itself, such that "base bias" means "the DC voltage applied to the base."

BPT—Bipolar transistor, a three-lead device consisting of an emitter (E), a base (B), and a collector (C); the most common type of discrete transistor; includes 2N3904, 2N3906, 2N2219A, etc. Transistors amplify, oscillate, and function as electronic switches.

breadboard—A fixture consisting of a matrix of holes connected to electrical conductors, into which electronic parts can be plugged to make circuits.

breakdown voltage—The reverse bias voltage at which conduction occurs; intentional in zener diodes, unintentional and undesirable in most semiconductors.

bridge—Four diodes wired such that a DC or AC voltage applied between two terminals emerges from the other two terminals. Has the property of rectifying an AC input or making a DC input insensitive to polarity.

bridge-tied load (or BTL)—A means of connecting two power amplifiers in which the load is wired between the output terminals and in which the signal is antiphase between the two outputs. The output stage of the MC34119 uses the BTL configuration.

bug—A surveillance device; aka gimmick, maguffin, "it."

bus—A good translation is "electrical path sharing a common potential"; speak of "the ground bus" or "the positive supply bus"; spelled "buss" in some texts.

bypass—When speaking of the power supply, synonymous with "decouple"; also means to provide an AC path around, as in ". . . emitter resistor R4, bypassed by C3."

C—Capacitor, as in C5, C8, etc.

CCW—Counterclockwise.

CW—Clockwise.

cap—Short for "capacitor."

carrier—Short for "carrier frequency"; a signal that bears another signal. Carrier is usually several times the upper limit of frequency to be recovered. On FM radio, the station's frequency gives the frequency of its carrier. Information modulated onto the carrier shifts the frequency a maximum of 75 KHz above or below the carrier.

coax—Short for coaxial cable.

coaxial system—Existing on the same axis; when speaking of coaxial laserbug systems, the receiver and the laser mount together and share the same optical axis; compare split systems.

collector current—When speaking of a single-transistor, common-emitter amplifier, the current flowing through the collector resistor; abbreviated IC. Important in bipolar transistors because transistor noise voltage varies inversely as the square root of IC; transistor noise current varies directly as the square root of IC. To determine IC, measure the voltage drop across the collector resistor; use that value and the collector resistance calculate current using Ohm's law.

collimator—A lens or lens system that narrows a beam of light.

Colpitts & Hartley—Namesakes of the inventors of two popular oscillator circuits.

common mode rejection ratio—Abbreviated CMRR; the extent to which a differential amplifier can ignore common-mode signals; for example, an op amp whose CMRR is rated 120 dB will generate a 1Êv output from a 1V common-mode input.

comparator—A circuit that compares one voltage to another, and changes its output state depending on the relationship of the two; has the effect of sensing a change in voltage, as in an off-hook phone sensor, or in converting sinewaves to squarewaves, as in a carrier current receiver.

corner—short for corner frequency.

darlington—Two transistors wired in series on signal die to act as a single transistor with extremely high DC beta.

DC—Direct current.

deviation—When speaking of FM systems, the percentage change in the carrier induced by the audio input.

DEW Line—Distant early warning line; a ring of radar stations once maintained by the United States to detect Soviet nuclear bombers.

diode—A unidirectional conductor.

dithering—The process of stimulating a sensor with a low-level, wideband, noisy signal to lower its response threshold.

DIP—Dual inline package; the most common package for integrated circuits. Pins are spaced on 0.1″ centers beside each other, and 0.3″ centers across from each other. Most consumer-level DIPs are plastic; "cerdip" means ceramic DIP, usually for military and high-temperature applications.

DMM—Digital multimeter, an electronic test instrument common since the early eighties. Display liquid crystal, read DC volts, AC volts, DC current, resistance in ohms; some add capacitance, transistor beta, AC current, audible continuity tester. Replaces the old vacuum tube voltmeter.

drain current—Symbol ID; the FET equivalent of collector current; ID bears the same relationship to FET noise voltage and noise current that IC does to bipolar transistor E_n and I_n (see collector current).

DSP—Digital signal processing.

dual supply—Noun meaning "a supply consisting of V+, V-, and ground"; compare to single supply.

duty cycle—When speaking of a squarewave, the percentage of time spent in a specific state (usually HIGH). A 1 KHz squarewave train with a 10 percent duty cycle spends 100µs HIGH, 900 µs LOW; a 50 percent duty cycle, 500µs HIGH, 500µs LOW, etc.

E—Symbol for voltage or electromotive force.

E_n—Input noise voltage.

EPROM—Erasable programmable read-only memory.

empirically—Adverb meaning "by trial and error."

fall time—When speaking of an optical sensor, the time needed for the output to fall to baseline following removal of the optical stimulus.

Faraday cage—A container or shield which RF energy cannot penetrate.

FET—Strictly speaking, a junction field-effect

transistor, or JFET. The "J" is often dropped. FETs have three leads: source (S), gate (G), and drain (D). These correspond, respectively, to the emitter, base, and collector of a bipolar transistor. Source and drain leads are interchangeable on most FETs.

fin—Five dollars.

first oscillator—In a superheterodyne receiver, the first local oscillator.

floating—Adjective meaning "not referred to ground."

forward bias—Verb and noun; to forward bias an electronic component means to apply voltage that causes or is expected to cause forward conduction; in the case of an LED, application of positive voltage to the anode, negative voltage to the cathode, causes current to flow and the LED to emit light.

forward drop—The drop-in voltage that occurs when current flows through a diode or other semiconductor junction.

frequency—The rate at which something occurs, usually expressed in Hertz (cycles per second); and multiples: kilohertz, megahertz, gigahertz, etc.

gig—A bugging job.

giga—Prefix meaning "times 1 billion" (×10⁹).

GND—Ground; on single-supply circuits, corresponds to the negative battery terminal.

harmonics—When speaking of RF bugs, or radio transmitters in general, harmonics refer to multiples of the fundamental tone. The 2nd harmonic is twice the fundamental; the third three times, and so forth. Harmonic generation is undesirable in some cases, deliberate in others.

headroom—The maximum peak-to-peak voltage swing possible before clipping occurs.

heatsink—A metal clip attached to the lead of an electronic part during soldering to absorb heat to prevent damage to the part; also, a metal fixture permanently attached to a part to soak up heat generated by the part during normal operation.

Hertz (or Hz)—Cycle per second; 60 KHz = 60 kilohertz = 60,000 cycles per second; 10.7 MHz = 10.7 megahertz = 10.7 million cycles per second.

HIGH—A DC potential at or near V+; often capitalized.

I—Symbol for current.

I$_n$—Input current noise.

IF—Intermediate frequency; pronounced "eye-eff"; the frequency derived by mixing two radio signals; the most common IFs are 455 KHz and 10.7 MHz. (See superheterodyne, local oscillator.)

impedance—Symbol "Z"; the net resistance to the flow of alternating current.

inverting input—Input whose output is antiphase to the input; usually labeled "—" on a schematic symbol.

junction capacitance—In a bipolar transistor, junction capacitance is that which exists inside the transistor; the amount depends on transistor type; ranges from a fraction of a picofarad to tens of picofarads. Important for many reasons, but in an RF core, junction capacitance (1) interacts with tank capacitance to determine carrier frequency, and (2) changes under the influence of audio fed into the base, and by that means alters the oscillation frequency.

K—Kilohms; a thousand ohms; "×1,000"; 22K = 22,000 ohms.

kale—Cabbage, lettuce, moolah, lucre, sheckels, pesetas, zulaks, coin, greenbacks, dinero, dough, centavos, grease, money.

L—Inductor, as in L1, L3, etc.

LC network—An inductor wired in series or in parallel with a capacitor.

local capacitance—"LC"; a specific type of stray capacitance; local generally means that produced by proximity of objects to the circuit under consideration. An LC bug tuned on the bench will change frequency if used as a body wire, because proximity to the body alters local capacitance. Crystal-controlled transmitters resist the effects of local capacitance better than LC bugs do.

local oscillator—"LO"; an oscillator, often inside a radio receiver, that generates a signal for the specific purpose of mixing with another signal to derive an intermediate frequency. (See IF, superheterodyne.)

LOW—A DC potential at or near ground; often capitalized.

M—Megohm; a million ohms; "times 1,000,000"; 2.2M = 2,200,000 ohms.

mah—Short for "milliampere hour"; one means to specify battery capacity. Can deliver 450 ma for one hour, or less current for proportionately longer time. Lithium with 5,000 mah capacity should be able to run a 3 ma bug for two months.

mega—Prefix meaning "times one million," e.g., ×106; megahertz = millions of hertz.

mH (or mh)—Millihenry; a thousandth of a henry; a common unit of inductance, derived from the henry (H).

micro—Prefix meaning "one millionth;" $\times 10^{-6}$.

middled—As in "getting middled," a gambling outcome in which bettors on both sides of the play win; the house, or bookie, loses.

milli—Prefix meaning "one thousandth"; $\times 10^{-3}$.

MOSFET—Metallic oxide surface field-effect transistor.

nano—Prefix meaning "one billionth"; $\times 10^{-9}$; as in "nanoseconds" or "nanometers."

nagra—The brand name of a European-made tape recorder once favored by federal law enforcement agencies.

network—Two or more parts wired together, as in "LC network" or "RC network," generally understood to perform a specific task, as "lowpass network R1-C12" or "decoupling network L4-C8."

nicad—Nickel-cadmium rechargeable battery.

noninverting input—Input whose output is in phase with the input; usually labeled "+" on a schematic symbol.

nonpolar—As of a capacitor; an electrolytic cap insensitive to polarity connection; also known as a bipolar cap.

nv—Nanovolts.

OFF—A nonconducting or inoperative state; when referring to a transistor or a conduction path, often capitalized, e.g., " . . . to bias Q1 in an OFF state that causes the collector to go HIGH."

offset—As in, "DC offset." Generally, any point in the circuit that does not exist at ground potential is spoken of as having a DC offset, the voltage relative to ground that exists at that point. An offset matters because its presence demands orientation of a polarized coupling cap such that the positive terminal faces the more positive DC offset. The electronic literature tends to speak of DC applied to the input of a stage as a bias, while DC present at the output of a stage is spoken of as an offset.

ON—A conducting or operative state; often capitalized, e.g., ". . . to bias Q1 in an ON state that causes the collector to go LOW."

one-shot—An electronic circuit that responds to an input stimulus by generating a single output pulse.

oscilloscope—An electronic test instrument that displays voltage on the vertical scale versus time on the horizontal scale.

pair, the—Telco/bugger slang for the twisted-pair phone line.

pa—Picoamps.

P.A.L.—Police Athletic League.

parasitic—As in "parasitic capacitance" or "parasitic inductance"; electronic traits that exist by the nature of the thing.

p-p—"Peak-to-peak"; the amplitude of an audio signal is often spoken of as "volts peak-to-peak" (V_{p-p}).

pF—Picofarad, 10^{-12} farad; a common unit of capacitance; called a micromicrofarad (μμF or mmF) in older texts; often abbreviated "p" on schematics.

photodiode—A photosensor consisting of a light-sensitive diode.

phototransistor—A photosensor consisting of a light-sensitive transistor.

pico—Prefix meaning "one million-millionth"; $\times 10^{-12}$

PIN photodiode—A type of photodiode whose hallmark is extremely high speed when properly biased.

pinout—A diagram relating the internal connections of a device to its external leads.

pix—Photographs.

pot—Slang for potentiometer, a 3-terminal variable resistor; the middle terminal is called the *wiper*.

quad coil—Short for "quadrature demodulator

coil"; a high-Q LC tank, often contained in a single part, used in narrowband and some wideband FM demodulators.

R—Resistor, as in R1, R34, etc.

ramp generator—A circuit that generates an electrical potential that rises from a low value to a high value, then returns instantly to the low value, at which point the cycle repeats.

rectifier—A diode used specifically as a unidirectional conductor.

repeater—A device that receives and retransmits a signal, and which might or might not alter the transmission medium; might or might not demodulate the signal.

resonance—Applied specifically to an inductor connected to a capacitor. Wired in parallel, they exhibit a resonant frequency at which impedance goes theoretically infinite; wired in series, they exhibit a resonant frequency at which impedance goes theoretically to zero. The same equation defines both points. (See Appendix III: Basic Bug Math.)

reverse bias—(verb and noun) To reverse bias an electronic component means to apply voltage that is not expected to cause current to flow. In the case of an LED, application of a negative voltage to the anode *reverse-biases* the LED, and no current flows. Some electronic parts are designed to operate in reverse-bias mode, such as PIN photodiodes and zener diodes.

RF—radio frequency; also short for radio-frequency energy.

RF flooding—The practice of getting RF into a target area, usually by some wire conduit, such as telephone line. Will acquire audio being reflected off metal objects.

rise time—When speaking of a photosensor, the time needed for the sensor output to respond to an optical input.

R$_s$—Source resistance.

rt—Square root.

sampling theorem—The mathematical explanation for aliasing; explains why the signal impressed on a carrier cannot be greater than carrier / 2 without the production of undesirable artifacts.

scannerista—Buggers' term for a militant scanner user who deliberately seeks out clandestine transmissions.

Schottky diode—Diode having a lower forward voltage drop than that of a conventional silicon diode; used for higher efficiency in switching power supplies and to prevent saturation of silicon switching transistors.

scope—Short for "oscilloscope."

second source—Refers to identical parts manufactured by different companies. For example, Precision Monolithics invented the OP-27 op amp but licensed manufacture to Motorola, a *second-source* supplier; second sourced parts are often cheaper than primary sourced.

semiconductor—The material that transistors, diodes, and integrated circuits are made of; most common is silicon; prior to 1965, many transistors were based on germanium; newer transistors use gallium aluminum arsenide.

single supply—A supply consisting of V+ and ground; compare to dual supply.

spectrum analyzer (or SA)—A device that senses RF energy and displays amplitude vs. frequency on a video screen.

split system—When speaking of a laserbug system, a split system is one in which the laser and the receiver are separated; compare to coaxial system.

squarewave—A squarewave isn't a wave at all, but the sum of an infinite series of sinewaves; for example, a 1 KHz squarewave is the sum of a 1 KHz sinewave plus 1/3 the third harmonic 3KHz ; plus 1/5 5 KHz the fifth harmonic; ad infinitum. Thus, squarewaves are rich sources of interference at frequencies higher than their own, explaining why digital equipment throws off so much RF hash; and the perfect input to an RF frequency multiplier.

stray capacitance—Capacitance that accompanies the proximity of leads to a device, such as an op amp; sometimes referred to as parasitic capacitance; distinct from local capacitance.

stripline—Method of circuit-board design used

at and above VHF, in which copper circuit traces act as inductors and capacitors in place of discrete parts.

superheterodyne—A type of radio receiver design that mixes the received signal with a signal generated by the receiver in a local oscillator, to derive an intermediate frequency equal to the difference between the signal frequency and the LO frequency. This new frequency can yield intelligence directly or can undergo additional stages of mixing/downconversion. The number of mixing stages is often used to define the receiver, such as single-conversion, dual-conversion, and triple conversion. Each conversion delivers gain, and each additional stage improves the receiver's selectivity.

tank—An inductor in parallel with a capacitor, usually used to achieve resonance. At resonance, impedance becomes theoretically infinite.

telco—General slang for the telephone company, in whatever incarnation.

tera—Prefix meaning "times a million-million"; $\times 10^{12}$.

thermal noise (aka "Johnson noise")—Noise produced by atomic movement in materials above the temperature of absolute zero.

transconductance—Simply, the change in conductance per unit of drive; base current in the case of a bipolar transistor, gate voltage in the case of a FET.

μF—Microfarad; 10^{-6} farad; a common unit of capacitance.

μh—Microhenry; 10^{-6} Henry; a common unit of inductance.

UHF—Ultra-high frequency.

Varactor—A diode specially made for use as a voltage-variable capacitor.

V—Symbol for volts.

VCA—Voltage-controlled amplifier.

VCF—Voltage-controlled filter.

VHF—Very high frequency.

vig—Short for vigorish, the percentage a bookie collects on losing bets.

V+—Pronounced "vee-plus"; on a schematic or wiring diagram it means "the positive power supply."

V-—Pronounced "vee-minus"; on a schematic or wiring diagram it means "the negative power supply."

walk test—In counterbugging, the practice of an operator wearing headphones connected to the output of a sniffer equipped with an audio feed, walking through the sweep area while carrying a radio or himself making noise likely to be heard through the headphones if a bug is near.

wavelength—1 / frequency; for light, expressed in nanometers (nm). Visible light falls in the range ~440–700 nm; infrared is >700 nm; ultraviolet is <440 nm.

X—Symbol for reactance, often specified as capacitive reactance (Xc) or inductive reactance (Xl).

Z—Symbol for impedance.

zener—A noun and a verb; the noun is short for "zener diode," a special diode used as a voltage regulator or white-noise generator; zeners come in 1.8 to more than 200 volts. As a verb, zener means "to use as a zener diode." Many common transistors behave as zener diodes when reverse-biased.

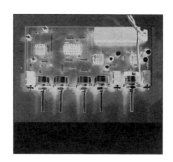

References

ARRL Antenna Book. American Radio Relay League, 1994, ISBN 0-87259-473-4.

ARRL Handbook (1994). American Radio Relay League, 1993, ISBN 0-87259-171-9.

ARRL UHF/Microwave Projects Manual. American Radio Relay League, 1994, ISBN 0-87259-449-1.

Barlow, Murray, and Bruce Barlowe. *Build Your Own Spectrum Analyzer.* Science Workshop, 1992 (no ISBN; for info on book/analyzer, send SASE to: Science Workshop, Box 310, Bethpage, NY 11714).

Baumgartner, Fred. "Build This Spectrum Monitor." *Radio-Electronics,* September 1989, pp. 33–42, and October 1989, pp. 46–48.

Best of Analogue Dialogue, 1967 to 1991. Analog Devices, Inc., 1991.

Bigelow, S. J. *Understanding Telephone Electronics (3rd Ed.).* Butterworth-Heimann, 1997, ISBN 0-7506-9944-2.

Carr, Joseph J. *Secrets of RF Circuit Design.* TAB Books, 1991, ISBN 0-8306-8710-6.

Crown Boundary Microphone Application Guide. Crown International, Inc., 1990.

Hayward, W. and Doug DeMaw. *Solid State Design for the Radio Amateur.* American Radio Relay League, Inc., 1986.

Heath Electronics Course. Heath Company, 1982, ISBN 0-87119-064-8.

Jung, Walter G. *Audio IC Op-Amp Applications, 3rd Ed.* Howard W. Sams, 1987, ISBN 0-672-22452-6.

___. *IC Op-Amp Cookbook, 3rd Ed.* Howard W. Sams, 1986, ISBN 0-672-22452-6.

___. *IC Timer Cookbook, 2nd Ed.* Howard W. Sams, 1983, ISBN 0-672-21932-8.

Kesteloot, Andre, and Charles Hutchinson. *The ARRL Spread Spectrum Sourcebook.* American Radio Relay League, 1991, ISBN 0-87259-317-7.

Lancaster, Don. *Active-Filter Cookbook.* Howard W. Sams, 1975, ISBN 0-672-21168-8.

___. *TTL Cookbook.* Howard W. Sams, 1974, ISBN 0-672-21035-5.

Linear Products Handbook (Vols. 1 & 2). Analog Devices, Inc., 1988.

1990 Linear Applications Handbook: A Guide to Linear Circuit Design. Linear Technology, Inc., 1989.

Manufacturers' Data Sheets for the following integrated circuits: SSM2017, SSM2120 (Rev. A). Precision Monolithics, Inc., 1989.

Maxim Analog Design Guide, Vols. 4, 6, 7, 8, 9.

Maxim New Releases Databook Volume III. Maxim, Inc., 1994.

Maxim New Releases Databook Volume IV. Maxim, Inc., 1995.

Maxim Product Data Sheets on CD-ROM, 1997 Edition, Maxim, Inc., 1997.

Melen, Roger, and Harry Garland. *Understand IC Operational Amplifiers*. Howard W. Sams, 1986, ISBN 0-672-22484-4.

Moell, J. and Thomas N. Curlee. *Transmitter Hunting: Radio Direction-Finding Simplified*. Tab Books, 1987, ISBN 0-8306-2701-4.

Motorola Linear and Interface Integrated Circuits, Rev. 2. Motorola Semiconductor, Inc., 1988.

Signetics Linear Data Manual Volume 1: Communications. Signetics, Inc., 1987.

Sporck, C. (Ed.) *Linear Applications Handbook*. National Semiconductor Corp., 1986.

Sporck, C. (Ed.) *Linear Databook, Vols. 1, 2, and 3*. National Semiconductor Corp., 1986.

United States Patent 3,632,886. "Quadrasonic Sound System."

United States Patent 3,835,255. "Matrix Decoders for Quadraphonic Sound System."

United States Patent 3,944,735. "Directional Enhancement System for Quadraphonic Decoders."

United States Patent 3,971,890. "Method and Apparatus for Quadraphonic Enhancement of Stereophonic Signals."

United States Patent 4,018,992. "Decoder for Quadraphonic Playback."

United States Patent 4,063,032. "Constant Power Balance Controls for Stereophonic and Quadraphonic Sound Systems."

United States Patent 4,361,736. "Pressure Recording Process and Device."

Zetex Discrete Component and Linear IC Applications Handbook, Zetex, Inc. June, 1996.

Parts Sources

Crystek Crystals
2351 Crystal Drive
Ft. Myers, FL 33907
Custom-cut crystals. Free catalog.

DC Electronics
Box 3203
Scottsdale, AZ 85271
Parts include: NE570, canned RF coils, MAR-6 MMIC, meters, XR2206, MC3340, MC1350, TL07X, MC3357, MC3317X series; 455 KHz Mouser IF transformers used in some carrier current devices, DTMF decoder chip.

Digi-Key
Box 677
Thief River Falls, MN 56701
Carries an exceptionally wide assortment of integrated circuits from National Semiconductor, Maxim, Linear Technology, Burr-Brown, and others; electret mics, ultrasonic transducers (40 KHz–200 KHz), IR LEDs, phototransistors, PIN photodiodes, laser diodes. Free catalog.

Edmund Scientific Company
101 East Gloucester Pike
Barrington, NJ 08007
Sells aluminum parabolic dishes great for directional mics; lasers, optics. Edmund sends the general merchandise catalog on request, but

items of interest to buggers are in their specialized catalogs (optics, lasers), available by specific request.

Hosfelt Electronics
2700 Sunset Blvd.
Steubenville, OH 43952
Many semiconductors, meters, cases, printed circuit fabrication materials. Free catalog.

Jan Crystals
Box 06017
Ft. Myers, FL 33906
Custom-cut crystals. Free catalog.

Mouser Electronics
2401 Hwy 287 N.
Mansfield, TX 76063
Sells all the miniature audio transformers listed in this book, IF transformers used in many carrier current designs, canned RF coils, MC3317X op amps. Free catalog.

(Mouser, Hosfelt, and DC Electronics stock the NTE line of replacement semiconductors.)

PAiA Electronics
3200 Teakwood Lane
Edmond, OK 73013
SSM2120, SSM2107.

Radio Shack

General-purpose electronic parts; entry-level printed circuit materials, telephone pickup coil.

Statek

512 N. Main St.
Orange, CA 92668.
Custom-cut crystals. Free catalog.

Yes, Virginia, all the prototypes were destroyed. . . .

If you liked this book, you will also want to read these: